If You're So Smart, Why Aren't You Rich?

A Guide To Investing Fundamentals

BEN BRANCH

Westport, Connecticut
London

Library of Congress Cataloging-in-Publication Data

Branch, Ben, 1943–
    If you're so smart, why aren't you rich? : a guide to investing fundamentals /
Ben Branch.
        p. cm.
    Includes bibliographical references and index.
    ISBN 0-275-99028-1 (alk. paper)
    1. Investments.   2. Stocks.   3. Investments—United States.   I. Title: Guide to
investing fundamentals.   II. Title.
    HG4521.B6462 2006
    332.67'8—dc22   2006004345

British Library Cataloguing-in-Publication Data is available.

Library of Congress Catalog Card Number: 2006004345
ISBN: 0-275-99028-1

First published in 2006

Praeger Publishers, 88 Post Road West, Westport, CT 06881
An imprint of Greenwood Publishing Group, Inc.
www.praeger.com

Printed in the United States of America

The paper used in this book complies with the
Permanent Paper Standard issued by the National
Information Standards Organization (Z39.48-1984).

10 9 8 7 6 5 4 3 2 1

Contents

Part III: MARKET TIMING

Introduction

If this title has caught your eye, you probably don't need any convincing. You would rather be rich than poor. You also know that one way to improve your financial situation is to save and then invest what you save. Saving may not be easy, but everyone knows how to do it: Spend less than you earn. Investing is also easy to describe. Anyone with some available savings can put it to work by investing. Put the money in a savings account at a bank and you become an investor. Take a little bit of savings and do a little bit of investing for a little bit of return, and you have made a start, but only a start. If you really want to become rich by saving and investing, you will need to begin to save some serious money and invest it for a serious return.

I shall leave to you the task of figuring out how to motivate yourself to undertake a serious savings program. This book focuses on the second matter: How to invest for a serious return. First, let's understand what a realistically serious return is. An analogy will help.

Football is often described as a game of inches. Scoring, first downs, and in/out-of-bounds decisions frequently come down to a matter of inches or even fractions of an inch. A similar concept applies to investment management. With investing, however, a *basis point* (see Glossary following Conclusion), one-hundredth of a percentage point of return, replaces the inch as the unit of measurement. The difference between outperforming and underperforming the market may turn on accumulating a few additional basis points of return in each of a number of places. Apply the power of compounding to enough incremental basis points of return, and the difference becomes increasingly noticeable, particularly as the holding period is lengthened.

The primary objective of most investment managers is to earn an attractive return on their portfolios. A portfolio's return performance is typically measured relative to some benchmark market index. For example, the performance of the S&P 500 index (an index of the stocks of five hundred major U.S companies) is thought to reflect what the stock market has done. An average investor who picks stocks at random ought to do about as well as the S&P 500 index. Consistently outperforming the appropriate market average is not an easy task, however. Most financial economists believe that securities markets (stocks, bonds, options, futures, and so on) are relatively efficient. The more effectively the market prices securities, the more difficult undervalued investments are to identify. An *efficient market* prices assets accurately vis-à-vis what is known about their underlying intrinsic values. In other words, the market processes the publicly available information effectively so as to produce prices that accurately reflect the available information. *While the market does not always get it right, it does seem to put a realistic price on most securities most of the time.* Those pockets of inefficiencies (or anomalies) that do turn up tend to be of modest size and duration. Accordingly, investors who seek to outperform an appropriate benchmark return consistently need to exploit a host of relatively minor opportunities. Exploring how to take advantage of these relatively minor opportunities constitutes the primary focus of this book. Taken one at a time and even as a group, these minor opportunities do not provide a panacea. And yet, paying careful attention to these little things offers the best chance most investors will have to achieve superior performance. Patience and the power of compound interest will take care of the rest.

To a very substantial degree, winning in investing is a matter of not losing. Much of what we know about successful investing is not so much how to make a killing but how to avoid being killed. Learning what strategies and practices are unlikely to succeed and then properly applying that knowledge is a large part of formulating a winning investment strategy.

Financial markets are much too uncertain and volatile for any risk-taking investor to hope to avoid losses entirely. Be assured that: *If you take risks, sooner or later you will incur losses.* You will purchase securities whose market prices decline; sometimes the decline will occur shortly after your purchase. In some years your portfolio's total market value may decline. Indeed, on occasion almost everything you own may trade for less than your cost. Risk-taking by its very nature implies that investment portfolios will lose value at least some of the time. Recognizing that you will experience some losses from time to time does not mean that you should just accept such losses as part of the ups and downs of being an investor. While you cannot avoid losses entirely, you can and should do what you can to avoid *unnecessary* losses. Much of what you will learn from reading this book is how to avoid what an experienced, well-informed investor would recognize as an obvious mistake. *Avoiding unnecessary losses will enhance your overall return every bit as much as getting an edge on the market in the relatively rare instances where that is possible.*

This book is designed for those who want to learn how to enhance their investment performance. You should find my book to be both interesting and relatively easy to read. Jargon, complex mathematics, and difficult theoretical concepts are avoided as much as possible. Both experienced and relatively less experienced investors should be able to improve their investment skills significantly by reading and applying the principles discussed herein. I do assume that you have at least a little bit of experience with investing and money management. If you are an absolute beginner, you may find the going a bit rough in spots. Even so, you may want to give it a try.

My book is designed for those who are interested in earning serious returns on serious money. Successful investing requires a commitment of time and a willingness to accept a certain amount of risk. Do not proceed with an active investment program unless you are willing to put some time in and take some risks. If you view investing as too much like work, you should probably hire an investment manager or put most of your investable resources into one or more mutual funds or similar types of investment vehicles. Similarly, if you are extremely risk-averse, active portfolio management is probably not for you. Buy treasury bills or FDIC-insured CDs and sleep at night. *You should always sell down to the sleeping point.*

My book is divided into three parts, each of which is further divided into a number of chapters. Each chapter contains a set of rules that relate to a particular topic. You can begin by sorting through its various sections to see what topics are covered. The table of contents will provide you with a useful overview. Then you can choose to read some parts and not others. You are encouraged to skip around if you like. Not every topic covered herein may appeal to you. Each rule is presented as part of a self-contained easy-to-read set of material. Ideally, you can identify an interesting segment (rule, for example) and read about it while drinking a martini. In most cases, you can finish the segment before your glass is empty.

I myself have been an active investor for more than forty years and a professor of finance and economics for more than thirty. I have written several books and numerous articles on various aspects of investing. I have always managed my own portfolio. Like most serious investors, I have taken my share of hits. But, I have tried to learn something worthwhile each time my investment decisions have turned out poorly (or well). As one who both teaches and undertakes research in the area of investing, I am also very familiar with the academic literature on the subject. For example, I read both the *Wall Street Journal* and the *Journal of Financial Economics*. In what follows, I shall share with the reader insights that have, in the aggregate, allowed me to achieve a significant degree of success as an investor. I hope you find these insights as helpful as I have.

Investing involves three types of activities: selection, timing, and execution. In other words, the investment process involves *what* to buy or sell, *when* to buy or sell it, and *how* to buy or sell it. Most resources on investing, such as books, articles, seminars, videos, or websites, focus on the latter two topics, selection and timing. Both matters are a central part to the investment process. And yet the third activity, execution, should not be neglected. Accordingly, each of these three areas of investing is treated here: investment mechanics, investment selection, and market timing. First, however, we need to explore an important preliminary: the power of compound interest and how it relates to your investment program. Understanding how compound interest works is so important that the rest of the chapter is devoted to it.

THE POWER OF COMPOUND INTEREST

Two important interconnected keys to getting rich slowly are patience and the power of compound interest. A patient investor avoids micromanaging his or her investments. Such investors allow their portfolios' values to grow without undo interference. Many investment strategies take time to work. You should give them that time. Don't expect too much too soon. If you do, you are almost certain to be disappointed.

The power of compounding your returns is amazing. It has been said that if the Native Americans had invested the $20 that the Dutch paid them for Manhattan at a reasonable rate of return, they would have earned enough to buy the island back. And indeed compounded at 9 percent over 360-year period, $20 would have grown to $59 trillion, no doubt more than enough to repurchase Manhattan and all of its improvements (plus all the securities listed on the New York Stock Exchange). Compounding does indeed work wonders.

Let's explore how compounding works. Suppose you invest $100 in an account that pays you $6 a year (a return of 6%). At the end of a year you will still have your original $100 plus an interest payment of $6. Your investment portfolio is now worth a total of $106. Invest the $106 total for another year and your original $100 investment will have grown to $112.36. You earned $6 more on the original $100 and $0.36 on the first year's $6 in interest. In the third year your total will amount to $119.10, reflecting an annual income of $6.74. Of this amount $0.74 represents *interest-on-interest*. That is where the compounding comes in. You earn return in year two on the accumulated total from year one. The process continues. By the fifth year your investment has grown to $133.82 and $179.08 by the tenth. Invest the money for twenty years and the total grows to $320.71, more than three times the $100 that you started with.

Compounding results from reinvesting the already-earned interest payments so that they will earn still more interest. If the $6 interest payment had been withdrawn and spent each year, the $100 investment would, over the twenty-year period, have produced a total of $120 in interest payments ($20 \times $6 = $120) and still be worth only its original value of $100. You would have your beginning $100 and have received an additional $120 in interest payments, for a total of $220. By reinvesting the interest payments, your total grows to $320.71 in twenty years. That sum includes more than $100 of interest-on-interest. Compound the sum for another ten years and the

The Power of Compound Interest		
Value of $100		
After:	Compounded at 6%:	Not compounded:
One year	$106.00	$106
Two years	$112.36	$112
Five years	$133.82	$130
Ten years	$179.08	$160
Twenty years	$320.71	$220
Thirty years	$574.34	$280
Forty years	$1,028.56	$340
Fifty years	$1,842.00	$400

accumulated total grows to $574.36, almost six times the original amount. This sum compares quite favorably to an accumulated total of $280 that would result if the interest payments were not reinvested. Clearly, reinvesting your investment earnings and thereby allowing your returns to compound has a very positive impact on your investment portfolio's accumulated value. Moreover, that compounding impact increases with time.

Having explored the power of compound interest applied to an *initial sum,* let's now consider the impact of incorporating a savings element into the *investment program.* If, instead of investing a single sum of $100 for twenty years, you invested *$100 a month* for twenty years, what would be the result? At the end of the first year you would have put aside $1,200 and earned a little bit of interest. What if you continue to put aside $100 a month for twenty years? If you earn 6 percent on the money, the total would grow to $44,142, of which $20,142 would be accumulated interest. Continue the process for another ten years and the total grows to $94,870, including $58, 870 of accumulated interest.

Now let's assess the impact that the rate of return has on the value accumulated. The preceding calculations assume that you earn 6 percent on your investment. Six percent is a relatively attractive return. But suppose you could earn a higher rate of return. Clearly, the rate of return that you earn on your investment makes a difference in how much you are able to accumulate. The higher the rate of return, the faster the sum grows. Let's see just how much a 2 percent increase in return affects the compound value. Suppose that instead of earning a 6 percent return on the money, you could earn 8 percent. At the 8 percent rate, the twenty and thirty-year totals increase to $54,944 and $135,936 (almost $100,000 of which represents accumulated interest).

Recall that these totals are the result of putting aside $100 a month. Saving and investing $100 a month would represent a good start. But putting aside a larger amount would be even better. Double the savings rate and all of the

---

The Power of Compound Interest and Savings I

Saving $100 a month

$100 a month @ 6% grows to: $100 a month @ 8% grows to:

$44,142 in 20 years $54,944 in 20 years
$94,870 in 30 years $135,936 in 30 years

---

totals double. If you can afford to save $500 a month, the totals are five times as great. At 6 percent you would have $220,710 after twenty years and $474,348 after thirty. At 8 percent the twenty and thirty-year totals become $306,666 and $817,800 respectively.

To assess the impact of a 2 percent increase in returns, let's compare the two thirty-year totals. Using a 6 percent rate of return, $500 a month for thirty years grows to $474,348. If the rate of return is increased to 8 percent, the thirty-year compounded total increases to $817,800. Thus we see that increasing the rate of return from 6 percent to 8 percent almost doubles ($817,800 versus $473,348) the value of the thirty years' accumulation. Clearly the rate of return that you are able to earn makes a substantial difference in how large a total value your portfolio will achieve.

The value of your portfolio will grow even faster if you can *periodically increase* the amount that you save and invest. As your career develops, you should receive both promotions and raises. Your rising income level should allow you to grow the amount that you put into savings each year. Suppose that you set up a savings program in which you periodically increase the amount that you put aside. In other words, you not only save a regular amount, but you increase the amount that you save at a regular predetermined rate. Suppose you start with $100 a month, increase the amount by 6 percent each year, and invest it to earn 6 percent each year. At the end of twenty years your total becomes $76,970, and in thirty years $206,766. If you can grow your savings and compound your money at an 8 percent rate, the twenty- and thirty-year totals rise to $111,864 and $362,232. Begin with $200 a month and those totals double. Start at $500 a month with an 8 percent rate and the

---

The Power of Compound Interest and Savings II

Saving $500 a month

$500 a month @ 6% grows to: $500 a month @ 8% grows to:

$220,710 in 20 years $306,666 in 20 years
$474,348 in 30 years $817,800 in 30 years

The Power of Compound Interest and a Growing Contribution Rate

$100 a month at 6% when the contribution also grows at 6% becomes:
    $76,970 in 20 years
    $206,766 in 30 years
$100 a month at 8% when the contribution also grows at 8% becomes:
    $111,684 in 20 years
    $362,232 in 30 years
$500 a month at 8% when the contribution also grows at 8% becomes:
    $558,000 in 20 years
    $1,810,000 in 30 years

---

total grows to almost $2 million in thirty years. *Thus, beginning with $500-a-month savings rate, earning 8 percent on the money, and increasing the monthly amount set aside at an 8 percent rate per year, you would approach multimillionaire status in thirty years.* The preceding statement reflects nothing more than arithmetic. It does, however, illustrate a feasible path to getting rich slowly.

We see from the above discussion that a relatively modest savings program can, through the power of compound interest, produce impressive results for a patient investor. Setting aside $100 a month or even $500 a month is well within the range of many aspiring investors. The average long-term return on stocks has been in the range of 9 to 11 percent. Thus earning 6 to 8 percent on your investments, while taking no more than a modest amount of risk, should be a realistic objective. True, taxes may reduce the return. If, however, the savings program is part of a retirement plan, the money will grow untaxed until you start to draw it out. Even if the portfolio's income is subject to taxation, careful tax management can substantially reduce the tax bite. Thus earning 8 percent after taxes is not an unreasonable objective. Many investors should also be able to increase the amount that they put aside as their professional career progresses. If you are a high achiever on a fast track professionally, an 8 percent growth rate in your earnings and savings should be well within reach. A modest savings program, patience, and a decent rate of return is all that is required to become reasonably wealthy. You supply the savings and patience, and I'll give you some ideas on how to achieve an attractive rate of return on your investments.

Is $500 a month a realistic initial savings goal? The answer to that question will vary with individual circumstances. Perhaps you believe that putting this much money aside each month is an unrealistic objective. Maybe it is. But consider the following: Suppose you and your spouse have a combined income of $60,000 a year. Five hundred dollars a month amounts to $6,000, or 10 percent of that income. That may seem like a large fraction of your income to try to save and invest. But if you own your home and make mortgage payments of, let's say, $1,200 a month, you are already putting aside at least $200 a month in amortization of the loan balance. If your house appreciates at 3 percent a year and you put 25 percent down, your investment in your home will be growing at 12 percent a year ($4 \times 3\% = 12\%$), well above our 8 percent target. Moreover, as you pay down the principal on your mortgage, the percentage of your mortgage payment that is applied to loan amortization (as opposed to interest) will increase. That mortgage pay-down of $200 a month takes care of two-fifths of your savings/investment program. Will your home's value appreciate at 3 percent a year? Maybe or maybe not. But from 1975 to 2003 the average house's market value increased at a rate of 5.6 percent. So, by recent historical standards, a 3 percent appreciation rate may actually be conservative.

Now for the other $300, consider the impact of taxes. You are already likely to be in at least the 25 percent tax bracket. If not, you will probably be there before long. That means that if you put $300 a month into a tax-sheltered retirement account (e.g., IRA, Keogh, 401K, etc.), you will reduce your tax bill by at least $75 a month. That tax savings takes care of another chunk of your savings/investment program.

Under the above circumstances, the out-of-pocket costs of a $500-a-month savings plan is reduced to $225 a month, or two thousand seven hundred dollars a year. That sum represents 4.5 percent of a $60,000 annual income, still a lot of money. But to put it into perspective, 4.5 percent is less than the amount already deducted from your salary for Social Security. Thus we see that beginning a savings/investment program by setting aside $500 a month should be well within reach for many readers of this book. Now let's turn our attention to how you might go about achieving that 8 percent (or better) return.

I
INVESTMENT MECHANICS

A useful place to start learning about investing is with the basics. Little could be more basic to investing than the mechanics of how to buy and sell securities. And yet most investment resources ignore or only lightly treat this important topic. I shall not make that mistake.

This section addresses four topics related to understanding and making effective use of various aspects of the mechanics of the investment markets. First, we discuss several issues that involve implementing security market trades, and the choice of brokers is discussed. Second, options contracts, including puts and calls and how to use them to buy and sell securities, are explored. Third, the uses of leverage and margin borrowing are considered. Finally, the complex but important topics of taxes, tax shelters, and tax management are addressed. Enhancing your understanding of each of these matters should help you manage your investment portfolio more effectively. If you are a relatively inexperienced investor, mastering these investment mechanics issues is especially important. Even if you are a relatively experienced investor, you still may be able to learn some useful tricks.

1

Securities

Buying and selling securities and other types of investment assets is different from, and more complicated than, buying and selling most other types of goods and services. The vast majority of the items that you buy as a consumer are purchased directly from the seller (e.g., supermarket or department store) at a fixed price. That fixed price is set by the seller. You pay the price that the seller sets or you don't buy from that seller. You can shop around or wait for a sale, but at the end of the day, you still have to deal with whatever price the seller sets. The prices of securities, in contrast, (e.g., stocks or bonds) are not set by either the seller or the buyer. They result from competition in the marketplace. That is, security prices are determined by the direct interplay of supply and demand. Such prices are literally changing from moment to moment. Moreover, buying and selling securities rarely involves a direct exchange from the seller to the buyer. You must almost always utilize the services of a broker. And this broker will charge you a commission for facilitating your trade. Finally, the vast majority of security market transactions take place either on an exchange or through an organized over-the-counter market.

An exchange, such as the New York Stock Exchange (NYSE), provides an established centralized market for trading a specific list of securities. Such *listed* securities have qualified for trading on that exchange by applying for listing and meeting a set of prespecified criteria. These criteria include the company issuing the securities having: at least the required minimum amount

of capital, number of publicly traded shares outstanding, past record of profitability, and so on. Most relatively large companies list their securities on the
NYSE. Somewhat smaller companies may choose to list on our second national
exchange, called the American Stock Exchange, or AMEX. Regional exchanges
located in various cities (Chicago, San Francisco, Philadelphia, Boston, etc.)
round out the list of U.S. exchanges. Many foreign exchanges also permit U.S.
securities to trade. During the trading day, European markets open well before
those in the United States, while Asian markets continue trading long after U.S.
markets have closed. Something close to twenty-four-hour trading takes place
in many different assets (e.g., U.S. Treasury securities, gold, crude oil, actively
traded U.S. and foreign stocks).

Most publicly traded securities (by number but not by dollar value) are not
listed on an exchange. These securities are bought and sold in a less organized
trading arrangement called the over-the-counter (OTC) market. Almost but
not quite all of the OTC market is under the supervision of the National
Association of Security Dealers (NASD) and are part of the market called
NASDAQ. In this NASDAQ/OTC market, individual dealers located throughout the country "make a market" in selected unlisted securities. Such dealers
make a market by standing ready to trade on either side of the market and
quoting prices at which they are willing to buy and sell. NASDAQ provides an
electronic connection among these dealers. Some exchange-listed securities
also trade over the counter in what is called the *third market*. Small, obscure
securities not listed for trading by NASDAQ may trade in a relatively inactive
OTC market known as the *pink sheets* market.

A variety of mechanisms has been developed to facilitate the trading of
securities. These mechanisms are designed to allow those who are interested in
buying a particular security and those who are interested in selling that same
security to find and conduct business with each other. Special arrangements
have been developed for those who seek to buy or sell large amounts of a
particular security.

In order to manage their buying and selling of securities effectively, investors
need to understand the various ways that securities are traded. A poorly executed security market trade can cause you to pay too much for an investment
that you buy or receive too little for an investment that you sell. The difference
between an effectively or ineffectively handled transaction can have a significant
impact on your portfolio's overall return. I shall now discuss several rules designed to help you obtain the benefits of executing your trades efficiently.

To make the bid-ask spread work for you, use limit orders.

In order to buy or sell a security (such as a stock or bond), you need to
explain to your broker what you want to do. You do so by giving him or her
an *order* that contains the information needed to implement your trade. All

such orders will identify the specific asset and the amount of it to be traded as well as whether the asset is to be bought or sold. The vast majority of securities trades are implemented with what are called *market orders*. Such orders call for an immediate execution at the best currently available price. The order will be sent to the marketplace (exchange, NASDAQ, etc.) where the security is traded. Other investors will already be present in the marketplace offering to buy or sell the security at various prices, which they have prespecified. If trading in that particular security is active, a number of different orders will already have been entered but not yet executed. Potential buyers (sellers) will be offering to pay up (sell down) to a prespecified price. For example, would-be buyers may be offering to pay as much as $31.15 for the stock. Would-be sellers may be offering to sell the same stock for as little as $31.50. An interested investor observing this market would see buyers available at $31.15 and sellers available at $31.50.

A market order to buy will usually result in a purchase at the *ask,* which is the lowest currently available offer (from someone else) to sell. In the above example, someone is offering to sell at $31.50. Similarly, a market order to sell will generally be executed at the *bid,* which is the best currently available offer (from someone else) to buy. In the above example, someone is offering to buy at $31.15.

The bid will almost always be below the ask. Otherwise the two sides of the market would trade directly with each other. Such a trade would remove both the buyer and the seller from the marketplace. This process of matching buyers with sellers would continue until no one wanted to sell for as low a price as anyone was willing to pay. At that point, a gap would appear between the bid and ask prices.

The difference between the bid and ask is called the *spread* or *bid-ask spread.* In the above example the spread would be $31.50 − $31.15 = $0.35. The level of trading activity in the security largely determines the size of the bid-ask spread. For less actively traded securities, the spread can be quite wide. For actively traded securities, competition tends to drive the spread down to a narrow range. The arrival of decimal trading (as opposed to fractional pricing, in which the minimum increment was typically at one-eighth of a dollar, or 12.5 cents) has tended to reduce spreads. Most securities prices can now be quoted to the penny. For options the minimum increment is five cents.

Those who use market orders to implement their transactions generally will find that they have bought at the ask and sold at the bid. Such an investor incurs not only a commission (the broker's fee for processing the order), but also the adverse impact of the bid-ask spread. Suppose a stock is quoted at $20 bid, $20.30 asked. If you entered a market order to buy the stock, you would probably pay $20.30 A market order to sell the stock would likely be executed at $20.00. With a market order you are almost certain to pay a higher price if you are buying than the price you would receive if you were selling. The difference between the bid and the ask in this instance is 30 cents ($20.30 − $20.00 = $0.30). Depending largely on how actively it trades, the spread on the $20 stock could range from no more than a few pennies all the way up to a dollar or more. Our example of a spread of 30 cents is in line with what you might encounter for a stock that trades in a moderately actively market. A spread of 30 cents on a $20 stock amounts to about 1.5 percent of the value of the trade. That 1.5 percent may not seem like a lot. If, however, a spread of such a magnitude is incurred on each trade, the impact will quickly add up. A 30-cent spread amounts to $30 on a hundred shares and $300 on a thousand shares.

One way to save a few basis points in transaction costs and thereby enhance your return would be to reduce the adverse impact of this bid-ask spread. Rather than relying on market orders, you could utilize more sophisticated trading techniques (to be explained), which have been designed to facilitate trading at more attractive prices. If those techniques allow you to save as little as fifty basis points (0.5%) on each trade and even if you hold stocks for an average of two years (a long time for many investors), their use will enhance your annual return by 0.25 percent. The more actively you trade, and the larger the spreads, the more money you are likely to save by executing trades more efficiently.

As previously noted, most trades are implemented with market orders. Using market orders to buy and sell securities is simple and easy but may result in your receiving less or paying more than is necessary. Less experienced investors are especially likely to use a market order for their trades. Stockbrokers also generally prefer that their clients use market orders. Such orders are certain to be executed and thereby result in a commission for the broker. But you can often do better on price by using a different type of order. A more opportunistic way to trade securities involves the use of a more flexible order type. A *limit order* provides that greater degree of flexibility. It allows you to specify the highest price that you will pay to buy or the lowest price that you will accept to sell your security. Using a limit order to implement your trade may allow you to reduce the adverse impact of the bid-ask spread. In the current example (bid = $20; ask = $20.30) you could enter a limit order to buy the stock at $20.01 or to sell it at $20.29. Such limit orders would place you in the front of what had been the market (by a penny). You would then be waiting at the front of the line hoping to enter into a trade with the next incoming market order. In a somewhat more aggressive strategy, you could enter a buy order below the current bid or, if you are looking to sell, a sell order with a threshold price a bit above the current ask. If the market encounters some selling (buying) pressure, the market price could decline (rise) to the threshold level specified in your order. Such an order to sell (buy) would be executed only if the market for the stock were to rise (fall) a bit. So for the current example, with a bid of 20 and ask of 20.30, you might offer to sell (buy) at 20.40 (19.85). Such an order would, when entered, be 15 cents above (below) the current ask (bid). By placing your order at that level, you would be positioning yourself to take advantage of what you hope will be a rise (fall) in the stock's price. Clearly such a hoped-for rise (fall) may or may not occur. The further away from the current market price that you place your order, the less likely you are to trade. On the other hand, the more aggressive your limit order placement, the better the price you will receive if you do trade.

Most limit orders are structured so that they will remain available for execution throughout the day in which they are entered. If, however, the limit order remains unfilled at the end of that day, the order expires. Such limit orders are called *day orders*. Alternatively, the order may be structured to remain on the books until execute or canceled (a *good till canceled* or *GTC* order). Such a GTC order would remain available for execution day after day until it either results in a trade or the investor instructs his or her broker to cancel the order.

Carefully analyze the relevant facts in order to set the threshold price on your limit order advantageously.

When you enter a limit order, you must specify the threshold price at which the order is to be implemented. Determining where to place your limit order's threshold price is an important strategic decision. If you are seeking to buy, you want to set your threshold price as low as you can and still purchase the stock (or possibly other security). Similarly if you wish to sell, you want to set the threshold as high as you can get away with and still sell the stock in a timely manner. Deciding where to set the threshold price level on a limit order involves both analysis and guesswork. You should start by gathering as much relevant trading information as you can. Determining the current daily and weekly trading ranges (high, low) for a given stock may provide you with some idea about where to place your order. Stock price movements do not generally follow any particular pattern. Still, stocks do often seem to trade within a price range, at least for a time. A particular stock's price may, for example, move back and forth between a range for the bid and range for the ask. The more volatile the stock, the wider the range. So identifying the recent range of trading is a useful place to start in trying to decide where to set the threshold price on a limit order.

Suppose that you wish to buy 100 shares of SS stock with a current quote of 15.30 bid and 15.45 asked, a daily high/low of 15.60 to 15.23, and a weekly high/low of 16.00 and 15.05. Where might you place your limit order for maximum advantage? Several possibilities present themselves: With a current bid of 15.30, entering an order of 15.31 would put you at the front of the line for any incoming market orders to sell. As long as no one enters a higher bid, you would continue to hold that front-of-the-line position until your order was filled. With an actively traded stock, such an order would very likely be filled. An offer in the 15.20–15.30 range, while below or equal to the current bid, would still be likely to be executed if the stock retraces its price levels of earlier in the day (prior low of 15.23). A weekly low of 15.05 suggests that any threshold price above 15 might have a reasonable chance of being executed, that is as long as the stock stays in the same range it has been in. So we see that, given this set of information, you might choose to enter a limit order to buy at prices ranging from 15.01 up to about 15.31 depending upon how willing you are to risk that your order will not be executed. A similar analysis would apply to the placement of the threshold price for a sell order. The lower (higher) you place the threshold on your limit order to buy (sell), the better the price you will pay (receive) if your order results in a trade, but the smaller the chance that your order will in fact be filled. Limit orders do not assure an execution. For an actively traded stock, however, the odds of a well-placed limit order being executed are generally quite good.

Another guide in the placement of limit orders is to get in front of *focal point numbers*. A focal point price is one where orders tend to congregate. They are price levels toward which the threshold price of the typical investor tends to gravitate when placing an order. For example, if a stock is trading in a range centered around 20, relevant focal points would be 19, 19.50, 20, 20.50, and 21. Such numbers have the look and feel of being clear, clean, and round. An investor is much more likely to decide, "I will sell my stock when it gets to $20," rather than, "I am waiting for the stock to reach $19.97." Such an investor is likely to place his or her limit orders accordingly. If you are looking to sell, you might take advantage of the situation by entering a sell limit order at 19.99. At that price you would be just a penny below 20.00, where a substantial number of sell orders may have already accumulated. Your offer to sell at 19.99 would have to be executed before any of the orders to sell at 20 could be filled. Limit orders entered at identical prices are to be executed in the order of their receipt. A new order to sell at 20 would be placed in line behind all of those orders that preceded your order. Some shares of the stock could trade at 20 without your order being filled. Similarly, a buy order at 19.51 would be appreciably more likely to be filled than one at 19.50, where limit orders may have already started to accumulate.

Finally, you should check the stock's recent volume history to see how frequently it trades. A stock that typically trades tens of thousands of shares daily will generally have a narrow spread. Because it trades actively, a strategically placed limit order is very likely to be executed. A stock that trades only a few hundred shares a day is likely to have a wider spread, but limit orders on such stocks are less likely to result in trades. And yet the wider spreads of less actively traded stocks may make limit orders particularly attractive to use in such situations.

> **Market and Limit Orders**
>
> *Market Order:* Must be implemented immediately at the best currently available price.
>
> > A market order to buy will usually be executed at the *ask* price (the lowest currently available offer to sell).
> > A market order to sell will usually be executed at the *bid* price (the highest currently available offer to buy).
> > The ask will almost always be higher than the bid.
> > The difference between the bid and the ask is called the *spread* or the bid-ask spread.
>
> *Limit Order:* The trader specifies the minimally acceptable price level at which his or her trade can take place. Unless this level is reached, the order will not be executed.
>
> > A limit order to buy specifies the maximum price that the investor is willing to pay.
> > A limit order to sell specifies the minimum price that the investor will accept.
>
> *GTC Limit Orders:* Good until canceled. GTC orders remain on the books until they are either implemented or canceled.
>
> *Day Limit Orders:* Canceled at the end of the trading day if they remain unexecuted.

When obtaining a quote, be sure to ask for full details, including "size."

If you ask your broker for a quote on a security, he or she will usually report the last price at which the stock was traded. If you obtain your quote from the Internet, you will generally see only the last reported trade price, with a fifteen-minute delay. You can subscribe to any one of a number of services that provide real-time quotes (e.g., pcquote: http://marketsmart-real.pcquote.com), but you must pay a fee for the service (about $10 a month). The last reported trade price, whether real-time or fifteen-minute-delayed, is not always representative of the current state of the market or, more important, the price at which you can trade. For example, the last reported trade could have taken place at the bid. If you enter a market order to buy, you will probably pay the ask, which will be above the bid by the amount of the spread. Indeed, the last trade price may be a stale quote from hours or even days earlier.

To trade effectively, you need access to a full set of relevant information on the current state of the market for the security that interests you. You should base your trading decisions on as much relevant up-to-date market information as you can obtain. In particular, you need to know not only the current real-time bid and ask prices, but also the *"size."* The "size" is the amount of stock bid for at the current bid level as well as the amount offered for sale at the current ask level. Information on size may provide some indication of where the stock's price is going to move next and thus where to place a limit order.

Suppose you contact your broker to request a quote on a stock that interests you. You are told that it has a bid of $18.25 and an ask of $18.40. That much of a quote provides you with some idea of the range where the next trade is likely to take place as well as the price level at which you might be able to buy or sell a small amount of the stock. Such a quote does not, however, provide you with any indication of the market's depth or potential direction. Information on size, in contrast, may help with these matters. For example, a size of 25×1 (2,500 shares bid and 100 shares offered) suggests that buying interest is much greater than selling interest. A bidder (or perhaps several bidders) is (are) seeking to purchase a significant quantity of stock, but no large would-be seller is visible. Indeed, the very small size offer to sell 100 shares may be from the *specialist* (the person on the exchange charged with making a market in the stock). If the stock typically trades about 1,000 shares in a day, a bidder seeking to purchase 2,500 shares may eventually need to raise his or her bid in order to get some action.

If, in the above situation, you also want to buy the stock, you would have a strategic decision to make. One approach you might utilize would be to enter a limit order of $18.26, a penny above the bid. Entering that kind of order is called *pennying*. Placing such an order may put you in the front of the line. Pennying frequently works well when the other would-be orders are small. Pennying may well be worth a try, even when you are competing with a large order. Often, however, the large buyer offering to pay $18.25 will turn around and penny you with a bid of $18.27. The two of you could then play penny Ping-Pong with the bid. As each of you is raising the other's bid by a penny, those on the sell side will see what is going on and may well raise the ask. And meanwhile, you would not have bought any stock. Under these circumstances you might consider using alternative strategies. You could, for example, either enter a limit order well above the current bid or just to pay the ask. Yet another approach to consider,

---

A Full Quote

Last: Last price at which the stock was traded.
Bid: Highest currently available offer to buy the stock.
Ask: Lowest currently available offer to sell the stock.
Size: Amount of stock currently bid for and offered for sale. A size of 10×20 means that 10 lots of 100 shares each (1,000 shares) are bid for, and 20 lots (2,000 shares) are offered for sale at the current bid and ask prices respectively.
Volume: Number of shares traded so far today.
High: Highest trade price reached today.
Low: Lowest trade price reached today.

particularly if the size of the bid is small, is to match the existing bid. Thus if the current bid is $18.25, you can also offer to buy stock at $18.25. That bid level puts you behind the earlier bid but does not set up a penny Ping-Pong.

On the other hand, if you are looking to sell stock and a large buyer has appeared, you may want to offer your stock at a somewhat higher price than otherwise. In any case, you should ask for a detailed quote before you enter an order. More knowledge on the state of the market is always better than less. Effective use of that knowledge can help you trade more efficiently. And the more effectively you implement your trades, the higher your return.

Don't be too aggressive in your limit order placement.

Patience and the use of limit orders can help you to obtain a better price on many trades. You do not, however, want to miss out on an attractive investment opportunity because you were holding out for a few extra cents per share. Suppose you have reason to believe that the price of a stock in which you are interested is to about to make a major move. Perhaps the company will soon announce earnings that you believe will be better than the markets expect. Perhaps you think the company is an attractive takeover candidate and likely to receive an offer. In either case the stock's price could quickly start to move up. Clearly you don't want to wait around with an aggressively placed limit order and thereby risk not buying into an attractive investment situation. You can still use a limit order to buy the stock, but you should enter it with a limit price threshold at or near the ask. That way you are still likely to buy the stock but you have protected yourself against the possibility of an adverse price change between the time your order is entered and when it is executed.

Understand the uses and limitations of stop loss orders.

The vast majority of orders to buy or sell securities are either market or limit orders. Several other types of orders exist, but are much more rarely used. The *stop loss order* is one such order type. On relatively rare occasions it may be advantageous to employ such an order. Stop loss orders, like limit orders, are contingent orders. Such orders are implemented only if a pre-specified threshold price level is reached. Limit orders are generally entered in an attempt to take advantage of a hoped-for favorable price move (down if you seek to buy, up if you seek to sell). Stop loss orders, in contrast, are designed to provide protection from an adverse price movement (e.g., down if you already own the stock).

To understand how stop loss orders work, consider an example. Suppose you purchase 500 shares of XYZ at a price of $20 per share for a total cost of $10,000. While you hope to make a profit on the investment, you would also prefer to limit your potential losses. Perhaps you would like to put a floor that would limit your losses to no more than 20 percent, or $2,000 of the $10,000 that you have invested. In other words, you want to ensure that you preserve at least $8,000 of the $10,000 that you put at risk when you made the investment. In this type of situation you could use a stop loss order. Such an order can be designed to provide a degree of protection against a large loss. For example, you could enter a stop loss sell order with a stop loss threshold price of 16. If a decline in the stock's price triggered your stop loss order, selling out your position at 16 would yield proceeds of $8,000 (less commissions), thereby recovering about 80 percent of the amount that you invested.

The contingent stop loss order would be entered into the books of the specialist. As long as the market price stays above 16, the stop loss order would not cause a trade to occur. If the stock's price either rises, stays at 20, or falls a couple of points but remains above 16, the sell order would remain on the books, unimplemented. If, however, the stock does drop to 16 or lower, the stop loss order immediately comes into play. If and when the market price first touches 16, the stop loss order requires that the stock must immediately be sold at the highest currently available price. The price received for the stop loss sale could be exactly 16, but it may be a bit lower. For the stop loss order to be implemented, the stock must have already dropped from 20 to 16. If the stock continues falling, the very next trade after it touches 16 will be below 16. Sometimes the sudden and unexpected release of bad news causes a stock's price to drop like a stone. If such bad news has just been released, the stock could quickly sell through this stop loss threshold. The next trade after the stop loss order is triggered by a trade at 16 could be 15 or lower. Most of the time a stop loss order, if implemented, will result in a trade at a price that is close to the stop loss threshold. But such a result is not guaranteed.

A stop loss order is used to protect the investor from an adverse price change, usually to limit exposure to a potential loss. Sometimes, however, a stop loss order is used to protect an existing gain. Suppose that the stock you bought at 20 (and entered a protective stop loss order for at 16) rises to 30. For a stock trading at a price of 30, a stop loss order with a threshold price of 16 is rather far away from the market. Having such a stop loss order in place at that level is essentially irrelevant. If you want to continue to protect your position, you could probably safely raise your stop loss threshold to 25. If the stop loss order is later implemented at 25, you will almost certainly sell your stock at a profit (above 20). If the stock's price continues to rise, you can continue to increase the threshold price level of your stop loss order. If, for example, the stock's price rises to 40, you could put in a stop loss order at 35. This strategy of raising your stop loss price threshold as your stock's price increases is called the *crawling peg* approach.

Stop loss orders may seem like an attractive mechanism for limiting your loss exposure while leaving open the potential for gain. You should realize, however, that *the market never gives anything away*. A stop loss sell order will indeed ensure that if the prespecified price is reached, your stock will be sold. But this type of order also has some drawbacks. It's protection is bought at a price.

First, the price that you receive will depend upon the state of the market at the point when the order is activated. Sometimes the relevant stock's price may blow through the stop level with such force that the very next trade after the stock first trades at the threshold price is much lower still. Indeed, if bad news is released after the market has closed, the stock may open well below its previous close, and perhaps well below your stop loss threshold price.

Second, because stock prices often fluctuate widely, having a stop loss order in place may cause you to sell out your position too soon. You may buy a stock and see it fall dramatically and then rise just as dramatically. If your stop loss order is implemented by the dramatic price decline, your position will be liquidated. You will have limited your losses. You won't, however, remain an owner even if this volatile stock rebounds.

Continuing with our prior example, the stock that you bought at 20 could fall to 15 and then rise to 25 on its way to 40. Your stop loss order with a threshold price of 16 would have limited your loss when the stock was falling but also prevented you from earning a profit when the stock's price turned around and rose dramatically. To reduce this type of threat, you should not set your threshold price too close to the current level. The more volatile the stock, the greater is the threat of being whipsawed by a down and up price move.

Third, stop loss orders are structured to work efficiently only for stocks that trade on exchanges. Stocks that trade on NASDAQ are not well suited for stop loss orders. Your broker may accept the order but will not guarantee its execution. NASDAQ stocks do not have a specialist to keep track of such orders (stop loss or limit). No one among the multiple market makers of OTC stocks is identified as responsible for implementing stop loss orders.

To minimize your current tax liability, use "versus purchase" orders.

You are required by the IRS to report the profit or loss on any investment asset sale on your tax return. Your results from this trade will have an impact on your overall tax liability. To determine that profit or loss, you must report what you paid for the asset that you sold. Your cost for tax purposes is called your *tax basis* in the investment. The tax basis is the amount that is subtracted from your sales proceeds in order to determine the size of the capital gain or loss that you must report on your tax return. If all of the initial position was acquired at the same time for the same price, the basis is easy to determine. It is the total amount paid (including the commission) for the investment. If you sell only a part of your position, the total amount of the basis is prorated. If the total position was acquired for different prices at different times, different bases apply to different parts of the position. If the entire position is sold, the basis is the total cost of the position regardless of whether or not it was purchased all at once. Sometimes, however, only part of a position is sold. When that happens, identifying which per share cost to use for the basis is not clear-cut. This is one type of situation where understanding investment mechanics can help you save some serious money.

The IRS permits you to determine the taxable basis in one of three ways. Normally the cost of the longest-held position is identified as the basis. Alternatively, the average cost may be used. If, however, the earliest purchase is not also the highest cost, using it as the basis will cause you to report a higher taxable gain (or smaller taxable loss) than would be the case if a more advantageous basis had been selected and applied. Similarly, using the average cost will result in a higher tax liability than necessary, if the position was acquired for different prices over time.

Versus purchase orders provides the investor with a third way of determining the basis. Using a versus purchase order allows you to specify for tax purposes which unused cost basis to apply to a particular trade. You simply instruct your broker to enter the order as versus purchase and then select the unused basis that you wish to apply (normally the highest cost). Suppose, for example, that you bought five separate 100-share blocks of stock at prices of 12, 17, 23, 19, and 27, and then sold 100 shares at 30. Your reported taxable gain could be anywhere from $1,800 (basis of 12) to $300 (basis of 27). In this example, if you used the *first in, first out* (FIFO) approach (the approach that the IRS would expect you to use if you did not employ a versus purchase order), you would report the highest taxable gain possible for this set of facts. Reporting the highest gain will cause you to pay the greatest amount in taxes. Using a versus purchase order to minimize the reported size of the gain (or maximizing the reported loss), allows you to reduce your *current* tax liability.

Calculating the Basis: An Example

Shares Purchased	Price Per Share	Basis
100	12	1,200
100	17	1,700
100	23	2,300
100	19	1,900
100	27	2,700
Total		$9,800

Average Cost   9,800/500 = 19
Basis if the cost of first purchase is used $1,200
Basis if the highest cost is used $2,700

Reported gain on sale of 100 shares at 30

Average cost basis	3,000 − 1,900 = $1,100	Tax @ 15% = $165
First cost basis	3,000 − 1,200 = $1,800	Tax @ 15% = $270
Highest cost basis	3,000 − 2,700 = $300	Tax @ 15% = $45

This strategy of minimizing your current reported gains will, to be sure, use up the lowest basis. You can use the high-basis trades for tax purposes only once. As a result, you will have to report greater gains and incur larger tax liabilities when additional shares are sold at a later time. Nonetheless, you are usually well advised to use this strategy to put off the higher tax liability. *Paying lower taxes now and putting off the higher tax liability until later is like receiving an interest-free loan from the IRS.* Read on.

Defer tax liabilities when possible.

Deferring tax liabilities is very generally advantageous for the investor. Using a higher basis, when it is available, allows the investor to report a lower tax liability currently and put off the realization of a greater tax liability into the future. Putting off having to pay taxes until the following year will thereby free up, for a year, the amount of money that was deferred. As a result, you can save a year's interest cost on that sum of money.

Most investors are also borrowers in one capacity or another. You may, for example, owe money on an auto loan, home equity loan, credit card loan, and/or margin debt. If so, you will be incurring an interest charge on each of these debts. If you defer what would otherwise be a current tax liability, you can (and perhaps should) use the freed up funds to pay down such a debt, particularly the one with the highest interest rate. Suppose you are carrying a credit card balance of $1,000. Deferring a tax liability for a year could free up enough money to allow you to pay off that debt. You will save $180 in interest cost (assuming an 18 percent rate). In effect you earn an 18 percent after-tax return on that transaction. If you (wisely) don't carry a balance on your credit card, perhaps you do at least have an auto or home equity loan balance that you can pay down. Even if you don't have any outstanding debts that you could pay off or pay down, having an extra thousand dollars to invest for a year is at least worth the amount of interest (or other return) that you could earn on the freed-up funds.

Another advantage to deferring a tax liability may apply. Moving a tax liability into a subsequent year may also mean that the tax rate applied to the income will be lower when the tax is due. Indeed, if you are nearing retirement, putting off a tax liability until after you have retired could place you in a lower tax bracket when you begin to receive your (typically lower) retirement income. If, however, you expect to be in a higher tax bracket next year, you may want to use the lowest reportable basis in order to accelerate the tax liability and thereby take advantage of this year's lower rate.

Be aware of the existence of stop limit, all-or-nothing, and fill-or-kill orders. You may occasionally find them to be useful.

We have already discussed the three primary types of orders: market, limit, and stop loss. We have also explained how an order can be specified as day,

GTC, and/or versus purchase. For the sake of completeness, we shall now explore three other variations in orders: *stop limit orders, all-or-nothing orders, and fill-or-kill orders*. Very rarely will the typical small investor need to use these variations. Nonetheless, you might as well have them in your bag of tricks.

Stop limit orders are much like stop loss orders. With a stop loss order, if the relevant stock trades at or through a particular prespecified threshold price, your contingent (stop loss) order to sell or buy is immediately converted into a market order. Thus, if you have a stop loss sell order on a stock with a threshold price of 21, your stock will be offered for sale (at the highest currently available price) immediately after the next time that the stock trades at 21. Your stock may be sold for 21. If, however, the market for that stock is moving quickly, it may end up being sold at a lower price. A stop limit order is structured to avoid this scenario. Once the stock trades at 21, a stop limit sell order with a threshold price of 21 would activate the entry of a limit order at 21. Your stock would be offered for sale at 21. Using this type of order would protect your position from being sold out at a price lower than 21. But the stop limit order would not ensure that your position was liquidated. The market could trade right through your threshold price level without stopping to allow your stop limit order to be executed at the prespecified limit price.

An all-or-nothing order requires that your securities be traded as a single block. Suppose you want to sell 700 shares of a particular stock. Normally, if you enter a limit order to sell the block at a prespecified price, anytime a buyer appears at that price for as little as 100 shares, part of your block will be sold. You would often be able to sell most or all of your position one piece at a time during the course of the day. On other days, however, you may achieve only a partial sale and, as a result, you would frequently be left with the remainder. Selling pieces at a time over the course of several days is likely to result in a higher total commission charge than what would be incurred if all of the trade occurred on a single day. Moreover, you may just want either to liquidate your entire position or, if that is not possible, hold on to all of it. To be sure of selling (or buying) the entire amount or if not, none at all, you can enter your order as all-or-nothing. Such an order must be executed as a single block or not at all. With such an all-or-nothing order, you give up the chance of selling (buying) all of your position a piece at a time, but you achieve the certainty of knowing that if you do trade, you will sell (buy) it all at once.

Generally, limit orders are entered as day or GTC. A rarely used third option is to enter the order as fill-or-kill. A fill-or-kill order is to be presented to the market, and if it is not executed upon its arrival, it is immediately canceled.

Stop limit, all-or-nothing, and fill-or-kill order types are only seldom useful to the small individual investor. You may never need to use them or, if you do, you will find them useful to employ only on rare occasions.

Stop Limit, All-or-Nothing and Fill-or-Kill Order

Stop Limit Order: A contingent order to buy or sell at a prespecified price. The order becomes executable when a prespecified threshold price is reached.
All-or-Nothing Order: An order that must be filled in its entirety or not at all.
Fill-or-Kill Order: A limit order that must either be executed upon reaching the floor or if this is not possible, it must immediately be cancelled.

Use discount/Internet brokers in order to minimize commissions.

The brokerage commission that is assessed on a given securities market trade can vary enormously depending upon which type of broker is used. The commission charge can amount to a substantial percentage of the monetary value of a transaction, particularly on a small trade. Full-service brokerage firms (Merrill Lynch, Solomon Smith Barney, etc.) generally charge the highest commission rates. They utilize a formula based on both the number of shares and the dollar value of the trade. The formula produces a commission charge that increases at a decreasing rate as both the number of shares and the dollar value of the trade rises. Thus the commission on a large-value trade is greater in dollar terms, but less as a percentage of the trade's monetary value than that of an otherwise similar, smaller-value trade. Similarly, for two trades having the same dollar value, the one involving the largest number of shares would incur the highest commissions. For modest-sized trades, the commission charged by these firms can easily amount to 2 to 3 percent of the money involved, and even more for very small trades and/or low price per share stocks. Furthermore, many full-service firms have commission minimums of $35 to $50. Applying such a minimum to very small dollar value trades can result in commission charges equal to 5 to 10 percent or more of the money involved in the trade (e.g., a $35 commission on a $300 trade). Indeed, *penny stocks,* stocks that trade for less than a dollar per share, can be particularly costly to buy and sell. Penny stocks typically not only incur high commissions, but also have large spreads.

As Table 1.1 illustrates, the highest full-service commission rates (in percentage terms) apply to small dollar value trades of low-price stocks. This table shows that a full-service firm's commission on a 100-share trade of a one- to five-dollar stock amounts to about 20 percent of the cost of the stock itself. A 1,000-share trade of a one (five)-dollar stock still incurs a rather high 7 percent (4.3 percent) commission. Commission rates decline to the 2 percent range on 500-share trades of stock priced at $20 per share or higher.

A commission is charged on both the purchase and the sale of a securities position. So if you end up paying commissions of 2 percent, 7 percent, or 20 percent on a trade, the corresponding round-trip cost for both buying and selling the position amounts to 4 percent, 14 percent, or a whopping 40

TABLE 1.1.   Typical Full-Service Commissions

Price Per Share	100 Shares	500 Shares	1,000 Shares
$1	$20.60 (20.6%)	$70.00 (14%)	$70.00 (7%)
$5	$50.00 (20%)	$120.00 (4.8%)	$218.45 (4.3%)
$10	$50.00 (10%)	$171.95 (3.4%)	$293.86 (2.9%)
$20	$65.02 (6.5%)	$247.36 (2.5%)	$433.77 (2.2%)
$50	$110.50 (2.2%)	$443.28 (1.8%)	$669.00 (1.4%)
$100	$110.50 (1.1%)	$552.50 (1.1%)	$988.55 (1.0%)

percent of the security's principal value. Such costs, particularly at the high end, could take a huge bite out of any gross profit (or perhaps turn it into a loss) that might be made on the transaction. Clearly commission costs are a drag on portfolio performance that need to be managed carefully and effectively.

Discount brokers charge less than full-service brokers. Rates vary, but discounts of 30 to 50 percent or more from the standard rates of full-service brokers are common. Full-service brokers will provide similar discounts to customers who give them a substantial amount of business. The lowest commission rates, however, are generally those charged by Internet brokers. Rather than applying a formula that can result in a large commission rate on sizable trades, Internet brokers generally charge a set fee of as little as $7 per trade. Clearly $7 per trade is much less than the $50 minimum that some full-service brokers charge. Similarly, the commission on a large dollar value trade may amount to several hundred dollars at a full-service firm compared with $7 at an Internet broker.

If Internet and discount brokers process trades for so much less than full-service brokers, why do so many investors still use full-service brokers? What do the full-service brokers have to offer in return for their much higher commission rates? A full-service broker is a flesh-and-blood account manager. This person is trained in the areas of financial planning, portfolio management, and investment selection. The brokerage firm itself has a research component that generates analysis and recommendations on the set of stocks that the firm covers. The firm is also involved in underwriting, which may allow the investor access to new issues and the like. You should not, however, expect to be allocated any of the hot new issues. These tend to go to the firm's favorites. Clearly, you need to decide whether the extra services available from a full-service firm are worth the extra cost. Often you will find that, once you gain a bit of experience, you have relatively little need for their help.

One could have the best of both worlds by opening accounts at both a full-service firm (for occasions when the extra service is needed) and at an Internet broker (when all that is needed are the tools to implement a trade).

Such an approach, however, makes sense only for investors who have relatively large accounts.

Avoid unnecessary trading.

Transaction costs are incurred every time you undertake a trade. These transaction costs include commissions, transfer fees, and the impact of bid-ask spreads. Additionally, for a large-size transaction, an order to buy may (temporarily) bid up the market price while a sizable sell order may push the price down. Each round-trip transaction (buy and sell) also has a tax implication. Unless the transaction involves securities that are part of a tax-sheltered retirement account (e.g., IRA), a tax will be due on the amount of any gain. If the gain is short-term (asset is held for less than a year), the tax liability is based on a much higher rate (your marginal tax rate on ordinary income, which could be as high as 35 percent or even more) than if the asset is held long enough to qualify for long-term tax treatment (a maximum of 15 percent). The more one trades, the greater are the transaction costs incurred and the greater are the tax impacts. Thus, overly active trading can have a substantially negative impact on returns.

You should limit your trading activity as much as you realistically can. If you trade excessively, your broker may make money (commissions) from your activity. But you probably won't. Moreover, a large number of small purchases and sales complicates record-keeping. If you don't already realize the importance of keeping well-maintained records, you will when you start to fill out your tax returns.

Take advantage of those dividend reinvestment plans that allow you to add to your holdings of a stock that you like.

Many companies offer their shareholders an opportunity to participate in a *dividend reinvestment plan* (DRIP). Such plans permit their stockholders to recycle their dividends into the purchase of additional shares or even fractional shares of the dividend-paying company. Some plans allow the shares to be purchased at a small discount (e.g., 5%) from the current market price. Under almost all such plans, little or no commission fee is charged on the purchases. Many plans also permit optional additional purchases. Thus DRIPs allow the shareholder to add to his or her position while incurring little or no transaction costs. Similarly, the sale of shares acquired in a DRIP will incur little or no commission charges if sold through the plan. The shareholder should participate if he or she wishes to acquire additional shares anyway, particularly where the stock can be bought at a discount. One caveat: Even though the dividend is being reinvested in the stock of the same company that paid it, income taxes are still due on the dividend-supplied funds that were used to buy more shares. The IRS always demands its cut.

*Block trades, tender offers, secondary distributions, and the super
DOT system are used for large trades. Understand how they
work and how they may impact the market.*

The vast majority of stock market trading takes place on an exchange or in
NASDAQ in the ordinary way, in small quantities of one or a few hundred
shares. The exchanges and NASDAQ are not, however, set up to facilitate the
execution of very large trades. A trade of up to several thousand shares can
usually be accommodated by the marketplace without undue difficulty.
Nothing more than standard trading mechanisms, such as market or limit
orders, are required in order for the trade to be implemented. If, however, ten
thousand or more shares are to be traded, the standard mechanisms often
do not work very effectively. The *specialist,* who manages trading in assigned
stocks on an exchange, is tasked with providing liquidity when temporary
market imbalances arise. If someone wishes to sell (buy) 500 or so shares and
no buyer (seller) is readily at hand, the specialist is expected to step into the
market and buy (sell). Specialists are expected (by the exchange) to buy or
sell at or close to the current price levels when no one else will. The specialist
does not, however, typically have enough capital to take (or enough shares to
sell) a substantial position in a large block of a single stock. Even if the
specialist does have sufficient capital available, he or she is unlikely to want to
assume the risks inherent in acquiring a very large position in a single stock.
Similarly, a sufficient number of readily available (nonspecialist) market participants willing to take a large enough position to absorb a sizable block of
stock may not be quickly available. Thus, the market can usually supply or
absorb up to a few thousand shares of most stocks without great difficulty, but
encounters problems with larger quantities.

Consider the hypothetical case of XYZ, a $20 stock that typically trades
5,000 or so shares a day. Dumping 30,000 shares of XYZ onto the market
could trigger a very substantial drop in the stock's price. A block of 30,000
shares of a $20 stock represents a total market value of $600,000 or so. That
sum represents about six times the value of an average day's trading in XYZ.
Six hundred thousand dollars is likely to represent a lot of money for those
who follow that particular stock closely. Some investors may be looking for a
buying opportunity. But they are unlikely to want or be able to come up with
such a sum quickly. The specialist is also very unlikely to want to risk that
much money on a single stock. A sufficient number of interested buyers may
be available on short notice to buy such a stock only if the price is much
lower. If you are seeking to sell such a large block, you don't want the process
of unloading your position to drive the price down dramatically. The lower
the price goes, the less you will receive for the sale of your position. You could
try to sell the block in pieces, a little at a time over the course of several days.
The marketplace, however, tends to recognize that a piecing-out sale is under
way when it sees a seemingly endless stream of sell orders. When that happens,

interest on the buy side tends to dry up. Once again, the market price would be driven down. And again, the more the price is driven down, the less value you, as a large seller, will derive from your position.

Mindful of the difficulty of using the normal market arrangements, the securities markets have developed several specialized mechanisms to sell (or buy) larger blocks of stock. These mechanisms are designed to mitigate the adverse market price impact of large trades. One such specialized mechanism relies upon an investment market professional called the *block trader*. To explore how block traders work, return to our situation where 30,000 shares need to be sold. Suppose the stock is now trading on the market with a bid-ask of 21.40/21.55 and a size of 10 × 10. Thus, a thousand shares are bid for at 21.40. You could indeed sell a thousand shares at that price. But selling only a thousand shares would leave you with 29,000 more shares to sell. Dropping 30,000 shares onto the market all at once could easily drive the price down into the mid-teens. Selling such a large block, if mishandled, would be very disruptive to the market. Such an approach might well result in a sale at a substantially lower average price than could otherwise have been obtained. Clearly you would prefer to avoid such an outcome. An experienced professional is needed in order to identify and seek out buyers who are willing to absorb the position. That is where the block trader comes in. He or she would be retained to undertake the task of identifying sufficient buying interest to facilitate the trade in a way that would not disrupt the market. The block trader could start by checking with the specialist in order to see how much potential demand is on the books (in other words, how many unfilled limit orders are available to purchase the stock at various prices). Institutional and large individual investors, particularly those who already have a position in the stock, could be contacted to see if any of them have an interest in adding to their holdings. The company itself might also be contacted in an effort to identify potentially interested investors. In this way the block trader would usually be able to generate some additional interest in the stock and thereby identify a number of potential buyers. After perhaps thirty minutes of calling around, the block trader would return to the seller with an offer to move the issue at a price somewhat below the current 21.50 price range. If enough interest was shown on the buy side, the block trader might propose to move the 30,000 share position at 21. A 50-cent-per-share discount ($21.50 − $21.00 = 50¢) to move a block of this size is likely to represent a significantly better result for the seller than the average sale price that would otherwise result. The block trader would receive a standard commission from both buyers and sellers as compensation for facilitating the transaction.

Block traders are able to handle positions in the tens of thousands, perhaps up to a hundred thousand or so shares. They cannot, however, be expected to find buyers (or sellers) for quantities that reach into the millions. Nonetheless, those wishing to sell such quantities do sometimes appear. For example, a foundation might need to sell several million shares of the founder's company, or an existing company may wish to raise capital by selling a large number of additional shares. Such a seller would not be able to use a block trader for such a large quantity. The block trader is simply not set up to handle trades of such a magnitude. Rather, the seller would need to utilize what is called a *secondary distribution*. An *underwriter* (investment bank/brokerage firm) or syndicate of underwriters would be assembled for the purpose of selling a large quantity of shares via a secondary distribution. The underwriters would offer the shares to their customers in a special sale at a specified fixed price. This offer price is usually set a bit below the range where the stock was trading before the offering. The buyer is not charged a commission directly, but the seller gives up a portion of the purchase price to the underwriter as an underwriting fee. The sale usually takes place over the course of a day. Prior to the sale, the underwriter prepares an offering statement designed to explain the terms of and relevant information on the offer to potential buyers. This offering statement must be approved by the SEC for relevance, accuracy, and completeness before the sale can proceed.

We have already seen that very large sellers need special help to accomplish their desired transaction. Similarly, substantial buyers often need special help to accomplish their purchase of a very large block of shares. As with the sale of a large block of stock, an attempt to use the standard market mechanisms to purchase a substantial quantity of stock would be very likely to disrupt the market. As the buyer bought more and more shares, sellers would tend to disappear and the price in the marketplace would be likely to be bid up higher and higher. The buyer would start acquiring shares at the current level. Sooner or later, however, the relentless buying might cause the price to rise so high that the overall cost of the purchase would be much greater than planned or expected. Experienced investors would conclude that someone was trying to acquire a significant position. They would then be inclined to hold out for ever higher prices. Indeed, the buyer might get part way into his or her buying program and realize that the total cost was going to be so great as to make following through with the full purchase unattractive. The use of a *tender offer* is designed to allow the buyer to avoid such problems. A tender offer is used to facilitate a very large purchase without unduly upsetting the market. Such a purchase offer may, for example, be structured to acquire shares by the company itself (*self-tender*) or may be used as part of a plan to take over control of a targeted company. As with a secondary distribution, an underwriting syndicate is organized to manage the offer. A price offered by the purchaser is set, usually at a level that is a bit above what had been the market price. The buyer specifies other terms, such as how many shares will be accepted and how long the offer is to remain open. The seller receives a net price, and the buyer pays a fee to the underwriter.

One more special trading mechanism to explore in this segment is the *super DOT system*. Sometimes traders wish to buy or sell a large number of different securities simultaneously. Such traders may, for example, wish to purchase

---

Mechanisms for Trading Large Quantities of Stock

Block Trader: Assembles one side of a trade involving 10,000 up to 100,000 shares in order to minimize market disruption and obtain a satisfactory price for the active side of the trade.

Secondary Distribution: An underwriting syndicate is assembled in order to manage the sale of a large quantity of stock (typically a million shares or more). The stock is sold at a fixed price that is usually set a bit below the predistribution level. The seller pays the underwriter a per-share fee for handling the marketing of the transaction.

Tender Offer: An underwriting syndicate is assembled in order to facilitate a large purchase, sometimes as part of a takeover attempt. As with a secondary distribution, the underwriters receive a per-share fee for their efforts.

Super DOT system: Facilitates the placement and execution of trades on many different securities simultaneously. Often used to implement an index arbitrage program.

(or sell short) each of the stocks making up the S&P 500 index in the proportions that correspond to those of the index. In essence, they want to buy (or short) a matched set of the index stocks for an overall price that reflects the level that the index is currently registering. Entering and executing 500 separate trades individually would take time. Before all 500 separate trades could be completed, the individual stock prices may have moved about quite a bit. Instead of assembling a portfolio of the securities making up the index at the expected cost, the actual cost could be rather different. Similarly, a set of trades designed to liquidate such a portfolio, if accomplished one position at a time (even if the entire process took only a few minutes), could result in a rather different set of prices from those prices that were available when the sale process began. Such a level of uncertainty is unacceptable where the trade is designed only to capture a rather modest price disparity. The super DOT system is structured to overcome this problem. It provides for the simultaneous electronic entry and implementation of many individual orders.

You, as an individual small investor, are not likely to be a seller using a block trader or secondary distributions; a buyer using a tender offer; or a trader using the super DOT system. You may, however, be on the other side of the trade or you may be on the sidelines but own or be interested in acquiring the affected stocks. Accordingly, knowing how these types of trades work may well be useful as background information.

2

Options: Puts and Calls

Normally someone who wishes to buy or sell securities will simply enter an order (market or limit) to do so. *Put* and *call* options, in contrast, are generally thought of as either stand-alone investment instruments to buy, hold, and sell, or as instruments to be used as part of a more complex position involving a combination of securities. And yet, options also provide an interesting and useful vehicle for both buying and selling stock. Utilizing options as an indirect means of trading shares of the underlying stock involves making a trade-off between the certainty of having the trade implemented and the possibility of achieving a better price on the transaction. If you use options as a trading vehicle, you give up a little bit of certainty in exchange for the prospect of obtaining a better price. Before we can examine the specifics of how this is done, we need to understand the basics of options. First, let's explore terminology. Some of the relevant option terms are defined in the box on page 26. Additional terminology will be introduced as the need arises.

Most option contracts provide a vehicle for the purchase or sale of stock (as opposed to some other asset). The standard stock option contract is written for 100 shares. Options can, however, be written on other types of assets such as bonds or even futures contracts.

Puts and Calls Defined

Call: A contract that provides the owner with the right, but not the obligation, to purchase a prespecified amount of an asset (e.g., stock) at a prespecified price (*strike price*) over a prespecified time period.

Put: A contract that provides the owner with the right but not the obligation to sell a prespecified amount of an asset at a prespecified price over a prespecified time period.

    An *in-the-money* call is one where the strike price is below the stock price.

    An *in-the-money* put is one where the strike price is above the stock price.

    An *at-the-money* put or call is one where the stock price equals the strike price.

    An *out-of-the-money* put (call) is one where the strike price is above (below) the stock price.

The seller or *writer* of the option contract (call or put) is paid a price for entering into the contract and thereby standing ready either to sell (call) or buy (put) the asset if the option is exercised.

Options investors pay for the privilege of being able to decide later whether or not to exercise the rights provided by the option contract.

When you own an option, you are the one who decides whether or not to exercise it. The option writer or seller, in contrast, must stand ready to perform under the contract when and if you choose to exercise. This ownership right of the option-holder has an important impact on the option's value. We shall now explore the topic of option valuation.

Option values (prices) can be decomposed into two components. The first component is the *intrinsic value*. That intrinsic value is the value that would be derived from the option if it was immediately exercised. In the case of a put, the intrinsic value is equal to the strike price less the stock price, as long as the difference is positive. If the difference is negative, the intrinsic value is automatically assigned a value of zero. As an example, a put with a strike of 30 and a stock price of 27 would have an intrinsic value of 3 ($30 - 27 = 3$). Those 3 points of intrinsic value reflect how much the stock's current market price exceeds the amount that the put option writer would be required to pay for the stock. If the put was immediately exercised, it would cause the buyer (put writer) to pay the seller (put owner) 3 more points per share than the stock sells for in the marketplace. The put option with a strike of 30 allows the holder of the option to sell stock to the put writer at a price of 30 regardless of the current market price. When the market price is 27, the put holder owns a contract giving him or her the right to sell the stock for 3 points more than the price that is currently available in the market. But of course, the stock price is very likely to be something other than 27 as the put approaches expiration.

Clearly, any option should be worth at least as much as its intrinsic value. An option will, however, almost always trade in the marketplace for more than its intrinsic value. The above intrinsic value price that usually obtains in the market is due to the attractive features that the option provides. These features include: (1) the ability to wait until just before the option expires before having to decide whether or not to exercise it, and (2) the ability to control a lot of stock with a small sum of money.

In the current example, if the put is sold for 5, that would price it at 2 points above its intrinsic value of 3. Since the stock itself sells for 27, the put sells for less than a fifth as much as the stock. Thus a speculator who wanted to place a large bet on the stock could use options to control more than five times as many shares with the same sum of money as with an outright stock transaction. Viewed another way, options provide what amounts to a high degree of leverage.

The difference between the market price of a put option and its intrinsic value (in the current example: $5 - 3 = 2$) is called the option's *time value*. This time value largely reflects the premium price that the option-holder must pay for the right to wait until the option's expiration date to decide whether to exercise or abandon the option. If the underlying stock's price moves in a favorable direction (up if a call, down if a put), the option's intrinsic value will rise (assuming it is in-the-money), which will almost always cause the option's market price to increase. If the stock's price does not move in a favorable direction, the option's market value will decline. The option may eventually become worthless. Your losses are, however, limited to what you paid for the option. As an option owner, you are allowed to wait until just before the option expires before you must decide what to do. That way you can wait until the last minute to see if the underlying stock's price is above or below the strike price before having to decide whether or not to exercise your option. The longer the option has to run, the more time the underlying asset has to move in a favorable direction and thus the more valuable is this right to sell it (put) or acquire it (call) at a fixed price. In the above example, if you bought the put with a strike of 30 for a price of 5 and the stock fell from 27 to 20, your option's intrinsic value would rise from 3 $(30 - 27 = 3)$ to 10 $(30 - 20 = 10)$. Clearly, you would want to derive value from this option. One way to extract that value would be to exercise the option (rather than allow it to expire unexercised). That is, you could use the put to sell shares having a market value of 20 for the put's strike price of 30. If you did not already own the shares, you could first buy them in the market at 20 per share and then use your put to sell the shares at 30. That would yield a profit of 10 per share (less commissions). A similar way to derive value from your in-the-money put is to sell it. It should sell for at least its intrinsic value or 10 per share. You should always be able to realize value from an in-the-money option by either exercising or selling it, just as long as you do one or the other before it expires.

Intrinsic and Time Values of Options

Intrinsic value is the financial benefit that could be derived from the option if it was immediately exercised.

For a call, the intrinsic value equals the stock price minus the strike price, if positive.

For a put, the intrinsic value equals the strike price minus the stock price, if positive.

If the difference is negative, the intrinsic value equals zero by definition. *Time value* for an option equals the amount that the option's market price exceeds its intrinsic value.

Out-of-the-money options, in contrast, are not advantageous to exercise. They lose most and eventually all of their value as they approach expiration. If, for example, the stock price rose to 35 before the put (with a strike of 30) expired, you would be best off letting the option expire unexercised. You would rather sell your shares in the open market at 35 than to put them to the writer at 30. The right to sell a stock at 30 when the market price is 35 is of little or no value, particularly if the option is about to expire.

As an option approaches its expiration date, its price tends to move toward its intrinsic value. In other words, as the time left before an option expires gets short, its time value tends to disappear. In the above example of a put with a strike of 30, if the stock's price did fall to 20, you could sell the put option for at least its intrinsic value of 10 ($30 - 20 = 10$). Since you paid 5 for the option, you would thereby have doubled your money. On the other hand, if the stock's price rose to 30 or more, the option's intrinsic value would fall to zero. If the stock price was above 30 on the day the option expired, the option would expire worthless. In this latter case, the most you could lose is what you paid for the option.

Option market values depend upon a number of factors including the length of the option's remaining life, its strike price, the underlying stock's price, risk level, and dividend rate as well as the market rate of interest (see Table 2.1).

Options almost always trade for at least their intrinsic value.

Options almost always sell for more than their intrinsic values. To understand why this is so, consider the alternative possibility. Suppose a call option (giving you the right to buy the stock at a prespecified price over a prespecified time period) could be bought for less than its intrinsic value. One could then buy the call, exercise it, and then sell the stock, thereby acquired for its market price. The result would be an instant profit. To illustrate this

TABLE 2.1. Factors Affecting an Option's Value

Factor	Call Direction of impact	Put Direction of impact
Strike price	−	+
Stock price	+	−
Volatility (risk) of underlying stock	+	+
Remaining life of option	+	+
Market rate of interest	−	+
Dividend rate on the underlying stock	−	+

point, consider the case of a call having a strike of 30 when the underlying stock sells in the marketplace for 35. This call has an intrinsic value of 5 $(35 - 30 = 5)$. Suppose you could buy the call for 3, which is 2 points below its intrinsic value. You could buy and immediately exercise it, thereby acquiring the stock for 30. Your total cost for the stock would be 33 per share. You would pay 3 for the call and 30 to exercise it $(3 + 33 = 33)$. You could simultaneously sell that stock for its market price of 35, thereby capturing a profit of 2 points (less commissions) per share $(35 - 33 = 2)$. You could profitably implement this set of trades over and over again. Just as long as the call option having a strike of 30 traded at 3 and the stock at 35, you could pocket a profit of 2 points per share (less commissions).

The opportunity to earn meaningful arbitrage profits very rarely occurs in the marketplace. When such opportunities do arise, arbitragers quickly rush into the marketplace in order to exploit them. Their arbitrage trading drives the prices back in line with the options' intrinsic value levels. As long as the option traded for less than its intrinsic value, arbitragers would buy the option. This buying activity would tend to bid up the option's market price. As the option's price rose, the gap between the option's market price and its intrinsic value would narrow. These same arbitragers would simultaneously sell the underlying stock, thereby tending to depress its price. As the underlying stock's price fell, that decline would also have the effect of reducing the call option's intrinsic value. Sooner or later the option's market price would no longer be below its intrinsic value. Accordingly, the trades of the arbitragers would tend to bid up the option's price while tending to push the stock's price down. Thus the actions of arbitragers should eliminate any arbitrage opportunities that do appear. The process should occur quickly as arbitragers scramble to take advantage of the mispricing before it disappears. That is why options almost always trade for at least their intrinsic values. Usually they trade for more than their intrinsic value if their expiration is not imminent. Accordingly, you can almost always count on receiving (paying) at least the option's intrinsic value when you sell (buy).

Put options may be used to buy stocks.

Suppose you have identified a stock that you would like to purchase. Further suppose that you have no reason to expect that the stock's price will move up dramatically in the near term. You could simply buy the stock on the market for the current market price. But you might consider another approach to acquiring the stock. You could write (sell) an in-the-money put (stock price above the put's strike price) on the stock that you want to acquire. If the put is exercised, you will end up purchasing the stock from the person who owns the put. Moreover, you will pay a lower overall price (strike price on the put less what you received for writing the put) on it than if you had initially bought the stock rather than written the put. If the put that you wrote is not exercised, you will still be paid for having written it. Once the put expires, you will have no further obligation to the put's owner.

Recall that a put gives the owner *the right but not the obligation* to sell the prespecified stock at a prespecified (strike) price over a prespecified time period. The writer of a put takes the other side of the contract. If called upon by the put owner, the put writer is obligated to purchase the stock under the prespecified terms of the put contract. By writing (selling) such a put, you must stand ready to purchase the specified shares from the put's owner at any time up to the date of the option's expiration. If, as the put is approaching expiration, the market price of the stock is appreciably below the put's strike price (in other words, if the put is in-the-money and just about to expire), the put is almost certain to be exercised. The owner always has an incentive to exercise the put as long as the stock price stays in the range below the put's strike price. Very rarely will in-the-money puts be allowed to expire unexercised. Failure to exercise an in-the-money option is like throwing money away. And yet, it can and sometimes (rarely) does happen.

Suppose that, in an effort to buy a stock, you wrote a put that remained in-the-money at expiration but was allowed by its owner to expire unexercised. As a result, the stock that you hoped to acquire by writing the put would not have been sold to you. The option owner's failure to exercise the put that you wrote is actually to your benefit. Since the stock's market price is now below the option's strike price, you would be able to purchase the stock in the open market for less than the put's strike price. But the strike price is the price that you would have had to pay if the put had been exercised. If you still want to acquire the stock, you should buy it at the market price or write another in-the-money put (and wait for it to be exercised).

Option holders have an incentive to wait until near expiration before deciding whether or not to exercise their options. As a result, the vast majority of option exercises occur in the last few days before the option is set to expire.

What are the advantages of using a put sale (rather than an outright purchase of the underlying stock) to implement a stock purchase? First, you are paid a sum of money (the put price less commission) up front for writing the put. Second, you delay paying the full amount of the stock's purchase price until the put is exercised. Third, and most important, your net cost, if you buy the shares, is less (by the amount of the put's time value) than what you would have paid with a direct stock purchase.

As a seller (or writer) of an option, you are paid a price that includes both the intrinsic and the time value. The intrinsic value plus the strike price equals the current stock price, the amount you would pay to buy the stock at its current level. The time value is the bonus that you, the writer, receive for using a put sale to implement a stock purchase. You write the put because you want to buy the stock. In the above example, you sell a put for 5, which, if exercised, requires that you purchase the stock for 30. If you bought the stock today, you would pay 27. But with the put sale you are paid 5 today and must pay 30 for the stock if and when the put is exercised. So if the put is exercised, thereby causing you to buy the stock, your net cost is 25 ($30 - 5 = 25$) rather than the current market price of 27. Furthermore, you save some financing costs by not paying the stock's full purchase price until the option is exercised. If, for example, the put has six months to run, you will not be called upon to pay the put's strike price (to buy the stock) for another six months. Finally, if you later decide you don't want to purchase the stock, you can extricate yourself from the obligation by buying an equivalent put to offset your short position. As long as you buy it back before the put that you wrote is exercised, your obligation will be extinguished. You don't need to buy back the same put that you sold, you just need to purchase one that is equivalent to (same strike price and expiration date) the one that you sold. This process of buying an offsetting option (either put or call) is called *covering* your option position.

This strategy of trying to buy stock by writing in-the-money puts is not devoid of risk. The strategy is designed to implement a purchase on the selected stock. That purchase takes place only if the put is exercised. In our example, the stock could rise above 30 during the time that the put, having a strike of 30, is still outstanding and unexercised (that is before the put expires). If around the date of the put's expiration, the underlying stock's price is above the option's strike price, the putholder will not exercise the option and therefore you will not be required to buy the stock. Your objective in writing the in-the-money put was to purchase the underlying stock. But the stock's price rises so high (above the put's strike price) that the putholder will not have an incentive to exercise the put that you sold. A rational putholder will choose not to sell you the stock for the put's strike price when they can sell it for a higher price in the market.

Remember, the putholder has the right but not the obligation to buy the stock at the strike price. In this instance, your put-writing strategy has not achieved your basic objective of acquiring the stock. You do, however, earn what amounts to a consolation prize. The money that you were paid for the put sale is yours to keep free and clear. Generally, that is not such a bad outcome. You were paid 5 for agreeing to buy the stock at 30, if asked. You ended up doing nothing because the put that you wrote was not exercised. In other words, you got paid 5 for agreeing to stand ready to do something that, in the end, you were not required to do. Still, if the stock's price rises to 40, you would probably prefer to have bought it at 27 (the price of the stock when you sold the put) rather than receive the consolation prize of the put-sale proceeds. So if you want to be absolutely sure of purchasing a particular stock, this strategy of writing in-the-money puts is not for you. On the other hand, if you are willing to take a chance that you will not buy the stock, but if that happens, you will be rewarded for trying, you may find this strategy to be of interest.

Call options can also be used to sell stocks.

Just as a strategy of writing an in-the-money put option can be used to buy a stock, a similar sort of strategy that utilizes the sale of a call option can be employed when you want to sell a stock that you already own. Rather than writing a put, you would write an in-the-money call. Suppose you own a stock that is now selling for 27. Rather than sell the stock immediately at the current market price of 27, you could write a call with a strike at 25. Such a call might sell for a price of 4. In this case, the call option has an intrinsic value of 2 $(27 - 25 = 2)$ and a time value of 2 $(4 - 2 = 2)$. As long as the stock's price is trading above 25 when the option expires, the option will be exercised and you will have sold your shares for a total of 29 $(25 + 4 = 29)$. This sum compares with what had been the market price of 27 that was available when you wrote the call.

Again, this strategy has a degree of risk. If the stock's price is below 25 at option expiration, the call will not be exercised and you will not sell your shares via the call that you wrote. But you still retain the proceeds (4) from the call sale. At that point you can write another call and wait to see if it is exercised, or you can just sell the shares at the currently available market price. Unless the stock has fallen more than two points below 25, you will still come out ahead (compared to having sold the shares directly). On the other hand, if the stock's price falls dramatically, the call will not be exercised and you will wish that you had sold the stock at a higher price when you could.

Writing an in-the-money call is a relatively conservative approach to using options as a stock-selling vehicle. Writing an out-of-the-money call represents a more aggressive strategy. Suppose, for example, you wrote a call with a strike of 30 for a market price of 1. If the stock rose from 27 to or above 30 before the call expired and stayed in that range at the call's expiration, the call that you wrote would be exercised. In this case, you would have to deliver your stock to the call-holder for the strike price of 30. As a result, you would derive a total of 31 per share $(30 + 1 = 31)$ from the sale of your position. If, however, the stock's price stayed below 30, you would still keep the 1 that you derived from the call sale. But the call would not be exercised and thus you would not have sold your stock. On the other hand, once this particular call expired, you could write another call option. If the stock stayed in the high 20s, you might receive another 1 point for the sale of a second call. You could continue to write calls on your position until one of the calls you wrote was exercised. That would be like earning a second dividend of a dollar a share on your position.

One further consideration for both call and put writers concerns the matter of collateral. When you write an option, you are obligating yourself to perform under the terms of the option contract. If you write a call against stock that you already own, the shares that you may need to deliver to the option-holder already sit in your account. The broker and brokerage firm who handled your call sale will be comfortable with the arrangement. On the other hand, if you write a put, you have obligated yourself to purchase the shares if the put is exercised. The brokerage firm handling the trade will demand that you either have enough cash or borrowing power (see margin) derived from other un-encumbered assets in your brokerage account to cover the cost of buying this stock if the put option is exercised. Similar rules apply if you write a call without owning the underlying shares (*naked writing*).

Neither buying stock by writing puts nor selling stock by writing calls is without risk. In both instances, a large adverse move in the underlying stocks' prices can render the strategy suboptimal. Still, using options as a vehicle for buying and selling stocks is a strategy worth a second look.

3

Sources of Credit

Investors often use borrowed funds to help finance the acquisition of the securities in their investment portfolio. Using other people's (borrowed) money to generate profits for yourself can be advantageous. Indeed, efficient debt management is an important aspect of effective investing. If you can earn a higher rate of return on your investments than you pay in interest to borrow the funds, your use of leverage will be profitable. Similarly, if you can use your investments as collateral to facilitate borrowing needed funds more cheaply than if you borrowed the same sum in another way, you are thereby reducing your cost of debt service. Both results are likely to be to your financial advantage.

Using the market value of your portfolio as collateral for a loan from your broker is called *margin borrowing*. You may utilize a margin loan in order to finance additional investments or other types of spending, or to pay down other debts. While margin borrowing has many advantages, it also involves some noteworthy risks. Leverage is a double-edged sword. Let's now explore its advantages, risks, and, most important, how to manage those risks.

Margin debt is almost always cheaper (a lower interest rate) than credit card debt. Pay off credit card debt with funds derived from a margin loan. Then be sure to pay off your credit card balance by each month's due date.

One of the benefits of having an investment portfolio is the ease with which you can use its market value as collateral for a margin loan. Margin loans do not require a credit check, or any specific repayment plan, and can be obtained on very short notice. Margin loans also do not incur prepayment penalties, or loan origination fees, and the interest rate charged is generally quite attractive. For those who have the collateral to borrow against, margin loans are a more advantageous source of credit than almost all of the alternatives.

Suppose, for example, that your investment portfolio has a market value of $10,000 and no debt against it. You could borrow up to 50 percent of the portfolio's value ($5,000) and use the borrowed funds for any legitimate purpose. The funds thereby obtained could be used to pay bills, pay down other debts, or just to spend on whatever. If the borrowed money is used to finance additional investing, the purchased securities would have the effect of increasing the market value of your portfolio, thereby increasing your borrowing capacity. Indeed, you could borrow up to a total of $10,000 on a portfolio with an initial market value of $10,000, just as long as all of the borrowed funds were used to buy more securities. That is, $10,000 of equity can support a $20,000 portfolio with $10,000 of margin debt. Thus, if you started with an unemcumbered $10,000 portfolio of stocks, you could buy up to another $10,000 of stock using the first $10,000 as collateral. As a result you would have a $20,000 portfolio with a $10,000 lien against it.

To qualify as collateral for a margin loan, the securities must meet certain standards. Typically, to be marginable, stocks must trade above some minimum price per share, like $5, and either be listed on an exchange or on the NASDAQ's national list.

The interest rate that brokerage firms charge on their margin loans is generally tied to a nationally established interest rate that is referred to as the *broker call loan rate*. This broker call loan rate is the interest rate brokerage firms must pay for the bank loans that they obtain in order to finance their own margin lending. In other words, the brokerage firms borrow from banks in bulk at the broker call loan rate and then lend to their margin loan clients individually. Their cost of funds, the call loan rate, determines how much they charge their clients for margin loans. This call loan rate is usually set a bit above or below the prime rate (the rate that banks charge their high-quality, low-risk customers). Depending upon the brokerage firm and the size of the loan, the rate charged on a margin loan may be as little as 0.5 percent to as much as 2.5 percent above the broker call loan rate. If, for example, the broker call loan rate was 5.0 percent, the margin loan rate charged individual customers would range from 5.5 to 7.5 percent. Most credit card rates are in the range of 1 to 2 percent a month or 12 to 24 percent per year. Clearly, substituting margin borrowing for credit card debt will save the borrower a substantial amount in interest charges. Moreover, to the extent that the money borrowed is used to finance investments, the interest charged can be utilized as an itemized deduction. This investment interest deduction may, however, be employed only to offset the tax liability on the taxpayer's dividend or interest income. Interest paid on credit card, personal, or auto loans, in contrast, is not deductible.

Margin debt is usually a more attractive way to borrow than other types of personal borrowing, such as auto or personal loans. Use it as a substitute source of credit when it is available.

Personal and auto loan rates, while rarely as expensive as credit card rates, are generally above the interest rates charged on margin loans. If you have sufficient collateral to do so, you are usually better off using the borrowing power of your investment portfolio to finance your automobile purchases with a margin loan than financing your car with a standard automobile loan.

Automobile companies do sometimes offer very attractive loan rates as a sales incentive (0% or 1% loans). Such deals require the auto company to subsidize the lender. Thus, the auto shopper may well be able to negotiate a better price on the car purchase by forgoing the cheap credit and financing the purchase elsewhere. One who has sufficient borrowing power to finance an auto purchase or to provide for other credit needs from margin borrowing should at least consider doing so if, as is usually the case, the interest rate is lower.

Margin borrowing power provides the investor/consumer with a useful backup line of credit.

Financial planners and investment counselors recommend that individuals hold a cash reserve for unexpected contingencies. Typically, a reserve equal to about six months of the individual's yearly income is suggested. This reserve would usually be held in a form that is able to be converted into spendable cash almost immediately (savings account, money market accounts, very-short-term CDs, etc.). Such a reserve is then available if needed, to cover unexpected/emergency expenses such as those arising from an operation, job layoff, auto accident, or wedding, for example. The ability to borrow an equivalent sum via a margin loan on your investment portfolio constitutes an effective substitute for an actual cash reserve. The availability of this backup line of credit thereby frees up reserve funds that would otherwise sit in a high-liquidity, low-yield account. The liberated funds can now either be invested in longer-term investments with higher potential returns or be used to pay down high cost debt.

Margin debt is not usually an effective substitute for fixed-rate mortgage debt, but it may be a reasonable alternative to a home equity loan.

Very few investors could borrow enough through their margin account to finance their home. Those few who could probably shouldn't do so. Similarly, using margin debt to pay down one's mortgage balance is rarely a good idea, even when the current margin loan rates are lower than the currently available mortgage loan rate. A mortgage loan can be and usually is structured to have a fixed interest rate. This fixed rate coupled with the amortization of principal results in a stable monthly payment amount. The borrower, therefore, knows that the mortgage payment will be the same amount each month. Such certainty is important for family budgeting purposes. An additional advantage to such a fixed-rate mortgage is that it can be refinanced at a lower fixed rate if mortgage rates fall in the marketplace. Margin loan rates, in contrast, are reset periodically as market interest rates change. That degree of interest rate uncertainty is generally not problematic for short-term, small-balance borrowings. For long-term, high-balance borrowing (such as with a mortgage), however, the risk of an adverse interest rate move is a much greater danger. Suppose, for example, you are paying $1,500 a month in interest (a mortgage payment of $2,000 including $1,500 in interest) to finance your home. An interest rate spike (for example, rates might rise from 6 to 10 percent in a short time period) could cause that monthly interest payment to rise to $2,500 ($3,000 total). An extra $1,000 a month in interest costs would blow a hole in many (most) family budgets.

While financing your home purchase with a traditional fixed-rate mortgage is usually preferable to other forms of financing, margin debt may still be a useful supplement in particular situations. Specifically, you might wish to use money borrowed on margin to facilitate taking out a lower-balance mortgage loan in at least two situations. Generally, the interest rate charged on a mortgage loan is often lower when the borrower makes a sufficiently large down payment. A larger down payment makes the loan safer for the lender. Thus, a mortgage loan with an initial balance equal to 80 percent of the property's appraised value may be charged a higher mortgage interest rate than one equal to 75 percent. Similarly, the borrower may be required to purchase mortgage insurance when the amount borrowed is above a certain threshold percentage of the property's market value and not otherwise. Mortgage insurance is put in place to protect the lender in the event that the borrower defaults. If the ratio of the collateral value of the property to the mortgage balance is large enough, the lender will not require you to purchase mortgage insurance. The high market value of the collateral provides the lender with sufficient protection. In the unlikely event that the lender must foreclose on the property, its sale should bring more than enough to pay off the outstanding mortgage balance. Thus, if the collateral-to-loan-balance ratio is high enough, mortgage insurance is not needed. Since it involves an extra cost and provides little or no benefit to the buyer, you should avoid buying mortgage insurance if you can do so. Accordingly, you may want to stretch your finances a bit in order to obtain a large enough down payment to avoid the cost of mortgage insurance and/or to qualify for a lower interest rate on your mortgage loan. In such circumstances, a prudent amount of margin borrowing may appropriately be used to help with the down payment.

While not an attractive substitute for a standard fixed-rate mortgage, margin loans are competitive with variable-rate home equity loans. Both margin and home equity loans offer flexibility. The interest payments on both may be tax deductible. Moreover, the interest rates charged tend to be relatively low for both types of loans. One major advantage of margin borrowing is the absence of any fees or other costs for setting up the credit facility. Home equity lines of credit, in contrast, typically require a title search. Title searches, which involve lawyers and title insurance, tend to be rather costly. Various other loan fees may also be incurred with a home equity loan. These fees can add up to a significant sum. So, if you don't already have a home equity credit line established, the choice between using a margin loan or a home equity loan may well favor the margin loan.

Limit initial margin borrowing to no more than 30 percent of your portfolio's market value.

One major drawback to margin borrowing (and not to most other types of borrowing) is the risk of receiving a *call* on the loan. A call on a loan is a demand by the lender for immediate repayment. The vast majority of standard loans have a prespecified term and loan repayment schedule. As long as the borrower makes the payments specified in the repayment schedule, the outstanding loan balance is extremely unlikely to be called prior to its due date. Margin loans, in contrast, do not have a prespecified time for repayment. They are extended for, what could be, an unlimited period. As long as the collateral is adequate, the loan is allowed to remain outstanding. The borrower is not required to adhere to any kind of specific payment schedule. Indeed, the monthly interest charges can simply be added to the principal as long as the collateral is large enough to support the loan. Margin loans are, however, always at risk of being called. Such loans are extended on collateral whose value will change over time. The securities that are used to collateralize the margin loan are continually trading at prices that reflect the changing interplay of supply and demand. Thus the securities collateralizing the loan are continually fluctuating in market values. The lender is fully protected only to the extent that the collateral value of the portfolio on which the loan is extended exceeds the amount borrowed.

Under current (2006) regulations (set by the Federal Reserve and not changed in many years), a margin loan's outstanding balance cannot initially exceed 50 percent of the market value of the stocks in the account on which it is based. Different percentages apply to bonds. Once a margin account's balance reaches this 50 percent threshold, no more can be borrowed on that collateral. An account with $50,000 in total collateral value could support up to $25,000 in initial borrowing, thereby leaving another $25,000 in equity. Your equity position is the residual left after the loan balance is subtracted from the account's total market value.

For a margin loan to remain secure, the collateral must maintain sufficient value so that the amount of the debt remains substantially less than the collateral's value. Security prices fluctuate, sometimes by large amounts. A margin loan may, when initially extended, be highly secure. The collateral value of the borrower's portfolio may be well above the required minimum. If, however, security prices fall sufficiently, that same account's collateral value may quickly deteriorate to a position where the equity in the account is at risk of being too small to support the margin loan. Margin lenders want to avoid finding themselves in the position of having extended a loan whose outstanding balance exceeds (or even gets close to exceeding) the value of the collateral pledged to support the loan (equity value in this margin account that is close to or below zero). Indeed, lenders always want to see a safe cushion of equity in the accounts that they lend to. *Margin calls* are designed to provide the lenders with a vehicle that they can use to avoid becoming undersecured. Such margin calls provide a type of early warning for outstanding margin loans that have come to be at risk. When triggered, a margin call provides a signal that the account may be approaching a deficit position. The borrower who receives such a margin call is required to take corrective action.

Consider as an example a margin account that, when established, has stocks in it with an initial market value of $50,000 and $25,000 in margin borrowing. This account would start out with an equity value of $25,000 ($50,000 − $25,000 = $25,000). At these levels, the account would be financed by 50 percent debt and 50 percent equity. If the market value of the securities in the account fell to $40,000 (a 20% decline in the account's market value), the borrower would still owe $25,000, but much of the account's collateral value would have disappeared. The decline in the value of the portfolio would be matched dollar-for-dollar by an equivalent decline in the account's equity position. At the $40,000 value level, the account would be above water by (have an equity value of) $15,000 ($40,000 − $25,000 = $15,000). At $15,000, the equity in the account corresponds to 37.5 percent ($15,000/$40,000 = .375) of the accounts' total market value. Most margin lenders issue a margin call (a *house call*) when the percentage of equity drops below 35 percent of the account value. Some wait until the equity percentage falls to 30 percent; the Federal Reserve *requires* a margin call (a *Fed call*) if the equity percentage declines below 25 percent. The account with 37.5 percent equity is just a bit away from the point where the margin borrower would be likely to receive a margin call (house call). Should the portfolio value drop another $1,600, the point for a margin call would be reached ($13,400/$38,400 = 34.9%). Once the margin call is issued, the brokerage firm would demand that the investor restore the account's equity position to at least the 35 percent level (assuming that is the firm's threshold). The investor could have effected the required restoration in any of three ways:

a. Pay off some of the loan balance with cash.
b. Add marginable securities to the account in order to increase its collateral value.
c. Sell securities from the account and apply the proceeds to reducing the loan balance.

Most margin borrowers cannot easily do either a or b, at least not within the few days that their broker gives them to implement their restructuring. Investors who receive margin calls are typically tapped out of loose cash and have already placed all of their marginable securities into their investment accounts. This leaves them with option c. The only available way most investors have for dealing with a margin call is to sell at least part of their holdings in order thereby to pay down their margin debt.

Receiving a margin call is always an unpleasant experience. Having to sell securities to meet a margin call is likely to be particularly painful. Such calls almost always arrive at what is a poor time to have to sell securities. Typically the market is well below its recent highs, and most or all of the investor's securities are selling at depressed levels. Margin calls usually force investors to sell shares that they purchased at high prices when the market was booming. When the margin call is issued, the investor almost always must sell securities at much lower price levels, perhaps at or near a market bottom. And, the required amount of selling is likely to be substantial. Selling to meet a margin call has the effect of reducing the total value (and thus the collateral value) of the portfolio. Accordingly, a substantial amount of selling is needed to restructure the account so that it will be in line with the required margin regulations.

To illustrate how a margin call can damage an investment portfolio, consider the following hypothetical case: Suppose, an account started out with $40,000 in securities and a $20,000 margin loan. What is the result if that account suffers a rapid 30 percent decline in market value? The account's total value would fall to $28,000. Its equity value would have fallen to $8,000 ($28,000 − $20,000 = $8,000). At that level, only 32.5 percent (8/28ths) of the account's value would be in the form of equity. To restore the account to a 35 percent equity position would require the sale of about $5,000 of stock. A sale of such a limited amount of stock would leave the account very vulnerable to further margin calls. If market values continue to fall, more margin calls would be likely. A sale of $12,000 worth of stock would be needed to restore the equity position to 50 percent (and thereby have some degree of protection against a further margin call). Selling $12,000 worth of securities would reduce the portfolio's value from $28,000 to $16,000 and margin debt from $20,000 to $8,000. Such a sale would reduce the value of the portfolio by over 40 percent. Having to sell this amount of stock in a depressed market is sure to be painful for the investor. Recall that the account began with $40,000 of securities and $20,000 in equity. Thus at $16,000 with $8,000 of equity, the account has lost 60 percent of its initial value.

Suppose the market recovers such that the portfolio's value rises by 30 percent, the same percentage that it fell. After meeting the margin call, the investor who started with a $40,000 portfolio has $16,000 worth of securities left in his or her account. Accordingly, a 30 percent increase in its market value corresponds to less than a $5,000 rise in the portfolio's value (0.3 × $11,000 = $4,800). That $5,000 sum is compared to the $12,000 loss when the $40,000 account declined by 30 percent to $28,000. This example illustrates an important point. Having to sell securities in order to satisfy the margin call, in effect, robbed the investor of a chance to recover fully when the market itself came back.

To reduce greatly the risk of a margin call, you should limit initial borrowings to significantly less than the maximum percentage allowed. Restricting initial borrowing to no more than 30 percent of the account value (as opposed to the allowed 50 percent) is a rather conservative approach. With a starting equity of at least 70 percent (1.00 − .30 = .70), a large, and therefore much less likely to occur, decline in portfolio values is needed to reach the point where a margin call is issued (35%). If you started with 50 percent equity, the chance of a margin call would be much greater. *If you can avoid a margin call in a major market decline, you will be much better positioned to recover when the market rebounds.*

If declines in the market values of the securities in your portfolio cause margin debt to rise to or above 40 percent of your portfolio's market value, sell securities in order to prevent your debt ratio from rising any higher.

Limiting initial borrowing to 30 percent of your investment account's value is a useful first step in protecting your investments from the ravages of a major market decline. As a supplemental rule I advise you to *take corrective action if and when your margin account's equity percentage falls to 60 percent* (borrowing reaches 40 percent) of the account's total value. By taking early action, you would have greater flexibility and more time to consider what and how to sell. The sooner you take corrective action, the less painful is the result likely to be. To paraphrase Benjamin Franklin: A sale in time may save nine.

Let's return to our prior example. The investor (e.g., you) with $20,000 in equity borrows not $20,000, but $9,000, yielding a starting portfolio value of $29,000. At that initial stage, you have about 30 percent borrowed (9/29, ≅ .30). Now suppose that your portfolio suffers a 30 percent decline. That would take the account's total market value down to about $20,000 (0.7 × $29,000 = $20,300). The equity value would decline to $11,000 ($20,000 − $9,000 = $11,000). You would then have a margin loan position of about 55 percent ($11,000/$20,000 = .55). At this 55 percent level, your account would still be quite some distance away from the point of receiving a margin call. You would not be required to do anything to protect your margin position. You would continue to be well secured. Still, to be on the safe side you might want to reduce the size of your margin loan. A sale of $2,000 worth of the stock would restore the equity percentage to over 60 percent and thus bring the margin borrowing level down to 40 percent of your portfolio's total market value. Now if the market recovers, you would be in a much better position to recapture your losses than would be the case if a higher percentage had been borrowed and later more needed to be sold in order to meet a margin call. If the market keeps falling, you may have to undertake some additional selling, but a lot less than would be needed if you had borrowed more initially.

These "30 percent initial" and "40 percent take-action" percentages are just guidelines. More experienced risk-tolerant investors may choose to use somewhat higher thresholds. Still, my basic point is valid: Margin borrowing can be risky and becomes most problematic when you are least able to deal with its most dreadful feature: the margin call. To avoid or at least minimize the danger of receiving a margin call, you should place some limits on how much margin borrowing you are willing to undertake and also be prepared to take early action if need be.

Two further points bear mentioning. First, the risk of a substantial value decline in a portfolio that is heavily concentrated in a few securities is much greater than it is for a well-diversified portfolio. If a large percentage of your portfolio is reflected in the value of one or a few stocks, you should be especially cautious about the use of margin. Second, low-priced stocks are particularly risky to rely upon as collateral for a margin loan. Most brokerage firms will not extend margin credit on very-low-priced shares. Many have a per-share threshold of $5. To explore this matter with an example, suppose you have some $7 stock in your margin account. As long as the stock's price remains above your broker's $5 threshold, the stock remains marginable. If the $7 stock's price falls to $6, its contribution to the borrowing power of the account declines, but remains substantial. If, however, the stock's price declines by a bit more than one more dollar (to below $5), the total value of that stock's position will be removed from the account's marginable total. This action could trigger a margin call even though the overall account value is well above the required threshold.

4

Tax-Sheltered Accounts

Y ou may not have thought about it this way, but you have an (uninvited) investment partner. This partner demands a share of all your winnings but refuses to cover more than a very small part of your losses. Your uninvited partner is, of course, the tax man. You are allowed to keep only that part of your portfolio's return that is left over after your taxes have been paid. The tax man insists on taking his cut whether you like it or not.

You may be surprised to realize just how much of your investment income goes out the door in the form of taxes. An important part of your investment education involves understanding the impact of taxes on your gross investment income and thus the portion of your investment income that you are permitted to keep. Having such an understanding enhances your ability to assess the advantages of those types investments that allow you to shelter part or all of your investment income from tax liability. Such an understanding also enhances your ability to analyze the trade-offs between fully taxed and tax-sheltered investment income as it applies to your own particular situation. The higher your taxable income, the higher your income tax rate (tax bracket). The higher your tax rate, the more important tax considerations become to your investment decision-making.

*Calculate your marginal tax rate so that you can accurately assess
the impact of taxes on your investment income.*

Clearly the taxes that you pay on your investment income have an adverse
effect on your return. To understand how much taxes reduce the return on
your investments, you need to understand the difference between your *marginal* and *average* tax rates. Your average tax rate is rather easy to calculate and
easy to understand. If, for example, you pay $12,000 in income and Social
Security taxes on an income of $60,000, your average tax rate is 20 percent
($12,000/$60,000 = .20). Thus a fifth of all that you earn goes to the government. You work all day Monday to pay your tax bill. The rest of the week, you
are working for yourself. As interesting as this average tax rate number may
seem to be, it is irrelevant for most investment analysis. Your average tax is a
blend of several tax rates that you pay under our progressive rate tax system.
You do not actually pay the average rate on any specific piece of your income.

The marginal tax rate is the rate that enters into most after-tax return calculations. Suppose you were to earn one more dollar of income. Your marginal
tax rate is the part of that additional dollar of income that must be paid as taxes.
Unless your investment income is a very large part of your total income, your
noninvestment income from wages, salary, and so on is the income level that
largely determines your marginal tax rate.

If you are fortunate enough to earn a handsome income from your job, you
should be able to derive a significant amount of investable funds from that
income. Your high level of base income does, however, have a downside. Such
an income level will place you in a relatively high tax bracket. The higher
your tax bracket, the less you get to keep of any additional taxable income
that you receive.

If, in addition to your salary, you derive some taxable income from your
investments, that investment income becomes part of your overall or *adjusted
gross income*. The amount of tax you must pay is largely determined by the
size of your adjusted gross income. Under most circumstances, your investment income (which is a component of your adjusted gross income) can and
generally should be viewed as extra income coming on top of your primary
sources of income (e.g., wages, salaries, pensions, etc.). Thus your marginal
or incremental tax is the rate that applies to your investment income.

Suppose you unexpectedly receive a sum of money that is over and above
your normal income. It is extra money that you could either spend or invest.
The funds might source from an unusually large tax refund, bonus from your
employer, inheritance, lottery winnings, or whatever. The funds are discretionary. They are not needed to meet ordinary living expenses. If you spend
this unexpected windfall, the money will be gone. If you invest these funds,
you will both retain ownership of the investment asset and earn an income on
it. But that investment income is very likely to be taxable. Knowing how
much your tax liability would increase if you earned that extra amount of

investment income would help you decide what to do with the money. This is where your marginal tax rate enters the analysis. The ratio of that extra tax liability to the extra investment income is your marginal tax rate. If, for example, you earn an additional $1,000 in interest income and your tax liability increases by $250, your marginal tax rate would be 25 percent.

To determine your marginal or incremental tax rate, you need to be able to answer the following question: If you earned an additional dollar of income, how much would your tax bill increase? You might think that the answer is easy to determine. If your income level put you in, say, the 25 percent tax bracket, the answer would seem to be 25 percent. You may well be correct, or at least approximately so. The issue may, however, be much more complex. First, the tax code has embedded within it a series of hidden taxes. At certain income levels, allowances for exemptions and itemized deductions begin to be phased out. If applicable, these phaseouts will have the effect of increasing your marginal tax rate above the bracket rate. So, above certain income levels, an extra dollar of income has the effect of increasing your taxable income by more than a dollar because it reduces the amount that you can subtract from your adjusted gross income to arrive at your taxable income. In addition, several deductions come into play only to the extent that their amount exceeds a percentage of your income (e.g., medical expenses, miscellaneous deductions). As your income level rises, this threshold rises with it. The effect of earning additional income may be to lower the amount of any deductions that you might otherwise be able to use to reduce that portion of your income that is taxable. If, for example, an extra dollar of income increases your taxable income by $1.10 and you are in the 25 percent tax bracket, the increase in your tax liability is 27.5¢ $(1.1 \times .25 = .275)$, or 27.5 percent of your additional income. Also, for an increasing number of taxpayers, the alternative minimum tax (AMT) may be triggered by the receipt of additional income of one type or another. If applicable, this AMT can increase your marginal tax rate substantially. Finally, you should not neglect the impact of state and local taxes. They can add 5 to 15 percent to the earner's marginal tax rate. The marginal tax rate that you calculate for yourself needs to take all of these factors (phaseouts, AMT, state and local taxes) into account.

Note, however, that *your marginal tax rate will always be less than 100 percent.* Even with all the bells and whistles of the federal tax system and the impacts of state and local taxes, you will still be allowed to keep at least a portion of any of the extra income that you earn. Some people mistakenly believe that if they were to earn a bit more, the extra income would put them into a higher tax bracket, thereby causing them to pay more in additional taxes than they would earn in extra income. This preverse result cannot occur. Even when earning an extra dollar puts you into a higher tax bracket, you pay that higher rate only on the last increment of income. The tax code is structured such that your first increment of taxable income is taxed at the lowest statutory rate. Then you move on to the next lowest bracket for the next level of income, and so on with higher levels of income. When your income places you in a higher tax bracket, only the income above the threshold that defines the beginning of that bracket is taxed at the higher rate. Suppose, for example, that your current level of income places you at the top of the 25 percent tax bracket and then you earn an extra $1,000. If your additional income pushes you into the 28 percent tax bracket on the last $1,000 of income, you would pay $280 in tax on that amount. The rest of your income would be taxed at lower rates.

You can compute your marginal tax rate in either of two basic ways. One approach starts by ascertaining your tax position to see if any hidden taxes apply. You would then take account of the impact of each of these provisions and add it to the basic tax rate. You would also determine if the AMT applied and what the impact was for state and local taxes (including an assessment of the deduction that such tax payments may allow on your federal taxes, if you itemize).

The second and far easier way to determine your marginal tax rate is to input your tax information into one of the computerized tax software programs such as TurboTax (turbotax.com). You would then add a hypothetical dollar to your taxable income and determine the impact. If, for example, a dollar of additional income would increase your tax liability by 35 cents, your corresponding marginal tax rate is 35 percent. Having a marginal tax rate of 35 percent would mean that you are allowed to keep only 65 cents of each additional dollar of fully taxable income. You would need to utilize the computerized tax software for both the federal and any applicable state and local income taxes to determine your overall marginal rate.

All of this may seem more complicated than necessary. You can take a shortcut under certain circumstances. If your income is below the level where the hidden taxes emerge (currently around $150,000 if you are married filing jointly) and if you do not qualify for the alternative minimum tax (check your last tax return to see if you had to pay the AMT taxes), then you can probably just take the federal and state brackets in which your income level places you and add them together. If you itemize your deductions (rather than taking the standard deduction), you would be able to reduce the net cost to you of your federal income tax by the tax benefit of the state income tax deduction. So, if your federal rate was 25 percent and your state rate was 6 percent, you would reduce the 6 percent by one-fourth and add the result to your federal rate. In this case, your marginal tax rate would be 25 percent plus three-fourths of 6 percent, or 4.5 percent. The total becomes 29.5 percent. That would mean that not quite 30 percent of every extra dollar earned on your investments goes out in the form of taxes. That is, if the investment income is in the form of ordinary income, you must pay a tax equal to about 30 percent of that investment income. So, for example, an investment that produced a fully taxable 10 percent return before tax would yield 7 percent ($.7 \times 10\% = 7\%$) after tax.

The accompanying table will provide you with some guidance in determining the level of your marginal tax rate. You simply estimate your taxable

2005 Tax Rates for Married Filing Jointly	
Taxable Income	Rate
0–$14,600	10%
$14,601–$59,400	15%
$59,401–$119,950	25%
$119,951–$182,800	28%
$182,801–$326,450	33%
over $326,450	35%

income (look at your most recent tax return and adjust the income number if necessary) and find the place where that income falls in the table. Note, however, that these are the rates for taxpayers who are married filing jointly (separate tables apply for different filing statuses) and ignores all the bells and whistles (ATM, phaseouts of exemptions and deductions, state and local taxes). Moreover, the IRS adjusts these threshold levels each year in order to offset the impact of inflation. So in subsequent years the dividing lines for each bracket will be increased as the price level rises.

Realize that not all investment income is fully taxed. Invest accordingly.

Investment income in the form of interest, rent, royalties, and short-term capital gains (and some dividends) is fully taxed at the investor's marginal tax rate. Long-term capital gains (realized) and most dividends are subject to special tax treatment that limits the rate to no more than 15 percent. The interest income on municipal bonds is tax-free (with very few exceptions). Unrealized capital gains are not subject to tax as long as the gains remain unrealized. Thus, depending upon the income source, your after-tax investment income may be equal to either 100 percent, 85 percent, or (1-MTR) percent of your before-tax investment income (where MTR = the marginal tax rate that applies to your ordinary income). If, for example, your marginal tax rate is 35 percent, an investment offering a 10 percent before-tax return would produce a 10 percent after-tax return if tax-free, 8.5 percent if taxed at 15 percent, and only a 6.5 percent after-tax return if fully taxed. Clearly, taxes can have a major impact on (after-tax) returns.

Utilize retirement and related accounts in order to shelter as much income as you are allowed to shelter.

A number of different government-authorized programs (e.g., IRA, Keogh, 410Ks, ESOP) allow investors to put tax-sheltered income into a qualified retirement savings account. In particular, employer pension plans, 401Ks,

ESOPs, regular IRA accounts, and Keogh accounts all allow the participant to contribute a percentage of his or her income, up to some maximum overall dollar amount, into a qualifying tax-sheltered account. Both the contributions that are set aside, and any income earned on those contributions, are sheltered from current federal income tax liability. No tax is due on either the income used to fund the payment or any investment income earned on the account until the funds begin to be withdrawn from the account (as retirement income). Funds may be withdrawn (without a penalty tax) beginning at age $59\frac{1}{2}$ and must begin to be withdrawn by age $70\frac{1}{2}$. Such withdrawals will be taxed as ordinary income.

These retirement tax shelters allow a substantial tax liability to be put off, possibly for many years. As a result, you are able to earn a compounding return on an appreciably larger sum of money than would be available if only after-tax dollars were available to be invested.

To see just how advantageous these retirement tax shelters can be, consider the following illustration: Suppose that you are in the 35 percent tax bracket and put $10,000 a year into a tax-sheltered retirement plan. In the first year your $10,000 contribution would reduce your tax liability by $3,500 (.35 × $10,000). Any return earned on the money put aside is also tax-sheltered. If you earn 10 percent on the money, your initial $10,000 contribution will return $1,000 in its first year. Thus your total tax savings in the first year is $3,500 on that year's $10,000 contribution. Assuming the investment income is otherwise fully taxable, you would also save $350 in taxes on your investment income. The total tax savings in the first year would come to $3,850 ($3,500 + $350 = $3,850). In the second year, your tax savings would again be $3,500 on the second $10,000 contribution, but an additional $735 on your investment income (35% of 10% of $21,000), for a total tax savings of $4,235. In the third year, your account grows to $33,100 and the tax savings is again $3,500 on that year's $10,000 contribution, and now saves about $1,160 in taxes on that year's investment income. So by the third year, the tax savings would offset almost half ($3,500 + $1,160 = $4,660) of the amount put aside. Again we see the impact of compounding, this time coupled with the addition of a tax shelter. Continue the calculation for a few more years and the annual tax savings will approach, and eventually more than offset, the amount being put aside. Indeed, by the eleventh year you would have accumulated more than $173,000, and all but $64 of that year's contributions would be offset by tax savings.

Bear in mind that the tax savings from such tax shelters is only a deferral. All of the money accumulated in the account will be subject to taxation at ordinary income tax rates when it is withdrawn. Moreover, this calculation assumes a 35 percent tax rate on all investment income and a 10 percent fully taxable return on all monies invested. These assumptions are rather aggressive. Results would vary for other assumptions. Still the basic point is valid. *Over time, a tax-sheltered account will tend to shelter a higher and higher percentage*

TABLE 4.1. After-Tax Cost of Contributions To a Retirement Account

Year	Beginning Portfolio Value	Yearly Contribution	Investment Income	Ending Value	Tax Savings	Net After-Tax Cost
1	$0	$10,000	$1,000	$11,000	$3,850	$6,150
2	$11,000	$10,000	$2,100	$23,100	$4,235	$5,765
3	$23,100	$10,000	$3,310	$36,410	$4,660	$5,340
4	$36,410	$10,000	$4,641	$51,051	$5,124	$4,876
5	$51,051	$10,000	$6,105	$67,156	$5,637	$4,363
6	$67,156	$10,000	$7,716	$84,872	$6,207	$3,799
7	$84,872	$10,000	$8,487	$103,750	$6,470	$3,530
8	$103,750	$10,000	$11,325	$124,579	$7,463	$2,537
9	$124,579	$10,000	$13,458	$148,037	$8,210	$1,790
10	$148,037	$10,000	$15,804	$173,841	$9,031	$969
11	$173,841	$10,000	$18,384	$202,225	$9,934	$64

of the annual contribution. Follow the program for long enough, and the annual tax savings (deferral) will more than offset the annual contribution.

Each type of retirement program has differing requirements for eligibility and maximum annual contributions. Qualified company plans are made available at the option of the employer. The plans may or may not require an employee contribution and may or may not allow for additional employee contributions beyond the minimum. Employees who have the resources should take full advantage of the tax shelter provided by their employer's retirement plan. To do so, they should put the maximum allowed amount into these plans.

Individual retirement accounts (IRAs) are designed to encourage retirement savings by employees having modest levels of earned income, particularly those whose employer does not provide their employees with a pension plan. Employees with higher income levels and their own company-sponsored plans do not qualify for an IRA.

Unlike the aforementioned plans, the so-called *Roth IRA* requires contributions of after-tax dollars, but imposes no tax liability on retirement money that is withdrawn from the plan. All of the other tax-sheltered plans provide a tax shelter for income going *in to* fund the plan. The Roth IRA plans shelter money coming *out.* As with the regular IRA, the Roth IRA is available only to those having modest income levels or no available employer plan.

Anyone who earns self-employment income can set up a *Keogh* plan. If you are also an employee covered by your employer's pension plan, you are still eligible to contribute to a Keogh on any self-employment income that you earn. Unlike IRAs, eligibility for Keoghs is not limited by one's income level. You can set up and contribute to a Keogh account no matter how high your income, just as long as some of your income is derived from self-employment sources.

Non–company sponsored plans, including Keoghs and both regular and Roth IRAs, must be carefully set up according to rather complex sets of government-established rules. Almost all such accounts are organized under a master plan established by a financial institution such as a bank, brokerage firm, or insurance company. The funds deposited in one of these institution-sponsored master plans may be invested in a variety of ways. Some plans allow the individual to manage the money directly. Others provide a menu of options such as several types of stock, bond, and money market funds.

Maintain a diversified retirement account. Don't let the value of the investments in any single stock, particularly your employer's stock, dominate your portfolio.

Those retirement/investment plans that encourage you to purchase your employer's stock (e.g., ESOPs) can place a large part of or even all your investment portfolio at serious risk. *While seeking the advantages of a tax shelter, you should not lose sight of the importance of diversification.* If your employer fails (e.g., Enron, WorldCom, UAL, Kmart, Adelphia, etc.), your job is very likely to be put at risk. In addition to losing your job, you could lose all of the money that you had invested in the company's stock. Accordingly, you should limit your investment in any one company to a relatively modest percentage of your total net worth (e.g., no more than 10%).

Allocate investments whose income is heavily taxed (e.g., bonds) to retirement accounts, while investments whose income that is taxed at lower rates (e.g., stocks) should be allocated to nonretirement accounts.

One caveat regarding these various types of retirement accounts: the tax reduction act of 2003 reduced the maximum tax rate on long-term capital gains and qualifying dividends to 15 percent. The tax rate is even lower for those in very low tax brackets. To qualify for the 15 percent rate on dividends, the income that funded the payment must be subject to the corporate income tax. The maximum statutory tax on ordinary income tops out at 35 percent. The effective top rate is somewhat higher as a result of the impact of hidden taxes. Accordingly, funds withdrawn from a retirement account (except for the Roth IRA) may be subject to a relatively high tax rate (your MTR). Investment income in the form of long-term capital gains and qualifying dividends, in contrast, is subject to the relatively low 15 percent rate, and even lower in some cases. Therefore, under some circumstances, particularly when one is already close to retirement, the tax-deferral advantage of having the income sheltered in a retirement account may be rather modest. One effective way to deal with this situation is to hold investments whose income is subject to high tax rates anyway (e.g., corporate and U.S. government bonds) in your retirement accounts while maintaining nonretirement accounts for more tax-advantaged types of income (e.g., municipal bonds, whose interest income is tax-free, and stocks whose income is in the form of dividends and capital gains).

Never let tax considerations override sound investment decisions.

Sheltering income from taxes is financially advantageous, as is postponing tax payments. But, you should never lose sight of your underlying investment objective: to maximize after-tax return while avoiding undue risk. *A poorly performing investment that lowers your tax bill is still a poorly performing investment.*

Managing your investment portfolio in ways that will reduce your tax liability is easy. Lose money on an investment and you will probably lower your tax liability in the process. If you are in a very high tax bracket, every dollar you lose may be able to save you as much as $0.50 in federal and state income taxes (the maximum amount in investment losses that you can deduct from ordinary income is $3,000 per year). But losing a dollar to save fifty cents in taxes still loses you a net of fifty cents. You would have been much better off if you had put the money in a safe deposit box, made a 0.0 percent return, and not saved anything in taxes. Better still, if you had made a modest positive return of, say, 6 percent and had to pay half of it in taxes, you still would have a positive after-tax return of at least 3 percent. So, whenever you look for tax savings, make sure that the end result is an attractive expected after-tax return. Many investments that are touted for their tax advantages are, in fact, very poor investments. Don't let the alleged tax advantages of an investment blind you to the overall picture. An attractive fully taxed return is almost always higher than an unattractive tax-sheltered return. See below.

Do not contribute funds to a tax-sheltered plan that you may need to extract prior to the point of allowed withdrawals.

While some emergency exemptions exist, most tax-sheltered plans do not allow penalty-free withdrawals until the owner reaches a specified minimum age. For IRAs and Keoghs, the minimum age to begin withdrawals without incurring a tax penalty is $59\frac{1}{2}$. You must begin your withdrawal program by age $70\frac{1}{2}$.

If you absolutely must withdraw funds from a retirement account prior to reaching the allowed age for withdrawals, you will be assessed a 10 percent penalty tax (unless the withdrawal qualifies under one of the allowed emergency exceptions). Thus, in addition to the regular tax liability that is incurred on funds withdrawn from a retirement account, another 10 percent penalty tax is assessed. If you end up having to withdraw funds and pay a penalty, you almost certainly would have been better off not to have put the money into the account in the first place.

*Certain types of assets cannot be purchased or held in a retirement
account. If you want to invest in such assets, retain a portfolio
of investments outside of your retirement accounts.*

While most types of investments, including stocks, bonds, and mutual
funds, can be held in a retirement account, several other types of investments
and investment strategies are not allowed. For example, collectibles, futures
contracts, options, and mortgaged real estate are not permitted in most types of
retirement accounts. Similarly, the use of margin leverage and short selling are
not generally permitted to take place in retirement accounts.

So, if you want to buy any of the types of assets or undertake any of the types
of transactions that are prohibited in a retirement account, you will need to
have sufficient funds to do so in a nonretirement account. It is, of course,
perfectly okay to have both a retirement account (or even a set of different
retirement accounts) and to have a fully taxed nonretirement account in which
you do things that you cannot do with retirement funds.

*Variable annuities also offer some modest tax benefits. Utilize these
annuities, however, only once you have taken maximum advantage
of tax-sheltered retirement accounts.*

Variable annuities, which are sold by insurance companies, also provide a
degree of tax-sheltering. Like mutual and closed-end funds, variable annuities
pool resources from a large group of investors into a common portfolio. The
net performance of the annuity portfolio is then attributed to the annuity
holders pro rata to their share of ownership. Unlike the other types of funds
(e.g., mutual funds), the realized return earned by a variable annuity is not
paid out to the holders each year. All of the annuity's income is reinvested in
the annuity itself. Also, unlike other types of funds, that internal return on the
annuity is not subject to tax on an annual basis. Rather than having to use a
portion of the investment's return to pay taxes, the total investment income is
available for reinvestment. As a result, all of the investment income is compounded. The income from an annuity becomes taxable only when the funds
are withdrawn. While this deferral-of-income-tax-on-earnings feature makes
annuities somewhat attractive on a tax basis, variable annuities do not either
allow contributions into the account with before-tax dollars, as is the case for
most other types of retirement accounts, or, as is the case with Roth IRAs, allow
tax-free withdrawals. Accordingly, these other types of savings vehicles tend to
be much more tax efficient than are variable annuities, which shelter only the
income on earnings but not the contributions themselves.

As a general rule, you should first contribute the maximum amount allowed
to fully tax-sheltered accounts. Only if you still have additional funds available
to invest should you consider moving on to something like a variable annuity.
The tax advantages of variable annuities are small compared to those of fully

tax-sheltered accounts. Moreover, the net return on the variable annuity is reduced by a couple of factors. First, you must purchase some life insurance protection as part of the product in your annuity account. Second, as with a load mutual fund, the annuity's sales force and portfolio managers will take out their sales and management fees. As a result, the net return to you will be appreciably less than the gross return on the fund's investments.

Be very wary of limited partnership tax shelters.

Financial promoters assemble and market a variety of types of investment vehicles in the form of limited partnerships (LPs). Limited partnerships, like corporations, restrict the investor's exposure to the amount invested. If a corporation or an LP goes bankrupt, the creditors are not able to seek recovery of their losses from the business's shareholders or limited partners. Unlike corporations, however, LPs are not subject to the corporate income tax. Corporations must pay taxes on their profits, and their shareholders are taxed on their dividends and capital gains. In this way the income of corporations is taxed twice. The LP's income flows through the LP untaxed at the partnership level. That income then becomes reportable on the LP investor's tax return. Thus the LP investor's investment income is taxed only once.

Many of these limited partnership investments are designed to produce tax benefits under certain circumstances. An LP can be structured to accumulate untaxed value internally while producing reportable tax losses up front. Recall that you are taxed only on *realized* income. Unrealized income is not taxed just as long as it remains unrealized. Accordingly, such shelters undertake a strategy designed to accumulate unrealized value enhancements while recognizing expenses and losses as incurred. On paper, the LP is throwing off losses that the LP owners may be able to use to reduce their tax liabilities. Thus the tax liability on capital gains and other types of income that the investor has in other parts of his or her portfolio may be offset by the losses that the tax shelter reports for tax purposes. So, for example, an investor with real estate that produces rental income may be able to offset the tax liability on that income with the losses from such a shelter.

Many LP tax shelters assemble portfolios of rental real estate as their investment vehicle. Such tax shelters generally rely upon timing differences in the recognition of expenses and income to create tax benefits for their limited partners. They seek to recognize for tax reporting purposes substantial expenses early in the life of the LP while realizing very little in the form of taxable income until the LP is near its scheduled time for liquidation. By deducting accelerated depreciation, interest expense, operating expense, and amortizing the partnership setup expenses, a limited partnership that invests in real estate may be able to report a loss for tax purposes (expenses in excess of rental income) in its early years. Because many of the reported expenses are noncash write-offs (depreciation, amortization, etc.), the partnership may still generate a positive cash flow. Nonetheless, these reported losses flow through to the tax returns of the LP investors. As the owned property appreciates, the value of that internal buildup becomes an unrealized gain. No tax is due on that gain until the point at which the property is sold. Once the property is sold, the net gain becomes taxable income to the investor but generally at the lower rate applicable to long-term capital gains. All of the above sounds attractive on paper; the scheme does, however, have a number of potential problems and drawbacks.

First, the promoters who put these deals together grab hefty selling fees from the investors' money as it goes in. Fees will also be charged by the organizers who set up the partnership, the brokers who sell the partnership units, and the brokers who handle the purchase of the assets that are put into the partnership's portfolio. For every dollar you invest in such a partnership, 20 percent or 30 percent, or even more, may stick to the fingers of the promoters and others in the form of fees and expenses. In other words, as little as 70 or 80 cents of each dollar put into the fund may actually be used to pay for the portfolio's assets. A further set of fees will be incurred at the partnership's termination. At a minimum, brokerage fees will be charged on the asset sales, and the managers are likely to collect a success fee as well. When you buy a security or mutual fund, in contrast, at least 94 percent of what you pay (load fund) goes to buy the asset and 6 percent or less (no load fund) goes to pay commissions and other sales fees.

Second, the managers of the partnership's assets usually pay themselves generous management fees. They will charge the partnership an annual fee that is usually equal to 1 to 2 percent of the assets under management. In addition, a success fee will be assessed on the partnership's income. The typical success fee extracts 20 percent of any gains above some threshold return (e.g., 6%). Thus we see that the promoters and managers take a hefty share of the return while placing little or none of their own money at risk. Unless the project turns out exceptionally well, these fees will reduce the investor's return to a rather ordinary level or worse. By comparison, an actively managed mutual fund usually charges a management fee of 0.75 percent and incurs expenses of about another 0.5 percent per year for a total of about 1.25 percent. For index funds the fees and expenses are even lower, averaging about 0.5 percent annually. Moreover, mutual funds do not assess success fees.

Third, once limited partnership ownership units are purchased from the promoters, they become very difficult and costly to resell. Most such partnerships are structured to exist for a lengthy period. Ten years is a typical life for a limited partnership fund. At the termination of this prespecified time period, the partnership's assets are liquidated and (after paying the managers their fees) the net proceeds are distributed to the partners. The units are not meant to be trading vehicles. Those who wish to sell their units prior to the windup of the partnership will encounter a very illiquid marketplace. Ownership transfers of partnership units normally require permission from the

---

Drawbacks To Limited Partnership Tax Shelters

1. High sales fees assessed by the organizer/promoter
2. Substantial management fees including success fees charged
3. Difficult and costly to sell prior to LP windup
4. Forward payments must be made by the investor, if called
5. Tax law changes could take away contemplated advantages
6. Use of reported tax losses is severely limited

---

general partner and/or the partnership group. The potential purchasers of the units almost always demand a very steep discount in order to induce them to buy into an ongoing limited partnership venture. Frequently, a discount of 50 percent from the LP manager's estimated valuations is needed to attract a buyer. Accordingly, you should *never invest in one of these LP deals unless you are confident that you can leave your invested funds with the partnership until its termination.* Only at termination is the full value of the underling assets (less fees due at termination) likely to be realized.

Fourth, many partnerships are sold with forward-looking payment schedules. Each investor agrees to pay a certain amount into the LP up front and then to contribute up to a defined amount of additional capital to the partnership when called upon to do so in the future. Failure to make the additional capital contributions can result in a forfeiture of all of the money that the unit-holder had already invested in the partnership. *Never invest in such an LP fund unless you are sure you will be able to make all of the forward payments as they come due.*

Fifth, the tax code in place (or thought to be in place) when the partnership was set up may be changed, thereby taking away some or all of the tax benefits contemplated by the plan. Similarly, the IRS may issue new regulations that remove or reduce the contemplated tax advantages. *Avoid investing in limited partnership tax shelters that seem especially aggressive in their pursuit of tax advantages.*

Sixth, the use of the losses thrown off by such funds is restricted. Only certain types of gains and income can be offset by the losses of these types of partnerships. Make sure you have enough of the type of income that the fund's projected losses can offset before you invest.

*Take advantage of the 15 percent tax rate on dividends,
but make sure that your dividends qualify.*

The tax reduction act of 2003 lowered the maximum tax rate on dividends from the rate applied to ordinary income (up to 35 percent) to 15 percent. This 15 percent rate on dividends compares favorably with the maximum of

---

Dividends Not Subject To 15 Percent Tax Rate Limitation
(Taxed as Ordinary Income)

REIT dividends.
Preferred stock dividends, where the preferred stock is actually
subordinated debt.
Dividends from money market mutual funds, bond funds,
and other types of fixed income funds.
Dividends from foreign corporations.

---

35 percent (or more) on most other types of income (e.g., interest income). As a result, the after-tax return on qualifying dividends is considerably closer to the before-tax return than that for bond interest (other than municipal bond interest). For example, someone in the 35 percent tax bracket would derive an after-tax return of 6.5 percent from a bond paying a 10 percent coupon. A stock with a 10 percent dividend yield would, in contrast, produce an after-tax return of 8.5 percent, a full two percentage points higher.

By no means do all dividends receive this favorable tax treatment. To qualify for the 15 percent rate, the corporation paying the dividend must also have paid U.S. corporate income taxes on the funds from which the dividend payments were derived. Under this provision, four sources of dividends do not qualify for the advantageous treatment. First, REITs are exempt from paying corporate income taxes as long as they distribute all of their income to their shareholders. Since REITs pay no corporate income tax, REIT investors must pay the full tax rate on their dividends. Second, most preferred shares are technically debt instruments. As debt instruments, the preferred stock issuer is allowed to deduct the dividend payments, technically interest payments, from their own taxable income. Since the preferred stock issuer does not pay taxes on the money used to make the dividend payment, the preferred shareholder must pay taxes at the higher rate that applies to ordinary income. In addition, the dividend distributions from many types of mutual funds do not qualify for the lower tax rate. For example, the dividend payment of money market and bond mutual funds, whose own income is in the form of interest payments, are taxed as ordinary income. Finally, dividends paid by foreign-based corporations that are not subject to the U.S. corporate income tax do not qualify. Accordingly, before you purchase a stock or mutual fund for its high dividend yield, determine whether the dividend qualifies for favorable tax treatment. Dividends that qualify are worth substantially more to the recipient than those that do not.

II
INVESTMENT SELECTION

W e now turn our attention to the important topic of investment selection. Deciding what to buy and what to avoid is clearly a central component of your investment strategy. The rules contained in this section do not, however, provide a detailed road map. Books with get-rich-quick schemes may sell a lot of copies, but the schemes always seem to have serious drawbacks. If investing is really that simple, why did the author waste time writing a book? Don't expect me to offer you any miracle guidelines. I don't have any. I don't believe that anyone else does, either. Getting rich slowly takes patience and hard work, but it is possible. If you want to get rich quickly, marry well or play the lottery and pray. If you are willing to settle for a shot at getting rich slowly, read on.

I shall, in what follows, offer some guidelines designed to help you make informed investment selection decisions. Much of what I have to say explores which investments and investment selection techniques should be avoided. Avoiding obvious mistakes is an important part of effective investment selection. The universe of possible investments is so extensive that staying away from certain problematic investment areas is not especially restrictive.

The first part of this section contains a list of general investment selection rules. This is followed by sections on more specialized topics related to investment selection including: mutual, closed-end, and similar types of funds; takeovers and risk arbitrage; debt securities; bankruptcy investing; rights offerings and share buybacks; and real estate.

————— 5 —————

General Investment Selection

his chapter deals with a variety of general approaches to making investment selections. The first rule focuses on having realistic expectations. Investment opportunities that seem too attractive are all too likely to have some hidden problems. The next several rules deal with two types of stocks: value and growth stocks. Both types have their proponents. Along the way a theoretical model, the dividend discount model, is introduced. Most of the remainder of the chapter deals with the value or lack of value of such matters as stock splits, analysts' recommendations, managers' ownership position in their companies, collectibles, tangibles, and IPOs. Finally, the need for approaching investing from a broad perspective is considered.

Be very skeptical of "investments" that promise returns that seem too attractive.

Expected returns on investments tend to vary with their risk. Higher-risk investments tend to offer higher potential returns than do less risky investment opportunities. Risk-averse investors can be induced to buy high-risk investments only if they expect the returns to be high enough to justify taking the risks. Investment opportunities vary all the way from being very-low-risk, low-expected-return investments to very-high-risk, high-expected-return investments. Long-term government bonds are viewed by most people in the investment community as having essentially no risk of default. Because of their high level of safety, such bonds usually offer returns in the mid to high single digits (depending upon inflationary expectations). Investment-grade corporate bonds (having a modest risk of default) are usually priced to yield no more than a couple of percentage points above the yields on government bonds of comparable maturity. High-yield, non–investment grade (junk) bonds are normally priced to yield several percentage points above investment-grade corporates. If, for example, inflation is expected to run at 2 percent, long-term government bonds might yield 5 percent, investment-grade corporates 7–8 percent, and high-yield junk bonds 11–15 percent. These *promised* rates of return exemplify what you can reasonably expect to be offered for the amount of risk that you are willing to tolerate. Note that these are the yields to maturity that the borrower promises to pay. Not all bonds pay what they promise to pay. Some default. Losses from default, to the extent that they occur, will cause the actual returns to be lower than promised. So, for example, if the junk bond portfolio suffers default losses equivalent to 3 percent per year (a reasonable average for default losses on junk bonds) and promised a yield of 12 percent, its default-adjusted average yield is reduced to 9 percent ($12 - 3 = 9$). If any bonds are sold prior to maturity, actual realized returns will also be affected by changes in market prices and interest rates.

Over long time periods, bond investors, even those willing to take substantial risks, are unlikely to achieve returns much in excess of 10 percent and may well be quite pleased with somewhat less. Similarly, long-term returns in the stock market have averaged 9 to 11 percent. These 9 to 11 percent returns are average rates that tend to be earned on relatively *risky* investments. So, if you are offered an investment opportunity with a projected return well above this 9 to 11 percent range (e.g., 20% or more per year), you should proceed with extreme caution, if at all.

Very high projected returns are likely to result from one or more of the following three sources:

- Extremely high risk
- Unrealistically optimistic assumptions
- Fraud

Some investments do have the potential for very high returns coupled with a great deal of risk. Some examples of high-risk investments that may, in individual cases, generate very attractive returns include: futures and options contracts with their high degree of leverage, defaulted bonds with some chance of a substantial recovery, wildcat oil wells that might turn out to be a gushers, and certain IPOs and penny stocks that have an intriguing story. But their high-risk level implies that those who assemble a portfolio of such investments are likely to own a lot of losers mixed in with their winners. If the overall portfolio return is to be attractive, the high returns on the successful portfolio components must be sufficient in number and magnitude to offset the losses on the unsuccessful components. One may still be able to achieve a bit of a premium return from a diversified portfolio of carefully selected high-risk investments. Profits on the winners in such portfolios may be sufficient to offset the losses on the losers. Such premium returns are, however, far from assured. *High risk is no guarantee of high returns.* Indeed, investments in high-risk assets are almost as likely to produce very poor results as very good results. That is why they are called *high-risk* investments.

Unrealistic assumptions are another problem. *Grant me my first premise and I can prove anything.* Let me slip one carefully selected assumption into the analysis and I can easily project extremely high returns. As an example, consider a very straightforward covered option writing strategy: You buy a stock at 25 and write a six-month call option for 2 with a strike of 30. The stock pays a dividend of $0.25 a quarter. What is the return on your covered option position if the option is exercised? Gain on the stock purchase $= 5$ ($30 - 25 = 5$); option price $= 2$; dividends $= 0.50$; total potential profit of $7.5 per share ($5 + 2 + .5 = 7.5$). A profit of $7.5 on an investment of $25 amounts to a 30 percent return in six months or 60 percent annualized. An annual return of 60 percent is fantastic! Achieve a return of even half that high for a few years and you will quickly become very wealthy. But don't count on it. The assumption that produced this return? That the stock's price rises high enough quickly enough so that the option is exercised. The stock's market price must move from 25 up to 30 or more in six months for the option to become in-the-money and therefore attractive to be exercised. It could happen. A five-point increase on a $25 stock is, however, a rather large move for a relatively short time period (20%, which is equivalent to 40% annualized). Only a small percentage of $25 stocks will move up to 30 in any given six-month period.

Six months from now the stock is much more likely to remain below 30 than it is to have risen from 25 to 30 or more. So what is your return if the stock's price stays below 30? What if the stock's price just stays at 25? The return is still attractive: $2 + 0.5 = 2.5$ on an investment of 25, a gain of 10 percent, which is equivalent to a 20 percent annualized return. What could go wrong? The company could fail to declare the dividend and the stock could fall to 20. A stock is about as likely to fall from 25 to 20 as it is to rise from 25 to 30. If the stock's price does fall to 20, you still retain the 2 points that you received from the option sale, but you are 5 points underwater on the stock. You would have a loss of 5 on the stock partially offset by 2 from the sale of the call. Thus you have a net loss of 3 points ($5 - 2 = 3$) on a stock position costing 25 (a loss of 12%, or 24% annualized).

Clearly the projected success of the covered option-writing strategy that I just outlined depends crucially on what happens to the market price of the underlying stock. The results projected for most, if not all, such strategies are dependent upon the underlying assumptions. You need to identify and then evaluate the reasonableness of each of these assumptions before you proceed.

Only if you are comfortable that the assumptions are realistic should you accept the feasibility of the analysis and resulting profit-projections.

High risk and optimistic assumptions are one thing. Fraud is quite another. If you invest in a high-risk venture or one based on unrealistic assumptions, you may get burned. But at least you have a fighting chance of achieving a reasonable result. Even if things don't work out as planned, you will usually be able to salvage something of value from the amount that you originally invested. So, for example, if you buy a junk bond that later defaults, you will end up with a claim in a bankruptcy proceeding. That claim may eventually produce a recovery equal to a portion (e.g., 20% or 50%) of the bond's face value. If you bought the bonds cheaply enough, your investment may even show a profit. If, in contrast, you buy into an investment fraud, you are almost certain to lose everything that you put at risk.

The most famous of investment frauds was concocted by one Charles Ponzi in Boston in 1919. Ponzi claimed to be able to purchase postal money orders in Europe at a steep discount and then redeem them in the U.S. for their full value. He said he needed capital from "investors" in order to purchase the money orders in bulk. He offered "investors" astronomical returns, such as 45 percent for an investment of sixty days. Mr. Ponzi could deliver these kinds of "returns" in only one way. He used the money brought *in* from new "investors" to pay *out* the monies that were due to old "investors." He also depended heavily upon the greed of existing "investors," who he urged to continue to let their money ride. He embezzled some of the funds entrusted to him in order to live high on the hog. The rest went to pay out the astronomical returns to those "investors" who demanded their promised payment. Eventually, a Boston newspaper reporter exposed his scam. Then everything came crashing down. Ponzi was convicted of fraud and sent to prison. He later died in obscurity in Brazil. But he did achieve a kind of immortality. The type of scheme that Ponzi was practicing soon came to be named after him.

Ponzi schemes utilize an investment pyramid. Such a scheme could, for example, take in a million dollars (50%) in period one, keep $500,000 for the scammer, and pay out $500,000 (50%) to "investors." Then take in $2 million in period two, keep a million dollars for the scammer, and pay out $1 million (50%). In period three the scheme would need to take in $4 million to stay on track. Soon the amount of new money needed to be raised to keep the scam going grows very large.

Contributions from new or existing suckers are depended upon to fund the ever-growing need for payouts. Such a scheme can last only as long as an ever-larger group of new participants (suckers) can be enticed into the program. Once "investors" begin to seek to withdraw their funds in significant numbers, the cupboard is quickly emptied and the Ponzi is exposed for the empty shell that it is. A very few participants who get out before the collapse may avoid a disaster. Under the bankruptcy code, however, even they may be required to put back the money (called a *preference*) that they got out near the end of the scheme. Usually the people who assemble these types of schemes have stolen and spent a large fraction of the money contributed by the participants. Little or nothing is left to be distributed to the disappointed "investors."

Clearly, you want to avoid getting sucked into a fraud such as a Ponzi scheme. But, how do you know if a particular investment opportunity is some kind of fraud? The first tip-off is a promise of an unreasonably generous (e.g., a 50%) return. The old saying, *If the offer seems too good to be true, it probably is*, remains a very useful guide.

Another guide: *Never invest in what you do not understand*. The fraud that was Enron is a good example of the type of company that many people invested in, even though they had little idea of its business model. Enron was said somehow to be in the business of buying and selling energy. And yet few if any of the analysts who recommended its stock really understood how Enron was supposedly producing the income that it falsely claimed to be earning.

A third guide: *Be aware of the kinds of schemes that have been used in the past*. One such example is based on the chain letter principle. Each participant must bring in two new participants to move up the chain. When the participant's name reaches the top of the list, he or she receives the contributions from each of the participants at the bottom of the list. Suppose the entrance fee is $1,000 and the chain has four levels, with each level double the size of the one below it. The person at the top of the pyramid will be above two at the second level, four at the third, and eight at the fourth. Put $1,000 in at the bottom and get $8,000 back when your name reaches the top level. Why not risk $1,000 to get back $8,000, especially if you think that you can talk two friends into coming into the pool? If they each find two friends who, in turn, find two friends each, you have gotten to the top to get your $8,000.

But if you take this route, you will encounter a couple of serious problems. First, this type of arrangement is illegal. Once the appropriate authorities realize what is being done, they will step in to stop it. If that happens before your name reaches the top, you are sure to have lost your $1,000. If you were one of the organizers rather than simply a naive participant, you are now in legal trouble. Second, these pyramids must grow very large very quickly and continue to expand at a rapid pace until they grow so large that they can no longer continue the rapid pace. Once they stop expanding, they quickly collapse. Finding enough suckers to keep the pyramid going and growing becomes increasingly difficult as time passes. Some people are skeptical of such seemingly easy money; they won't buy. Others are already in and waiting to see how they will come out. They already have as much money at risk as they want. Still others would like to, but just can't come up with the initial "investment." Finally, many people perform a bit of analysis and conclude that the scheme will soon collapse of its own weight. As a result, finding two friends to buy in is not always easy. Even if you do find the two willing participants, you have some obligation to these friends as a result of your getting them into the program. If the scheme disintegrates after you receive your $8,000 but before they get theirs, what do you say to them? Or, suppose it collapses one more level down? What about your friends' friends? Aren't you likely to know them, too? Sooner or later the schemes will collapse. Do you really want to be a participant in such situations even if you are lucky enough to come out ahead?

The above description of a pyramid scheme is simple and straightforward. Often the chain is more carefully disguised. A pyramid scheme does not need to involve money. It could call for contributions in savings bonds, ounces of gold, or bottles of wine, for example. Sometimes the scheme is embedded in a seemingly legitimate business (Dare To Be Great, for example, an ostensible marketing syndicate that was largely in the business of selling franchises to one group, which would then seek to sell more franchises to another group, and so on).

By no means are all investment frauds based on the chain letter or even the Ponzi scheme concept. Some of the most egregious schemes have relied upon the generous nature of many people. The advertised appeal is to make money by doing good. One such fraud involved the sale of what was touted as participation in a religious theme park to be called Bible City. Rural God-fearing folk throughout the Midwest were offered an opportunity to buy into the "project." In fact, no legitimate theme park was ever planned. The promoters were selling a giant fraud. The "investors," however, just could not believe that Bible City wasn't the real thing. Similarly, many frauds have been perpetrated by Mormons on other Mormons, who are particularly inclined to trust their fellow church people.

The most mundane medium may be the basis for a fraud, as the *great salad oil scandal* illustrates. In this instance, a dealer in fats and oils sought a bank loan using his salad oil inventory (a liquid asset) as collateral. When the loan officer checked the borrower's (salad oil dealer's) tank, it registered as full. The loan collateral was judged sufficient. Later, the bank was asked to double the size of the loan. When the loan officer came to inspect the facility and its collateral, he saw two tanks. Each was found to be full of salad oil. A third tank and then a fourth appeared and each was used to collateralize an addition to the loan. The process continued with additional tanks and additions to the loan. Eventually the pattern became too suspicious. A careful analysis revealed that a single tankful of salad oil was being pumped from tank to tank just in time to show each tank as full when checked. Clearly almost anything can be the basis for a fraudulent investment scam.

To sum up, promised or projected returns that seem too high should be taken as a red flag. Such anticipated returns are very likely to be due either to very high risks, to unrealistic assumptions, or to outright fraud.

Fad/growth/story stocks are particularly vulnerable to general market declines. Be cautious with such stocks, especially when the market seems frothy.

Two major schools of investment analysis approach investment selection from very different perspectives. The *growth stock* school prefers companies that are projected to show rapid increases in sales, assets, earnings, and eventually perhaps dividends. Growth stock advocates are willing to pay a high price relative to current earnings (a high *price earnings,* or *PE,* ratio) in order to buy stock in a company that they expect to grow rapidly. Such investors believe that the kinds of companies that they prefer as investments will grow much larger and be much more profitable in the future. They point to companies such as WalMart, Dell, Microsoft, or more recently eBay or Google as examples of the types of stocks they would like to have bought when these companies were just getting established. An early purchase of such stocks would indeed have produced phenomenal returns. The same was said about IBM, Xerox, and Polaroid in an earlier era. More recently, however, IBM has been a lackluster performer, Xerox has been struggling, and Polaroid had to file for bankruptcy. Strong performers of one era do not necessarily remain strong performers forever.

Value stock investors, in contrast, prefer to assemble portfolios of companies whose stock prices are low relative to their tangible intrinsic values. They focus attention on dividends, book values, and especially earnings (low PE) as measures of intrinsic value. While not averse to the potential benefits of growth, value investors are unwilling to pay a large premium for what they fear may be no more than a hope of high future growth rates. Value investors believe that the market often neglects the kinds of stocks that they prefer. This allegedly unwarranted neglect is exactly why these types of stocks appeal to value investors. Such "neglected" stocks are often underpriced precisely because the market is overlooking their virtues. When (if) the market rediscovers the favorable aspects of such companies, their stock prices will rise. Or at least that is what value-oriented investors expect (hope) to happen. Value investors subscribe to the so-called *theory of contrary opinion:* "Buy what the market doesn't like when it is out of favor because in time the market's view is likely to change." It is kind of like buying Christmas ornaments in January. By no means do all stocks identified as value stocks turn out to be undervalued any more than all supposed growth stocks turn in rapid growth. Value investors, however, believe that these types of stocks tend to be the better buys.

The debate between value and growth stock investors boils down to the following question: Do value stocks, on balance, outperform growth stocks, or vice versa? In other words, would a well-diversified portfolio of value stocks tend to outperform or be outperformed by a similarly well-diversified portfolio of growth stocks?

In some periods, the stocks favored by the growth stock school tend to do best. At other times the value stock school's choices are more in vogue. Some studies suggest that, for long-term holding periods, value stocks tend to be the better buy. The evidence for this conclusion is not overwhelming, however. What can be said with a significant degree of confidence is the following: *In a major market downturn, the stocks that tend to get hit the hardest are the very stocks that were bid up the most on optimistic expectation for their future growth.*

Accordingly, one of the worst times to own a heavy concentration of high-PE growth stocks is when the market is about to experience or is in the process of experiencing a dramatic fall. When the market's mood turns negative, it is likely to turn especially negative on those stocks whose story is largely in the future (growth stocks). So, when the market appears frothy, one should be especially cautious about owning high-PE speculative stocks. To implement this advice, however, you need to be able to identify when the market is nearing a top and about to experience a major decline. That is not an easy task. But it may not be impossible.

When, however, the PE ratio of the overall market is well above its normal range and when a lot of investors and many analysts are rejecting the old wisdom on the importance of assets, cash, and earnings, and when the IPO market is hot for concept stocks, the market can be described as frothy (e.g., the late 1990s). It may well become more overpriced before it changes direction, but change direction it will. It is just a matter of time.

Use the PE ratio as one index of how expensive a stock is.

Both value and growth stock investors utilize the PE ratio (the ratio of the stock's per-share price to its earnings per share) as a measure of a stock's relative price. A theoretical relationship called the dividend discount model (DDM) has been developed by the finance profession to explain the determinants of the PE ratio. This model is based on the proposition that the price of a stock equals the present (discounted) value of its expected future income stream. According to this model, a stock's PE ratio is a function of just three variables: its payout ratio, expected growth rate, and the appropriate discount rate. See below:

Dividend Discount Model

$PE = \text{payout} / (r-g)$
where:
payout $=$ dividend rate/earnings per share
$r =$ appropriate (risk-adjusted) discount rate
$g =$ expected long-term growth rate for dividends and earnings

---

Let's explore the operations of this dividend discount model with an example. Consider the case of a company that pays out half of its after-tax earnings in the form of dividends and has a market-determined discount rate of 12 percent applied to its expected income stream. Thus payout $= .5$ and $r = .12$. We can use the DDM to see how its expected growth rate will affect its PE. If the firm is expected to grow at 8 percent, the DDM formula solves as follows:

$$PE = .5 / (.12 - .08) = .5 / .04 = 12.5$$

If the expected growth rate is 10 percent, the solution for the PE becomes:

$$PE = .5 / (.12 - .10) = .5 / .02 = 25$$

For an expected growth rate of 11 percent, the formula yields a PE of:

$$PE = .5 / (.12 - .11) = .5 / .01 = 50$$

So we see in this example that expected growth rates of 8, 10, and 11 percent correspond to PEs of 12.5, 25, and 50 respectively. Thus, a stock with those characteristics (payout $= .5$, discount rate $= 12\%$) that generates an EPS of $1 could, for example, sell at 12.5, 25, or 50 depending upon its expected growth rate. The faster its earnings are expected to grow, the higher its PE. Clearly, the growth rate that the market expects a company to achieve plays a large role in the pricing of its stock. Small changes in expected growth rates can produce large changes in the market price. High PEs reflect market optimism about the firm's growth prospects.

A similar relationship obtains for the overall market. The more optimistic the market's view of the economy's growth prospects, the higher the major market indexes' PE ratios tend to be.

The stock market's expectations for a particular company may or may not be realistic. If the market overestimates a company's growth prospects, its stock's price will be inflated. Once the market realizes its error, the price will decline; perhaps by a lot. Suppose the market initially expects a stock's earnings to grow at an 11 percent rate with a PE of 50. Now assume that somewhat later the market reevaluates the situation so that it now expects the growth rate to be 8 percent. For the above example, the PE would fall to 12.5, or one-fourth the prior level. Indeed, stock prices can move around quite a bit as the market's expectations for future growth rates rise and fall.

PE ratios are also affected by both market interest rates and risk levels.

Recall that the dividend discount model's denominator is the difference $(r - g)$ where r is the appropriate market-determined discount rate and g is the market's expected long-term growth rate. For a given payout ratio, the smaller the difference, the higher the PE ratio. That difference $(r - g)$ will be affected by changes in either r or g. We have already explored the impact of g (the growth rate) on the PE ratio. Now consider the PE ratio impact of r (the discount rate). As r increases, so does the denominator $(r - g)$. An increase in $(r - g)$ lowers the value of the fraction, payout/$(r - g)$, which in turn is equal to PE. Thus the higher the discount rate, r, the lower the PE, holding the other variables (g and payout) constant. But what determines the value of r?

The discount rate, r, can be decomposed into two parts, the risk-free rate (RFR), and the appropriate risk premium (RP): $r = RFR + RP$. That is, when the market, through the interplay of supply and demand, establishes a market price, it implicitly assigns that investment a discount rate to be applied to its expected income stream. This discount rate is the sum of the economywide rate for riskless investments and an additional increment that reflects the risk level of the individual investment.

The market views government bonds as essentially being devoid of risk. Accordingly, the yields on these bonds should provide a rather reliable proxy for the risk-free rate. At any particular point in time, this market-determined risk-free rate is the same for all investments. Changes in the risk-free rate will affect the overall level of security market prices. The risk premium, in contrast, will vary from asset to asset depending upon the risk of the particular investment. Low-risk investments (e.g., high-grade corporate bonds) will have lower-risk premiums than high-risk investments (e.g., speculative bonds). Changes in the market's view of an individual investment's risk will influence its price. If the market believes that a stock has become more (less) risky, its discount rate (r) will go up (down) and its price will fall (rise), other things being equal. That is, as the risk premium (RP) changes, so will r, and in turn so will $(r - g)$, which in turn changes the fraction, payout/$(r - g) = PE$.

Thus we see from the prior discussion that individual stock values depend crucially on two factors:

1. The market's expectations for its future long-term growth rate.
2. The market's view of its risk.

Any attempt to uncover securities on which the market has placed an inaccurate value needs to take careful account of these two key factors: expected growth and risk. Stock values tend to rise with their expected growth rates and fall as their risk increases.

Another important ratio for stock analysts is the dividend yield.
Value investors focus on dividends as an important indicator
of intrinsic value.

The payout ratio (the ratio of dividends to earnings per share) is the third independent variable in the dividend discount model (PE is a function of r, g, and payout). Most investors, however, prefer to work with a different dividend ratio when it comes to exploring the relationship between dividends and stock prices. A stock's *dividend yield* is its current indicated annual dividend rate divided by its price per share. If a stock selling for $20 pays an annual dividend of $1, its current yield is 5 percent ($1/20 = .05$). A stock's dividend yield is one part of what is called its *total return*. The total return earned on a stock investment reflects the impact of both dividends and any appreciation in its price. Thus the total return is the sum of the dividend and price appreciation (which can be either positive or negative):

$$\text{Total Return} = (\text{Dividend} / \text{Price}) + (\Delta \text{Price} / \text{Price})$$
$$\text{where}: \Delta \text{Price} = \text{change in price}$$

If the $20 stock with a 5 percent dividend yield also experienced a price rise of $2 over the year, its return from price appreciation would equal 10 percent and its total return would be:

$$1/20 + 2/20 = 5\% + 10\% = 15\%$$

Dividends are an important source of investment income. For many stocks, the dividend yield is a large part of its total return. Furthermore, the dividend tends to be a more reliable form of return than the other total return component, the price appreciation. The price increase that the investor anticipated often does not occur, or if it does, the price rise takes place in fits and starts. Indeed, stock prices can, and all too often do, go down as well as up. To earn that part of the return that takes the form of dividends, in contrast, requires only that the firm continue to make the payment.

A company that has begun to pay a dividend on a regular basis is likely to continue to do so as long as the payments can afford to be made. Similarly, once a dividend has been increased to a given level, managers generally prefer to maintain the new higher rate rather than reduce it. The market generally views reducing or eliminating the dividend rate as evidence of a problem at the firm and a failure on the part of management. The firm's managers would much prefer to be able to increase their company's dividend rate from time to time. A rising dividend rate is generally viewed by the market as a sign of progress and tends to enhance the firm's stock price.

Clearly the managers' desire is to maintain their firm's dividend rate at least at its current level. Still, no law prevents managers from reducing or eliminating their firm's dividends. Unlike the coupon rate on a bond, paying a dividend is completely within the discretion of the firm's board of directors. If the board does not believe that the firm can afford to pay the dividend, or if it believes that the firm has better uses for the funds, the board has every legal right not to declare and thus not to pay a dividend. Unlike interest payments on debt, dividend payments are totally discretionary.

Many companies choose not to pay dividends. They may hope to pay them someday, but do not pay dividends currently. Such companies are generally either plowing all of their earnings back into the company in an effort to grow rapidly or are not generating sufficient free cash flow to afford to pay a dividend. Dividends require cash, which is often a scarce commodity, even for profitable firms. *Don't ever confuse profitability with liquidity.* A firm can report high profits but, because its funds are being used to finance a rapid rate of growth, can be very short on cash. A firm that grows rapidly generally consumes more cash than it generates. It must then raise additional capital in order to help fund its growth. Such a firm has no available cash to pay dividends.

Tax considerations also enter into the determination of a firm's dividend policy. If a company's earnings grow, its stock price is likely to rise. The income produced by that stock price increase will be taxable only if and when the shareholder sells his or her shares. Dividends, in contrast, become taxable upon receipt. Investors cannot avoid incurring the tax liability on any of the dividends that they receive even if they reinvest the payments in the dividend-paying company's own stock. Accordingly, investment income in the form of dividends may be somewhat less attractive to some investors (especially those in high tax brackets) than income in the form of unrealized price appreciation. Such investors tend to prefer to invest in firms that plow their profits into growth-producing projects rather than pay them out as dividends. Other investors prefer the cash income. They may look to those dividend checks as a supplement to their other sources of income. They gravitate toward firms that pay generous dividends because they prefer current income over an equivalent amount of potential price appreciation. The higher (lower) your marginal tax rate and the lower (higher) your need for current cash income, the less (more) attractive dividends will be for you. One of your important strategic decisions as an investor is to determine your preference for current income. If you opt for high-dividend-paying stocks and bonds with attractive yields, you will receive a substantial percentage of your return in the form of current income. That current income has the advantage of being immediately available for spending, but it also has the disadvantage of being taxed upon its receipt.

Avoid (or sell) stocks of companies that engage in reverse splits.

A *split* is a transaction in which the company alters the number of its outstanding shares without buying or selling any of its stock or altering the relative holdings of any shareholder. The act of splitting its shares has no impact on the company's assets, liabilities, or income level. In a stock split, the number of shares held by each shareholder changes proportionately. No one ends up with a greater or lesser ownership percentage of the company as a result of a split.

A split can be designed either to increase or decrease the number of shares outstanding. The vast majority of splits are *forward splits* in which the number of shares outstanding is increased. A two-for-one split, for example, doubles the number of everyone's shareholdings. Someone who owned 100 shares before the split now owns 200 shares. After the split, every shareholder has twice as many shares as before. The value-producing fundamentals of the overall company (payout ratio, growth potential risk, and appropriate discount rate) have not been changed by the increase in the number of shares outstanding. Accordingly, the post-split market price of the stock will typically fall to about half its pre-split level (thereby maintaining a constant market value for the company). The overall market value of a company's equity (over and above its outstanding debt) is equal to the product of the per-share price of its stock and the number of shares outstanding. With twice as many shares at half the price, the market value is unchanged.

Companies that split their shares generally do so in order to move their stock's per-share price into what they believe to be a more desirable price range. For example, many investors are likely to view a stock trading at $200 a share as, in some sense, too expensive. They would rather own 100 shares of a $40 stock ($4,000 worth of stock) than 20 shares of a $200 stock (also $4,000 worth of stock). Such investors may think that a $40 stock can more easily double to $80 than a $200 stock can double to $400. Accordingly, managers of a company with a $200 stock may be troubled with its high absolute price level. They may wish to take some action that will lower their company's stock price while maintaining the company's overall value. Splitting this $200 stock five-for-one will reduce the per share price to around $40 ($5×$40 = $200). Such a level may seem more appealing to the investment community.

This theory that a stock's price needs to be in the proper range to be fully appreciated by the investing public has not been supported by those financial economists who have studied the matter. Stock prices are largely determined by the firm's profit performance and growth potential. The number of its outstanding shares plays little or no role (other than scaling). Nonetheless, managers who make decisions about splitting their companies' shares do appear to believe that moving the stock price into the desirable range enhances its marketability and thus its price.

Forward splits are usually preceded by a price rise in the relevant stock. Over a period of time the stock's price may have increased from $15 to $50 and then to $90. As a result of this price increase, the stock has risen out of the range that the managers prefer. A three-for-one split would put the price of this $90 stock back to around $30. Such a forward split is designed to reduce the stock price to a level that is thought to be more attractive to investors.

The stock market has tended to rise along with the growth of the economy and the resulting increase in corporate profits. Most individual stock prices also tend to go up, at least in the long run. Thus individual stocks are much more likely to be rising above than falling below the desirable price range. As a result, most stock splits are forward splits designed to reduce the price per share by increasing the number of shares outstanding.

Stock prices can go down as well as up. Sometimes a stock's price falls so low that the company wishes to take some action to move it to a higher level. Perhaps a stock that had been trading for $15 falls to $5 and then to $1. This kind of dramatic price decline is likely to result if the company incurs a series of substantial losses, causing the market to sour on its prospects. At a price of $1 per share, the stock is referred to as a low-priced or *penny stock*. Low-priced stocks are generally viewed by the market as speculative and of low quality. Indeed, most brokerage firms will not allow stocks with prices below $3 per share to be used as margin collateral. Some have a $5-per-share marginability threshold. Stocks whose prices drop so low that they are no longer marginable tend to be less attractive to investors than those that remain marginable. Indeed, stocks that fall below the marginability threshold may trigger margin calls, putting further selling pressure on their price.

If the firm, whose stock sells for a low per share price, could increase its earnings and/or its dividend rate, that improvement in fundamental performance would probably lead to a higher price for its stock. Such an attempt to improve performance is difficult to implement, takes time, and often does not succeed. Accordingly, the firm's manager may choose to undertake a *reverse split* in order to move the stock's price up more quickly. A company having a stock trading for $1 that then engages in a twenty-for-one reverse split would hope to see its shares' price rise to about $20.

Neither forward splits nor reverse splits create or destroy any underlying company value. A company's total market value is based on its assets, earnings, cash flow, risk level, growth prospects, and other factors, not on the number of shares outstanding. And yet, as a general rule, *stocks that forward split tend to rise in price after they split, and those that undertake reverse splits tend to fall*. The companies that engage in reverse splits are thought to be signaling to the marketplace (unintentionally) that they do not have confidence in their ability to move the price up the old-fashioned way: by earning it. Those firms that forward split, in contrast, are signaling their confidence in the future growth prospects of the company.

Analysts' forecasts and recommendations are not what they seem. Read them with a very skeptical eye.

Most investment analysts are intelligent, well-trained, highly paid experts. They generally specialize in the stocks of companies in a particular industry, have access to senior managers in the companies that they follow, and often have particularized knowledge of their chosen industry's technology. If any outsiders working with publicly available information should be able to understand the companies and industry that they cover, investment analysts should. Does this mean that when an investment analyst (or even a group of investment analysts) recommends buying a particular stock, it is an attractive investment? Not necessarily, and indeed, not in general.

First of all, investment analysts' recommendations tend to be positively based. The vast majority of their recommendations are to "buy." Analysts rarely recommend a sale. Short sale recommendations are even rarer. At least two factors help account for analysts' reluctance to issue negative opinions on their list of companies. First, the analysts need to maintain cordial relations with the companies that they follow in order to maintain continuing access to knowledgeable insiders. Hard-hitting negative reports are likely to close those doors. Second, investment banks for whom the analysts work may be seeking business from the same companies that their analysts cover. Thus their employers will not want their analysts' recommendations to harm their own business prospects. Recent reform efforts are designed to remove this conflict of interest. Time will tell whether these reform efforts will be successful. In any case, most analyst write-ups are heavily biased in favor of *buy* recommendations. Indeed, anything less than a *strong buy* should be taken as a negative. An analyst who issues a *neutral, weak buy, hold,* or even *accumulate on weakness* recommendation should be viewed as issuing a *disguised sell* recommendation.

Do the biases and other problems present in many analysts' reports mean that you should ignore what they say? No. Such reports often contain useful information and insights. While the actual recommendation to *buy, hold,* or *sell* should be largely ignored (particularly if it is a *buy* recommendation), the totality of the report should be read and digested. Often the body of the report will reveal much more of what the analyst really thinks than is contained in the buy-hold-sell recommendation. Moreover, analysts in the aggregate tend to reflect the market's overall wisdom vis-à-vis the stocks that they cover. Accordingly, their views provide the investor with useful benchmark information on the market's consensus view of a particular stock. A buy decision on your part indicates that you tend to believe that the stock is undervalued by the market, and a sell decision reflects the opposite view. So you should buy (sell) a stock if you are even more (less) optimistic than the consensus view of the analysts.

If senior managers are selling their company's stock, you should probably avoid the stock or sell your own shares if you have any. If the senior managers are net buyers, that is a plus for the stock. You may want to buy it.

Trading on material, nonpublic information is illegal. When insiders such as senior executives or members of the board of directors buy or sell stock in their own company, they are not generally doing so because of any specific inside information. They are no more likely to want to risk being sent to prison for violating the law than you or I. Rather, when insiders are net buyers (sellers) of their own company's stock, it is frequently because they believe that things are (or are not) going well for their company. At other times they may be selling because they wish to diversify or need money for personal reasons. While far from a perfect forecaster, the buy/sell decisions of insiders do offer useful signals. If the insiders expect their company to have a bright future, they are more likely to be buying. If they view the company's prospects as bleak, the insiders are more likely to be selling. These insider trades must be reported to the SEC, which then makes information on their trading publicly available.

If senior managers have a large stake in a company, it may enhance the investment's attractiveness.

One way that managers signal their degree of confidence in the company that they manage is by their investment portfolio decisions. When senior managers own a large and growing stake in the company for whom they work, that level of manager ownership suggests that the company's prospects are attractive. The managers of such companies will share in its success and therefore have strong incentives to produce positive performance. If their holdings are small, their incentive to produce favorable performance for the shareholders may not be as great.

Similarly, the degree to which the managers take advantage of their positions to have themselves awarded high pay and executive perks is a useful indicator of how diligently they are working for the shareholders as opposed to how much they are doing to feather their own nests. The more out of line (on the high side) the executive compensation is, the less likely is the company to produce favorable performance for its shareholders. As an example, both Bill Gates, of Microsoft, and Warren Buffett, of Berkshire Hathaway, take very small salaries for themselves. Because of their large ownership positions in the companies that they manage, they have profited handsomely from their companies' success. These two gentlemen just happen to be the two richest humans in the United States.

A large manager stake in a company can help align shareholders' and managers' interests. A very large manager stake, however, often has a downside. A manager who owns a controlling interest (either individually or via a family group) may treat the company as if it is his or her own private firm (fiefdom). Such an attitude may impact dividend policy, reactions to takeover offers, decisions to retain unprofitable business units, the hiring of relatives, and so on. Such an ownership structure often works to the detriment of minority shareholders. Be wary of a company whose management owns a controlling interest in the firm. Such a company may be run for the benefit of the insiders rather than its public shareholders. A particularly egregious situation arises when the corporate structure allows the control group to retain a large percentage of the company's voting power with a relatively small percentage of stock ownership. This structure may be accomplished via special super voting rights shares. For example, super shares may be allocated ten votes compared to one vote for regular shares. Realize that such a structure permits the control group to run the company more or less as it wishes. Also be wary of companies that award inordinate amounts of stock options to their senior executives. Modest amounts of such options help align shareholder and manager interests. Large awards tend to dilute the nonmanager shareholders' ownership. Managers of well-run companies deserve to be rewarded for effective management, but there are limits.

Avoid collectibles as an investment, unless you are already an expert in the area.

Baseball cards, Beanie Babies, Cabbage Patch Kids dolls, and many other items (stamps, coins, antiques, antique and classic automobiles, etc.) have become collectibles. Such items may experience dramatic price increases when they are hot. Just about the time that the fad is beginning to lose steam, novice investors may be enticed into the market. Having seen prices double annually for each of the last several years, they may become involved, thinking that they have found the key to great wealth.

True, some collectibles do have a long history with significant periods of major price increases (paintings by old masters). In other cases, the fad dies back as quickly as it started (Cabbage Patch Kids dolls and Beanie Babies). As with the securities market, the past price history for a particular type of collectible provides little or no guidance to its future. Even well-established collectibles (coins, stamps, etc.) have a number of major drawbacks that limit their appeal as investments.

First, collectibles largely trade in a high markup *dealer market*. When you buy and sell stocks, bonds, mutual funds, options, and the like, you usually trade through a broker who earns a commission. That is, you are actually buying from the seller or selling to the buyer with the broker facilitating the transaction. The total impact of commissions and bid-ask spreads is, typically, no more than a few percentage points and often less than 1 percent of the asset's market value. With collectibles, which tend to be relatively unusual, one-of-a-kind items, you would generally buy from a dealer. Similarly, when you wished to sell part or all of your collection, you would be likely to sell to a dealer. Dealers constitute a very large part of the collectibles marketplace. Such dealers need to make enough money from their buying and selling of collectibles to be able to cover all of the costs associated with maintaining their store or other selling facility. In particular they need to be able to earn a return on the substantial sum of money that they have tied up in inventory. What he or she buys from you may sit on the shelves for months, or even years, before it is sold to another collector. These dealers will generally try to pay as little as they can get away with for what they buy. Indeed, many dealers make a substantial percentage of their profits by buying cheaply from uninformed sellers and quickly reselling to another dealer at a higher price. The dealer who buys may already have a collector lined up at a still higher price.

For collectibles, the difference between what a dealer will sell an item for and what he or she will pay for it can easily be 20, 30, or even 50 percent of the retail selling price. Most dealers will charge what the market will bear when they sell. To top it off, you will often have to pay sales tax on the purchase. This high markup represents a steep barrier to overcome for those who invest in collectibles. You may sometimes be able to reduce or even eliminate the markup by buying and selling at auctions, over the Internet, or directly with other investor/collectors at club meetings. Nonetheless, the average markup on your acquisitions will still tend to be high compared to the costs of buying and selling securities. As a result, the item that you purchase may need to appreciate by 20 to 50 percent before the dealer will buy it back for what you paid for it. It will need to appreciate even more if you are to earn a profit. That is a heavy burden for any investment.

Second, the value of most collectibles is very sensitive to the item's condition. A collectible item in like-new condition is worth much more than an otherwise identical item that has been well worn through heavy use. With coins for example, an uncirculated (shiny, no wear) particular coin is usually worth many (maybe hundreds of) times what a well-worn twin will bring in. This reality has several implications. Collectibles must be carefully maintained if they are to retain their original-condition value. You should never use what you collect for its original intended purpose. Quilts or oriental rugs that are used and soiled in the process will lose much of their collector appeal. Similarly, baseball cards that have become bent or soiled through mishandling are worth much less than those in pristine condition. Subtle differences in quality/condition can have a large impact on value. When buying an item, the dealer may assure you that the quality is high. When the dealer (sometimes the same dealer) is offering to buy it back from you, you may be told that the quality is appreciably lower. A large difference in value is at stake. Clearly, you need to be able to judge an item's condition yourself rather than rely upon what the self-interested dealer tells you. A high level of expertise is needed in order to judge a collectible's quality/condition reliably. Books are written on the subject. In some areas (e.g., coins), grading services have arisen to provide a certification-of-condition service. Evaluation of a collectible's condition is, however, inherently subjective.

Third, many collectibles are relatively easy to counterfeit. Such counterfeits are generally a simple matter for experts to detect. But they may not be so obvious for novice investors. Counterfeits are particularly likely to appear when the market price is high relative to production costs and where copies are easy to make. So, for example, a rare and valuable baseball card can be copied with a color printer and then, with a bit of cardboard, a stack of counterfeited copies can easily be turned out. The counterfeit won't mislead an expert, but it may well fool a novice. Similarly, the date on a coin such as 1944 can easily be altered to 1914 with a tiny grinding wheel. A 1944 D penny is common, while the 1914 D is rare. The "D" indicates that the coin was made in the Denver mint.

Fourth, collectibles tend to be subject to fads. These fads often grow into speculative bubbles and then end quickly and without warning. Once the fad has past, selling such collectibles for anything close to what you paid is difficult at best. The hobby (such as Beanie Babies) will continue to exist, but with a much lower level of popularity.

Fifth, collectibles do not produce any cash income (dividends, interest, rent, etc.). The only profit that can be derived from an investment program in collectibles must come from price increases (if any). Collectors derive enjoyment from having, adding to, and on occasion completing their collection. Investors, who are likely to be involved purely for the hoped-for profit, are much less likely to derive a similar benefit.

Sixth, while the supply of any specific collectible is generally fixed, the supply of similar items is not. So, for example, the supply of baseballs signed by Babe Ruth is limited to the number that he signed during his lifetime. The potential number of baseballs signed by home run champions is, in contrast, unlimited. Any type of collectible that becomes popular is likely to experience a growing supply of similar items made available to collectors. As more and more merchandise hits the market, the pressure on the prices of existing items increases. The Franklin Mint and similar concerns are known for producing just as many manufactured collectibles as the market will absorb. A growing supply is the enemy of scarcity and rising prices.

Seventh, collectibles require a certain amount of maintaining. Specifically, they must be stored and should be insured (fire, theft). Collectibles take up space. A large collection (e.g., antique automobiles) may take up a lot of space. Some types of collectibles, such as stamps and first editions of books, need to be stored not only in a safe place but under the proper climate conditions. Too much heat or humidity can be destructive. Since collectibles

---

Drawbacks To Investing in Collectibles

1. High markups (20, 30, 50 percent, or even more)
2. Condition, condition, condition (huge value impact)
3. Counterfeits (all too easy to make)
4. Fads/bubbles/busts (frequent, unexpected)
5. No cash income production (only potential price appreciation)
6. Expanding supply (manufactured collectibles)
7. Storage and insurance costs

are often valuable, they may need to be stored in a secure place such as a safe or safe deposit box. Insurance for valuable collectibles is available but costly.

None of the above implies that you can't make money investing in collectibles. If you discover an old attic filled with a treasure trove of nineteenth-century campaign buttons, you have found something of considerable value. Similarly, if you have been a collector of English porcelains for the past thirty years and really know your subject, you could make some money buying from those who are less knowledgeable. You may occasionally find a valuable piece available for a song at a flea market or garage sale. But, if you are a novice entering a particular collectible area as an investor, the odds are very much against you.

If you really do want to invest in a collectibles area, begin by becoming a true collector. Learn the hobby and come to appreciate it on a small scale with a commitment of no more than a modest amount of your funds. You should continue as just a collector for a number of months, or preferably years. Join a club and read some books about your new hobby. Then and only then will you be positioned to try to make money as an investor. Before actually investing any serious money in collectibles, try your hand at selling some of your existing collection. This effort should provide a reality check on your ability to exit the market.

Unless you have extensive expertise in the area, avoid tangible and other offbeat investments.

A good rule for all types of investors is *never to invest in something you don't understand.* With nonstandard investments, the rule should be don't *ever* invest unless you *really* understand the area *extremely* well.

Tangible investments include such items as gemstones, precious and strategic metals, raw whiskey, wines, and spirits. Much of what has already been said about collectibles applies to the market for tangibles: Markups tend to be very high (precious metals are an exception), no cash income is produced, the market can be faddish (blowing hot and cold), and dealers in the market are generally much more interested in selling than buying (unless they are able to buy very cheaply from an uninformed seller).

Consider diamonds as an example. Diamonds are beautiful stones with undeniable intrinsic value. Diamond prices have tended to rise over long periods of time. But the markup from start to finish is huge. Take a nice diamond ring that a jeweler would sell for $1,000 (after a 50% discount from the so-called appraised value) to a pawnshop and see just what you can get for it. You would be lucky to be offered $100. Then use a jeweler's loop to examine stones of various quality. How good are you at determining the three C's: clarity, cut, and color? A nice clean, white stone is worth many times the value of a slightly colored one with a modest number of carbon spots that are visible only under high magnification. Could you trust yourself to tell the difference?

Realize that the market for each of these tangible investments is largely composed of people who earn their living by doing business in the area. Those on both the buy and sell side of this market generally have years of experience and a great deal of their own money at stake. If such dealers are willing to sell some tangible asset to you for a price of X, they probably do not expect to have to pay you or someone else significantly more next year to replace it. Rather, they are selling to you for X what they can buy now for enough-less-than-X to make the sale worth their while. Moreover, if they thought the price was likely to rise dramatically in the next few months or years, they would probably be stockpiling the item in order to capture the anticipated profit for themselves.

Investing in nontangible, offbeat assets such as vacation time-shares, copyrights, Lloyds guarantees, Broadway shows, minor league sports teams, and so forth is even more fraught with danger for the unwary. Clearly, less experienced investors should generally avoid such potential investments.

Avoid the stocks of hot IPOs in the immediate aftermarket. Their prices very often come down substantially, once reality sets in.

When what had been a private company first sells stock into the public market, the sale process is called an IPO (initial public offering). The market for IPOs blows hot and cold. When it is hot (such as in the late 1990s), stocks with an exciting story (e.g., dot.com stocks) tend to rise dramatically on the day that the company goes public. Some stock prices double or even triple on the day of issue. In a few cases these price run-ups may be justified. Most of the time, however, the investment bank that assembles and brings the deal to market has already realistically assessed the pros and cons of the new company's market value. The investment bank/underwriter may want to price the new issue a bit on the low side in order to facilitate the sale. Neither they nor the company going public have an incentive to leave huge amounts of money on the table. The investment banker's fee is based on the amount of money raised. The greater the sale proceeds, the greater the underwriting fee. Why should a company that is offered to the market at $12 a share trade up to $30 on the first day? If it was really worth $30, why wasn't it priced in that range to begin with? Who has a better idea of the new company's value? The speculators who bid the price up in the post-IPO aftermarket, or the underwriter who, after extensive due diligence, brought the issue to market in the first place? The investment bankers who put a price on the issue do so only after a careful analysis of its risks and potential. Bringing new companies to market is a significant part of the investment banking business. Investment banks are generally staffed by experienced professionals. These experienced professionals can usually be expected to do a creditable job.

While investment bankers do have some expertise in bringing companies public, they can and do make mistakes. The new company could be worth more than the underwriters project. But, it could also be worth less. The underwriter's valuation is probably just about as likely to be too high as it is to be too low. If the initial valuations of these investment bankers were consistently too low, they would not be able to stay in business. Companies planning to go public would surely seek to avoid those investment banks that acquired a reputation for bringing their clients to market too cheaply.

Usually after these large post-offer price run-ups, the newly public company begins to report results that don't live up to the expectations of those who initially bid up the price. As reality sets in, the company's market price tends to fall back to, and often below, the original issue level. If you acquired your shares at the high aftermarket prices, you would have gotten burned. Accordingly, one should avoid these kinds of markets.

If making money by purchasing these hot IPOs in the immediate post-issue market is likely to prove costly, perhaps selling these hot stocks short may appear to be more appealing. The problem with such a strategy is one of timing and the potential for bad luck. Overpriced stocks can, and often do, take time before they come to ground. The short seller can get badly whipsawed as an overpriced stock is speculated to ever-higher levels of irrational exuberance. Moreover, a percentage of these speculative issues will turn out to be real winners on fundamental grounds.

Take an eclectic approach to investing.

Many different forces move the stock and bond markets. These market-moving forces can influence a wide variety of topics. Investors who wish to understand how these various matters impact the financial markets will find some degree of expertise in a variety of disciplines to be helpful. The following list is by no means all-inclusive:

• **Finance:** Investors need some knowledge of interest rates, compound value, present value, leveraging, valuation theory, portfolio theory, risk analysis, market microstructure, and many other finance concepts.

• **Economics:** Economic (monetary and fiscal) policy, the theory of the firm, scale economies, competition and monopoly, and many other economic concepts are relevant to many investment decisions.

• **Political Science:** Economic policy is made in an inherently political environment. Changes in fiscal policy generally require congressional action. The Federal Reserve's implementation of monetary policy is also subject to political forces. Similarly, trade, antitrust, regulatory, environmental, labor, and other areas of governmental policies are subject to many and various political pressures.

• **Law:** Legal issues subject to judicial action often impact investment valuations. Commercial, antitrust, bank, environmental, securities, bankruptcy, labor, pension, regulatory, and various other types of law often influence investment values.

- **Accounting**: Balance sheets, income statements, and statements of cash flow are all key financial statements designed to provide information on the economic position and performance of companies. The accounting process that results in the production of key numbers such as earnings per share contains much discretion and subjectivity. Understanding the process can help uncover misstatements that often arise as a result of overly optimistic (or pessimistic) choices.

- **Demography**: The greatest generation, baby boom generation, generation X, generation Y, and so on tend to have differing needs, tastes, and preferences. An understanding of how demographic trends will lead to changes in the market for various goods and services (three-wheel bicycles versus video games, for example) can help identify growth and nongrowth opportunities.

- **Psychology**: Market and investor psychology have an undeniable impact on investment performance. An understanding of one's own psychological makeup can, for example, help avoid some common errors of investing.

- **Science and Technology**: In this age of high tech, nanotechnology, high-energy physics, cyberspace, and so forth, knowledge of basic and applied science can be very helpful in understanding the economic positions of many types of firms.

- **Meteorology and Climatology**: Many industries such as insurance, petroleum, construction, and agriculture are sensitive to weather and related impacts (floods, earthquakes, volcanoes, tidal waves, etc.).

6

Mutual Funds, Closed-End Funds, and Other Types of Investment Funds

V arious types of pooled portfolio investment vehicles are designed to appeal to individual investors. If you want to obtain the beneÞts of diversiÞcation and professional management by having someone else manage part or all of your investable resources, you may want to consider mutual funds or similar types of investment companies. The following rules are designed to help you select a fund or funds that Þt your own particular needs. First, let s explore the various types of pooled portfolio investments. They all have certain similarities, but each has some unique features. Each of these types of investment companies pools the resources from a group of investors and uses these resources to assemble a common portfolio. Each individual investor owns a share of this common portfolio.

All of the above types of investment companies have two features in common:

1. They assemble and manage a common portfolio for the beneÞt of a group of investors, each of whom owns a piece of the portfolio.

2. They are organized in such a way that they are not subject to the corporate income tax. The investors in the pooled portfolios are taxed directly on the portfolios incomes. The double taxation of corporate income (proÞts taxed at the corporate level, and then dividends and capital gains income taxed at the shareholder level) is avoided.

Types of Investment Companies

Mutual Fund: Mutual funds make a market in their own shares. They do so by standing ready to buy and sell their shares based on their daily closing new asset value (NAV), the market value of the fund s portfolio divided by the number of shares outstanding.

Closed-End Fund: The fund allows the public market for its shares to determine the per-share price through the interplay of supply and demand. Most such funds are listed on an exchange or traded on the NASDAQ. The market-determined prices of the closed-end fund s shares will vary from its NAV. Usually such closed-end funds trade at a discount from their NAVs.

Exchange Traded Fund: Like closed-end funds, they do not make a market in their own shares. They allow the per-share price to be determined by market forces. Most are set up as index funds and trade on an exchange. Their market price closely tracks their real-time NAV as it changes throughout the day. Exchange traded funds provide the investor with a vehicle for taking advantage of intraday price ßuctuations.

Unit Investment Trust: Assembles a common portfolio of assets (usually debt investments) for the unit-holders. The net (of expenses) cash ßows from the portfolio are paid out to the unit-holders over time. The portfolio s composition is set at the trust s inception and not managed thereafter. As the debt instruments mature, the proceeds are paid out to the unit-holders. This process continues until all of the assets are liquidated and all of the funds are paid out. At that point this particular unit investment trust is dissolved. But, of course, you can reinvest the proceeds in another one.

Variable Annuity: Sold by insurance companies as part of a life insurance program. Unlike other types of funds, variable annuities are allowed to retain the portfolio s income and reinvest it without attributing a current tax liability to the annuity-holders. The annuity-holders tax liabilities are deferred until they liquidate their variable annuity positions.

Hedge Fund: Pools funds of large, sophisticated investors into a common portfolio. Unlike other types of pooled portfolio funds, hedge funds are structured to allow their portfolio managers to undertake many risky types of trades and purchase many risky types of investments. More speciÞcally, hedge funds are permitted to utilize leverage, sell short, purchase and write options and futures contracts, accumulate a concentrated position in a single security, and take an active role in managing companies in which they hold a position. Mutual and closed-end funds, in contrast, cannot do any of the above unless speciÞcally authorized in their charter (which is rarely the case).

Real Estate Investment Trusts (REITs): Assembles a common portfolio of real estate assets (developed property, land, real estate mortgages). The net income from their portfolio must be ßowed through to the REIT owners. The price of the REIT s shares are determined by supply and demand in the public market.

Avoid load funds. If you want to buy a mutual fund,
buy a no-load fund.

Mutual funds are sold in two basic ways, with or without a sales fee. *Load funds* are sold through an agent who is paid a commission for making the sale. That fee is carved out of the money that the investor pays to buy the mutual fund s shares. A standard load fund charges a sales commission equal to 6 percent of the purchase price paid by the investor. This load is used to cover marketing expenses, particularly the sales fee of the agent who handled the sale. As a result, only 94 percent of the investor s money (100 − 6 = 94) actually goes toward buying the fund s shares. Recall that the stock market averages a return of about 9 percent per year. Accordingly, a 6 percent load takes away the better part of an average year s return. The purchaser of *low-load* and *12 b 1 funds* also incurs a sales fee. In the case of low-load funds, the commission is typically 2 to 3 percent of the purchase price, and the 12 b 1 funds charge an annual fee. The lower sales charges of low-load funds are less of a burden than a full load of regular load funds, but still involve a sales fee that is carved out of the fundholder s initial investment. The 12 b1 funds annual fees may actually result in higher total selling costs than a typical load fund. *No-load funds,* in contrast, are sold directly by the fund (without an agent) to the investor. Since no sales fee is carved out, the entire amount of the purchase price of no-load funds is used to buy fund shares.

Ways Mutual Funds Are Sold

Load Fund: Sold through an agent who is paid an up-front selling fee. The load is typically 6 percent. A sliding scale is applied to large purchases such that very large purchases incur a reduced-percentage fee.

No-Load Fund: Sold directly to the investor by the fund. No agent is involved and no sales fee is charged.

Low-Load Fund: Also sold directly to the investor by the fund, but a small selling fee, usually 2 to 3 percent is incurred.

12 b 1 Fund: Sold through an agent who is paid an up-front commission. The fund charges its investors an annual fee designed to recapture the sales commission that the fund paid to the agent who handled the transaction. If a 12 b 1 fund s shares are redeemed prior to a prespeciÞed number of years, an early termination fee is also assessed.

All of these types of mutual funds can be sold back to the fund for the fund s NAV (sometimes less a redemption fee).

Redemption Fees: Some funds also charge a fee (typically 2%) when a fund s shares are redeemed.

Management Fees: All funds charge a fee for their management services. Such fees are typically 0.5 to 0.75 percent of the fund s asset value per year.

The average gross returns on the portfolios of load, no-load, low-load, and 12 b 1 fund shares are indistinguishable. Moreover, for every type of sales-fee fund that one might Þnd attractive, a comparable no-load fund can almost always be found.

Why pay the load? The one advantage to investing in a load fund is that such a fund affords you the opportunity to talk with the agent who handles the transaction. The agent has some specialized training and expertise in Þnancial planning, including such matters as taxes, trusts, estates, and cash management. Thus mutual fund agents will be able to help novice investors understand the pros and cons of various Þnancial products such as money market funds, tax-free bond funds, index funds, country funds, REIT funds, variable annuities, junk bond funds, and so on. Note, however, that such an agent is likely to show you only those products on which he or she is paid a sales fee (load funds). Moreover, they may have a short list of funds on which they receive incentive fees and are expected to push. Thus the agent s interests and yours may not be aligned. Still, the agent should be able to help you understand the trade-offs. The availability of this service may be sufÞcient reason for some investors to choose to buy their funds through an agent. Most reasonably sophisticated investors, however, have little need for the agents services.

Indeed, one who is sufÞciently interested in investing and money management to be reading this book is very likely to know or soon learn enough to be able to do without the agents help. One who does wish to obtain help from an expert might consider hiring a *fee only* Þnancial planner. Such professionals do not have an incentive to direct their clients to investments that have high sales fees. They are therefore less subject to conßicts between what is best for their clients and what provides them with the highest fees.

Avoid actively managed mutual funds unless you believe that the portfolio manager has superior ability. Buy index funds instead.

Most Þnancial economists believe that a concept/theory called *market efficiency* provides a useful Þrst approximation/description of how securities markets work. According to this theory (semistrong form), the market always takes proper account of the publicly available information in pricing investment assets such as stocks and bonds. That is, the actions of informed buyers and sellers are said to drive security market prices to the levels where they accurately reßect the underlying values. If markets are fully efÞcient, portfolio managers will not be able to select securities that outperform the average return on the market (e.g., S&P 500 index) with any degree of consistency. Nor will they be able to enter and exit the market at opportune times with any greater-than-random accuracy. According to this view, the investment selections and timing decisions of portfolio managers are about as likely to cause the funds that they manage to underperform as to outperform the market. Most Þnancial economists do not believe that the market is always and everywhere as efÞcient as the efÞcient-market hypothesis contends. They do, however, believe that the market tends to be relatively efÞcient.

Numerous studies have all come to more or less the same conclusion: The average mutual fund generates a return that is, after deducting its fees and expenses, a bit below the average returns on the market as a whole (e.g., the S&P 500). This Þnding implies that active fund managers efforts to select winners and time the market do not, in general, succeed in producing returns that are sufÞciently above the market averages to offset the cost impact of their fees and trading costs.

Extensive evidence supports the approximate validity of the (semistrong form) efÞcient-market hypothesis. These market efÞciency results coupled with the rather pessimistic Þndings on average mutual fund performance have led to the development, growth, and popularity of a type of investment company called an *index fund.* Such funds do not attempt to outperform the market averages. They do not attempt to time the market, nor do they try to assemble a portfolio of undervalued stocks. Rather, they seek only to assemble a portfolio whose per-formance comes close to equaling that of their chosen benchmark. Index funds assemble portfolios designed to mimic a particular market index (often the S&P 500). Because they are not trying to pick winning stocks and not trying to move in and out of the market at the most opportune times, they engage in much less trading than do actively managed funds. The passively managed index funds incur much lower trading costs and charge much smaller management fees than do actively managed funds. Moreover, with much less buying and selling going on, the realized taxable gains on an index fund s portfolio tend to be much more modest. Most of the index fund s gains remain unrealized and therefore not subject to tax. Thus in an efÞcient-market environment, index funds are likely both to outperform actively managed funds and throw off less taxable income.

Some circumstances may, however, tip the balance back in favor of actively managed funds. First, certain portfolio managers do appear to have superior ability (e.g., Warren Buffett, Peter Lynch, John Marks Templeton). Such man-agers may be able to produce a superior return by taking advantage of any residual market inefÞciencies, even if the average manager will turn in only average results. Second, the investor may believe that a particular sector (e.g., real estate) is especially likely to outperform the market. Such an investor will wish to take advantage of this expected superior performance by purchasing shares in a fund with that attribute. A few index funds may exist for some specialized sectors. The odds are much greater, however, for Þnding an actively managed fund that can provide the investor with exposure to a speciÞc, desired sector.

In choosing among index funds, select a fund that has a record of low expenses.

Most index funds track their chosen benchmark index rather effectively. Any differences in the performances of index funds tracking the same index largely relate to their level of operational efficiency. Index funds incur some expenses (commissions, management fees, etc.) in the management of their portfolio. The actual indexes (e.g., S&P 500) performances are computed without reference to any expenses. Accordingly, the funds net returns will typically be a bit below that of their benchmark index. Some funds will underperform their index by 0.2 percent. Others, suffering the drag of a greater expense ratio, will generate returns that are 0.5 percent below the index. Because of the dead weight of their expenses, all index funds are likely to underperform their benchmark index. Clearly you would prefer to own a fund that underperforms its benchmark index as little as possible. Funds that have the lowest ratio of expenses-to-assets will generally come closest to equaling the returns of their benchmark indexes. Those are the funds that you will find to be the most attractive (produce the highest returns for a given benchmark).

You incur taxes on investments in mutual and closed-end funds in two basic ways. Plan accordingly.

The fund itself generates taxable income as a result of the dividends it receives and the gains it realizes on its portfolio. That income must be distributed to the fundholders on an annual basis. The fundholders are responsible for any tax liability on the distributions. The fundholder cannot avoid incurring this tax. If you own shares of the fund at the time of the distributions (and not necessarily when the income is earned), you will incur the tax liability. Both you and the IRS will receive a statement (Form 1099) reporting the amount of such income. The fundholders will also be taxed on any gains realized on the purchase and sale of their fund s shares. This tax liability is, however, incurred only when the fundholder elects to sell his or her shares. Unrealized gains remain untaxed.

The fundholder can avoid (defer) the second category of tax liability (unrealized) by continuing to hold his or her shares, but cannot avoid the first (realized). Since index funds do not undertake nearly as much buying and selling as actively managed funds, they tend to impose much lower tax liabilities on their fundholders. This reduced exposure to a tax liability is a significant advantage for index fund investors.

Avoid buying shares of closed-end funds at their original issue price. This original issue price is above their NAV. The share prices of such funds usually fall to a discount from their NAVs once they are issued and begin trading on their own.

Unlike mutual funds, that buy their shares directly from and sell directly to their fundholders, closed-end funds do not make a market in their own shares. Rather, their shares prices emerge from the interplay of supply and demand in the public market. Many closed-end funds are listed for trading on an exchange. Those not listed on an exchange trade in the over-the-counter market (usually NASDAQ). Generally (but not always), the price established by the interplay of supply and demand is below the fund s NAV (net asset value per share). Financial economists have long debated why such funds tend to sell at a discount from their NAVs, but the evidence that they do so is overwhelming.

When a new closed-end fund is established, it must be sold to the public at a premium to its NAV. That premium (typically 8 to 10 percent) is needed to cover both the cost of organizing and setting up the fund as well as the cost of marketing its shares. Once the dust settles and supply and demand take over, the closed-end fund s shares are very likely to trade more or less as such funds typically do. That is, the fund s price will probably settle down to a discount from its NAV. If, for example, the fund was originally sold at a 10 percent premium to its NAV and once trading starts, the market price declines to a 10 percent discount, the investor could experience a 20 percent decline in the value of his or her investment. *So, one who is interested in investing in a closed-end fund that is about to go public should wait until the fund has had at least a few weeks (or months) of trading before buying any shares.* At that point, the fund s shares are very likely to be selling for signiÞcantly less than its NAV and therefore very likely to be selling for substantially less than its original offer price.

Do not invest in funds of funds. You can create your own and save.

The *fund of funds* concept is like a bad penny. It just keeps coming back no matter how bad an idea it is. As the name implies, a fund of funds is a mutual or hedge fund that invests in a diversiÞed portfolio of mutual funds or, in some cases, other types of funds such as hedge funds. By assembling a diversiÞed portfolio of funds, one can put together a rather ßexible and diversiÞed portfolio of portfolios. Each separate portfolio is diversiÞed within its asset class, and the portfolio of portfolios provides diversiÞcation across asset classes. With such a homemade fund of funds, the investor can easily shift his or her exposure to various market sectors by altering the relative portfolio weights. In a simple example, an investor could purchase shares in both a stock fund and a bond fund. When stocks (bonds) were thought to be the better value, the percentage of the portfolio invested in the stock (bond) fund could be increased and that on the bond (stock) fund decreased. If the components of the homemade portfolio of funds all reside in the same family of mutual funds (e.g., Fidelity, Vanguard, etc.), the investor can shift exposure from fund to fund with a phone call and usually without having to pay more than a modest fee ($5). As long as the investor is not engaged in frequent hair-trigger market timing, the fund s family is happy to accommodate the moves.

Funds of funds are, however, quite different from a homemade portfolio of funds. The fund of fund s concept is weighted down by the double impact of its fees and expenses. Each fund in the fund of funds portfolio has its own set of fees and expenses. Each component fund s net return is the result of deducting these costs from that gross return on the fund s portfolio. The fund of funds layers its own fees and expenses on top of those of its components. Thus the fund of fund s own fees and expenses are also subtracted from the gross returns. A single dose of fees is enough to tip the balance in favor of index (as opposed to actively managed) funds for many investors. The comparison becomes all the more insidious when two layers of fees are imposed by the fund of funds structure.

The managers of fund of funds contend that they are particularly adept at selecting well-managed (mutual or closed-end) funds and moving money in and out of various market sectors at opportune times. Ask yourself the following question: If these fund managers are so skilled at fund selection and market timing, why can t they use these same skills to manage their own mutual fund? Why make you pay two sets of fees?

If you want to take a position in a component of the market during the course of the day, consider the use of exchange-traded funds.

Exchange-traded funds are a relatively recent market innovation. They are essentially closed-end index funds that trade on an exchange throughout the day. Traditional closed-end funds also trade throughout the day, but at prices that can vary widely from their NAVs. Mutual funds are set up to trade once a day at their daily closing NAVs. In order to trade at that day s closing prices, you must place your order before the markets close. When you seek to buy or sell a mutual fund, you do not know what the per-share price will be until the end of the day. If you enter your order before 4:00 P.M. EST, you will know only what the prior day s closing NAV was. You will not know what that day s closing NAV will be until after the time that you have entered your order. Later in the evening (or perhaps the next morning), after the markets have closed, you may be able to learn the new NAV. That new day s closing NAV is the price at which you will trade.

Exchange-traded funds, unlike traditional closed-end funds, are structured so that their market prices almost never depart very much from their NAVs. Shares are created or destroyed as needed to maintain parity with their NAV. Their market prices track their NAVs throughout the course of the day. Exchange-traded funds are available on a number of different broad and narrow indexes. So if you want to trade on the basis of very-short-term expectations, you may want to buy and sell exchange-traded funds.

Invest some of your resources in mutual funds that hold portfolios of securities of companies located outside the United States in order to obtain their diversification potential, but be mindful of the risks.

DiversiÞcation involves spreading your resources across a number of different assets and asset classes. It is a much recommended and very useful method for managing risk. The risk-reducing benefits of diversification within U.S. markets are, however, limited. U.S. stocks all tend to be affected by conditions in the economy. Thus most individual U.S. stocks tend to move up and down with the overall U.S. market. So, for example, the movement of the U.S. stock market as reflected in the movements of the broad market indexes, such as the S&P 500 or Dow Jones industrial average, will have a substantial impact on the performance of individual U.S. stocks. Diversifying into other asset classes such as bonds and real estate can help reduce portfolio risk. Still, the performances of all of these markets are to some degree dependent upon the performance of the U.S. economy.

Diversifying outside the U.S. markets provides an additional opportunity to reduce risk. Just as the economies of other nations move in different cycles from those of the U.S. economy, the securities markets located outside the United States fluctuate in different cycles from those in the U.S. Sometimes the U.S. markets are rising when various foreign markets are falling, and vice versa. As a result, diversifying internationally can reduce risk by a greater amount than can be accomplished by diversifying exclusively within U.S. markets alone. Put another way, once you have obtained all of the risk reduction available from diversifying across U.S. securities, you can reduce risk still further by adding non-U.S. securities to your portfolio.

Investing in U.S.-based firms that have large international operations (e.g., Coca-Cola) does not provide the same degree of diversification benefit as investing in firms based outside the United States. The stocks of such U.S.-based international firms continue to move largely in sympathy with the U.S. stock markets.

Diversifying internationally is, however, appreciably more complicated than diversifying within the U.S. market. One who would do so needs to understand the various options that are available to accomplish this objective. Buying individual securities of companies based outside the United States is possible, but poses a number of hurdles. Those individual foreign securities that have actively traded American deposit receipts (ADRs) are the easiest to buy and sell in the United States. ADRs are warehouse receipts reflecting beneficial ownership of foreign shares. The actual shares are held in the name of the trustee who, for a small fee, sets up and manages the ADRs. These ADRs provide a convenient way for dealing with foreign taxes, currency translation, and avoiding the need to trade in a foreign country's securities markets. Still, investing in individual foreign securities is challenging for a number of reasons (e.g., the difficulty of obtaining relevant accessible information in English). Accordingly, many investors utilize international mutual and closed-end funds to provide them with exposure to the international securities markets. Both mutual and closed-end funds exist in the following categories:

While investing in foreign securities does have diversification benefits, a number of additional risks should not be overlooked. First, when you invest in foreign securities, you are subjecting your portfolio to *foreign exchange risk*.

Categories of International Funds

International funds invest in a diversiÞed portfolio of stocks of companies based in countries around the world. They tend to be among the most diversiÞed funds available. Some fund managers, like the gnomes of Zurich, try to move their money around seeking exposure in the countries with the hottest or most undervalued stock markets. Others simply try to hold a representative portfolio of international stocks with weights more or less reßecting the market capitalizations of the various stock markets around the world.

International funds with a theme also invest around the world but with a speciÞc concentration. For example, such funds may focus on a particular industry (telecommunications), region (Latin America), or country type (emerging markets). Investors who have a positive opinion about the relative potential of such themes may want to buy a fund that mirrors that exposure.

Country funds invest in a diversiÞed portfolio of companies based in a particular country. Country funds now exist for a large number of countries. Indeed, index funds are available for most countries that have their own stock markets.

Foreign bond funds invest in the debt securities of companies based outside the United States. International funds may be organized as either mutual or closed-end funds. Moreover, many hedge funds invest internationally.

If, for example, you invest in a fund that owns a portfolio of stocks of companies based in the European Union, their sales, proÞts, and stock prices will be denominated in euros. As the value of the euro ßuctuates relative to the dollar, these funds values in dollar terms will move up and down. In a period when the dollar s value is rising (falling) relative to the euro, securities priced in euros will tend to fall (rise) in dollar terms even when they do not fall (rise) in euro terms. Sensitivity to changing relative currency values is called exchange rate risk. Exchange rates can, of course, move in your favor. The fact, however, that exchange rates for different currencies can move in either direction adds an element of risk to international investing that is not present in domestic investing.

Dollar Value of an Investment Fund Worth 10 Euros Per Share

Exchange rate $1 = 1   euros → $8.
Exchange rate $1 = 1 euro → $10
Exchange rate $1 = 7/8 euro → $12.50
Exchange rate $1 = $3/4$ euro → $15
Exchange rate $1 = $5/8$ euro → $17.50
Exchange rate $1 = ½ euro → $20

The second type of additional risk associated with international investing is what is called *country* or *political risk*. Those who invest in U.S.-based companies are protected by the American legal system. They can rely upon the stability of the U.S. political system as backed up by the U.S. military establishment. Investing outside the United States, in contrast, may involve not insigniÞcant risks of economic loss resulting from the potential for political/legal turmoil. We in the United States are blessed with a relatively stable political system coupled with a legal system that does a rather effective job of enforcing rights to property and performance under valid contracts. While these kinds of protections exist in many other countries, they may be present only in weaker form. Moreover, local governments tend to be much more interested in protecting the property rights of their own citizen/voters than those of investors from outside the host country. Both violent revolutions (China, Russia, Cuba, Iran, etc.) as well as more peaceful change of government (Chile, Argentina, Mexico, Brazil, etc.) can result in a radical change in the investment climate. In some cases, foreign-owned property may be expropriated outright. In other cases, increased tax rates and/or restrictions on repatriation of proÞts limit the investor s upside potential. Political risk varies greatly from country to country. Political risk is much less of a concern for countries that have a history of stable economic development like Canada, the UK, and those in Western Europe than for many of the less developed countries of Africa, Latin America, or Asia.

Notwithstanding the risks inherent in international investing, the universe of securities available throughout the world provides a much larger set of investment opportunities than the constellation of securities originating in the United States. Moreover, stock and bond markets around the world are often rising when U.S. markets are falling (and vice versa). So, those who invest internationally have a much larger set of securities from which to choose and substantially greater diversiÞcation opportunities, coupled with the unavoidable acceptance of exchange and country risks not present in U.S.-only investing. Like virtually all other aspects of investing, international investing involves trade-offs.

Individual investment managers are another money management option. Unless you have a rather large portfolio, they are probably too costly for you.

One alternative to investing in professionally managed investment companies is to hire your own personal portfolio manager. Either approach assigns most of the day-to-day investment decision-making to a professional money manager. You might choose to work through the trust department of a bank or hire an individual manager who is part of a Þrm that is established as a separate investment management enterprise. Alternatively, you could set up a discretionary account with a brokerage Þrm. Depending upon the amount of money you have to invest, your investment manager may place your funds into a set of common investment pools (smaller sum), or may manage and maintain a separate portfolio just for you (larger sum). In either case, the manager will (or at least should) try to build an overall portfolio that matches your preferences for such objectives as:

- risk tolerance
- liquidity
- tax-sheltering
- capital preservation
- current income
- desired social policy

Individual money managers have one major disadvantage compared to the investment company option. Unless the sums to be invested are quite large, the fees of these individual money managers relative to the assets under management tend to be rather high. Two percent of assets plus expenses is a typical annual fee structure. Moreover, the performance of the typical individual portfolio manager tends to be no better than the market averages. Indeed, some unscrupulous portfolio managers have been known to embezzle their clients money, thereby greatly reducing the relevant portfolio performances. For all of these reasons, mutual funds and other types of investment companies usually provide a preferred way of having your funds managed by professionals, particularly if the amount to be managed is relatively small.

7

Investing in the Debt Market

Debt securities, primarily bonds, constitute the principal security market alternative to stocks. Bonds have many uses. This asset class that should not be overlooked by individual investors. Bonds were once thought of as almost exclusively in the province of institutional investors. More recently, however, bonds have begun to appeal to individual investors, even small individual investors. Indeed, the rather poor performance for stocks compared with the much stronger performance for the bond market over much of the 1999–2002 time period drew increasing numbers of small individual investors into the bond market. The markets do, to be sure, run in cycles. In 2003 bond market yields were at historically low levels and the stock market performed very well. In both 2004 and 2005, long-term interest rates were expected to rise, but when they didn't, bonds turned in a rather good performance.

The debt security market is itself divided into a number of sectors, including short, intermediate, and long-term; corporate, government, and state and local; as well as investment grade, junk, and distressed. While direct investment in debt securities is one way to participate, many investors prefer the convenience of mutual and closed-end bond funds.

*Understand and take advantage of the short-term end
of the debt securities market.*

The short-term end of the debt securities market is called the *money market*. The money market appeals to investors who prefer its safety and security, as money market instruments have little risk of default or significant price drops. Such securities are structured automatically to turn back into spendable dollars soon after they are purchased, usually with little risk of loss. A number of different types of underlying securities are designed to trade in this market. Treasury bills, debt instruments issued by the federal government for terms of up to one year, are the best-known money market instrument. Because of the government's power over tax collections and the money supply, Treasury bills are considered to be essentially devoid of risk. Because they are viewed as being especially secure, the rates offered on Treasury bills are below those of other money market instruments and generally lower than longer-term Treasury debt instruments as well.

Banks and other types of depository institutions issue marketable CDs (certificates of deposit), which constitute another significant piece of the money market. Such CDs are insured by the FDIC for up to $100,000 per holder per bank. As a result of this insurance, CDs can be very nearly as safe as Treasury bills. Those CDs that are not covered by FDIC insurance (that portion over $100,000) can default, but only if the issuer bank itself fails. Default losses on large CDs are rare, but they do occasionally occur. If the issuer (e.g., bank) fails, holders of uninsured CDs are likely to recover only a portion of their CDs' face value. This recovery percentage is determined by how much value of the failed institution remains relative to its debts. When a bank fails, it is seized by the regulators and then either sold to another bank or its assets are liquidated. The proceeds from this process are then paid out to uninsured creditors on a pro rata basis. Investors might recover anything from 0 percent to 100 percent of face, depending on how deeply insolvent the issuer of the CDs was at the time it failed. The FDIC makes up the shortfall for insured but not for uninsured creditors (e.g., depositors of the failed bank). Suppose you had $200,000 invested in CDs at an FDIC-insured bank that failed. If recoveries on the bank's assets permitted the FDIC receiver to pay out 80 percent of allowed claims, you would recover 100 percent of the first $100,000 and 80 percent of the remaining sum, or, in this case, a total of $180,000 of your $200,000 investment. The FDIC's insurance fund would make up the difference on the insured accounts. You would suffer a loss on the uninsured portion. The FDIC's insurance fund is financed from the premium payments made by banks that are members of the FDIC system. All commercial banks are required to be members of this system.

Those large corporations that the market views as being very secure are able to issue short-term debt instruments called *commercial paper*. Such paper is underwritten by investment bankers according to strict standards. Usually, backup lines of credit are required by the underwriter as take-outs. The commercial paper issuer must pay a fee for the backup line of credit. This fee adds to the cost of the funds. Still the total of the interest cost and the line of credit fee is generally below that of any alternative funding source. In the unlikely event that the commercial paper issuer cannot refinance the debt as it comes due, the take-out line of credit is tapped to pay off the maturing commercial paper. Accordingly, commercial paper almost never defaults. And on those rare occasions when it does, the underwriters are likely to be sued for failing to uncover the problem.

Two other components of the money market are eurodollars and bankers' acceptances. Eurodollars are dollar denominated deposits in financial institutions based outside the United States. Bankers' acceptances are company-issued IOUs that have been guaranteed by a bank. Such acceptances often arise as part of the payment process in an international transaction.

The vast majority of money market instruments, whether government-issued or not, are viewed by the marketplace as being extremely safe. Only very secure borrowers can issue and sell their own money market instruments. Moreover, these instruments (which by definition must pay off within a year) always mature soon after their issuances. Accordingly, very few issuers of money market instruments can get into very deep financial difficulty in the short amount of time between issuance and maturity. Defaults in the money market are extremely rare. Those issuers whose credit quality declines appreciably soon find the money market closed to them. Their outstanding money market instruments mature at a time when the issuers are usually still healthy enough to pay them off (often utilizing their backup banks' lines of credit). Therefore, these former issuers of money market securities cannot issue new ones unless and until their credit quality improves sufficiently.

Unlike bonds, which are structured to pay a coupon every six months and repay principal at maturity, almost all money market instruments are sold at a discount from their face value (par) and mature at par. They do not make coupon payments. The return or yield on such instruments is derived solely from the difference between their initial price and their par value, which is paid out at maturity. For example, a one-year T-bill might be issued at a price of $9,500 and mature at $10,000. The buyer of such an instrument will earn $500 on the $10,000 face value T-bill, for a discount yield of 5 percent.

Note that a discount yield (only one payment, which occurs at the bond's maturity) is a slightly different concept from the more familiar coupon yield (coupon payments every six months). For example, one could earn $5,000 on a $95,000 one-year investment for a 5 percent discount yield. A 5 percent coupon yield would result from earning $5,000 on a $100,000 investment. So we see that a 5 percent discount yield is slightly more attractive than a 5 percent coupon yield. In this particular example, earning a 5 percent discount yield on $95,000 is approximately equivalent to earning 5.26 percent on $100,000

$(0.05/95 = 0.0526)$. The actual computation is a bit more complicated because of the impact of the semiannual payment on the coupon bond.

One can participate directly in the money market by buying, holding until maturity, and sometimes selling the various money market securities. Most small investors will, however, find indirect participation in the money market to be a much more convenient approach. The minimum denomination of money market securities is high ($10,000 for Treasury bills, $100,000 for large, marketable CDs, and larger still for the others). Moreover, the market for individual investor participation is not well developed. Indeed, with the exception of T bills, the minimum denominations are very high and the markets are almost exclusively the preserve of institutions, large corporations, and large individual investors. Thus the money market is not well suited to direct participation by small investors. And yet many small investors would like to invest in the very safe short-term securities that make up the money market. Responding to this reality, a number of instruments have been developed to provide the small investor with indirect access to the money market.

One alternative to direct participation in the money market is to access the market via an intermediary such as a *money market mutual fund*. Such funds assemble and maintain large, diversified portfolios of money market instruments. The net returns (after subtracting fees and expenses) are passed through to their fundholders. Their fees and expenses typically amount to between 20 and 50 basis points annually. That cost is, however, a rather small price to pay for the convenience and diversification provided by money funds. Fundholders have immediate access to their funds via check-writing privileges. Because the portfolios are composed of very-short-term, highly secure debt instruments, losses on those types of diversified money market portfolios are almost non-existent.

To compete with the money market mutual funds, banks offer a product called a *money market account*. In addition to paying a yield tied to money market rates, these accounts provide check-writing privileges and immediate access to the investors' funds, much like money market mutual funds. Money market accounts are as easy to open and operate as standard bank accounts. Such accounts are FDIC insured up to the $100,000 maximum. This FDIC insurance makes these accounts even safer than most money market mutual funds. At times the interest rates offered by the banks are below, and at other times above, those offered by the money market mutual funds. Most of the time the money funds have offered the better rates. When, however, overall rates fall to very low levels (2003–4), the banks tend to be more competitive.

One special type of money market mutual fund is the *governments only* fund. This type tends to pay a slightly lower yield than the standard money fund. It does, however, have two significant advantages over other types of money market mutual funds. First, the portfolio of a governments only fund consists exclusively of government securities. Accordingly, it is even safer than other types of money funds. Second, the interest income from government securities is not subject to state income taxes. If you live in a state that has a high income tax rate, governments only funds may offer you a more attractive after-tax yield than the standard (taxable at the state level) money fund.

Money market mutual funds and money market accounts at banks are two major ways for individual investors with modest resources to participate in the very short-term debt securities market. *Short-term unit investment trusts* represent a third approach. Unit trusts own self-liquidating portfolios of short-term debt instruments. Because their portfolios are unmanaged, the fees and expenses of unit trusts are quite low. Accordingly, the investor's net portfolio return tends to be closer to the gross return on the portfolio than is the case for money market mutual funds. Unit trusts do, however, lack the convenience (e.g., check-writing privileges) of money funds and money market accounts. Unit trusts are structured to have a specific maturity such as six months from their date of issuance. At maturity the fund is liquidated and the proceeds are distributed. The only way one can access his or her funds prior to the trust's maturity is to sell the units in a market that is not especially liquid.

Yet another approach, *short-short funds,* maintain portfolios of debt securities whose maturities are longer than those held in money funds but shorter than four other types of bond funds. A money fund portfolio would have a weighted average maturity of perhaps sixty days. A short-short fund's average maturity, in contrast, might be six months or a year. By assembling a portfolio of investments with longer terms than a money fund, short-short funds may be able to obtain somewhat higher yields. Such longer terms do, however, involve the risk of taking some small losses if market interest rates rise and thus the market values of the short-short funds' holdings decline. Put another way, when market interest rates rise, the yields on short-short funds are slower to adjust upward than are the yields of money funds. On the other hand, when interest rates fall, short-short funds' yields decline more slowly than do money funds. Like other types of mutual funds, short-short funds are very liquid.

Finally, investors may choose to purchase small-denomination bank CDs, or hold other types of depositor accounts (e.g., savings accounts) at a financial

---

The Money Market for Small Investors

Money Market Mutual Fund: Convenience, diversification, very low risk
Governments Only Money Fund: Slightly lower yield than standard money funds; sheltered from state tax; very safe
Money Market Account: Bank product, FDIC-insured; very safe
Unit Investment Trust: Very low fees, unmanaged, illiquid
Short-Short Funds: Less liquid than money market mutual fund, but offers somewhat higher yields
Savings Accounts and CDs: Safe, FDIC-insured, liquid; shop for best yields

institution such as a commercial bank, savings and loan association, credit union, and the like. The traditional bank savings account (passbook or statement) tends to offer relatively low rates. Small-denomination bank CDs may be more attractive, but one needs to shop around in order to obtain the best rates.

For small individual investors, bond funds provide an attractive vehicle for entering and participating in this market.

Most bonds are sold in $1,000 face value denominations. A typical small purchase would involve at least five to ten bonds, or a $5,000 to $10,000 commitment. Rarely would you see bond trades involving less than five units. To be reasonably well diversified, a portfolio of bonds should contain a minimum of eight to ten separate issues. Thus, $40,000 (eight issues with $5,000 invested in each) to $100,000 (ten issues with $10,000 invested in each) would be needed to assemble a diversified portfolio of bonds. Most investors who participate in the bond market also own a portfolio of stocks. For such an investor to have equal amounts invested in a reasonably well-diversified portfolio of stocks and bonds, perhaps $200,000 in investible funds would be needed. Two hundred thousand dollars represents a substantial sum of money for most individual investors.

One attractive alternative to assembling your own portfolio of individual bonds is to purchase shares in a mutual or closed-end fund that owns and manages a portfolio of bonds. A small investor may start by buying as little as a few thousand dollars' worth of shares of a bond fund. The investor can then add to that sum over time. The bond fund's income can also be automatically reinvested in the fund. Bond funds (mutual or closed-end) provide such individual investors with the opportunity to participate in the bond market with as little as $500 to $1,000. Thus, for a relatively small sum, an individual investor can obtain all the diversification benefits of the fund. As with any such funds, fees and expenses are passed through to the fundholders. Thus the net return on the bond fund will always be below the gross return on its portfolio.

Bond funds come in many different varieties. Choose one that fits your needs.

Bonds are issued by three primary categories of borrowers: the U.S. Treasury (*governments*), state and local governments (*municipals*), and corporations (*corporates*). Short, intermediate, and long-term bonds are available for each type of issuer. All government bonds are regarded as being extremely safe. The risk levels of municipals and corporates can, however, vary substantially. Such bonds can and sometimes do default.

Bond funds exist for each of the categories outlined above. So, for example, you could buy a long-term government fund, an intermediate-term high-grade (low-risk) municipal bond fund, or a long-term high-risk (junk) corporate bond fund. As with stock funds, bond funds are available in both actively managed and index fund types. Bond mutual funds come in both load and no-load types. Closed-end bond funds are also available. Each type of fund has its own set of advantages and disadvantages.

Bear in mind that a rise in market interest rates corresponds to a decline in bond prices.

Almost all bonds are structured to make a fixed coupon payment every six months. Thus, a 7 percent bond promises to make a coupon payment equal to 3.5 percent of its face value, twice a year. The market value of this payment stream ($35 every six months on a $1,000 bond) depends upon the rate at which the marketplace discounts (present values) it. If, for example, the market were to apply a discount rate of 7 percent, the payment stream would be worth (have a market price of) $1,000, the same amount as its face value. Put another way, if the market price of the 7 percent coupon bond is $1,000, the market must be applying a 7 percent discount rate to the bond's promised income stream. If, however, the market-determined discount rate for this bond is higher than 7 percent, the present valuing process applied to the projected payment stream would result in a market price that is below the bond's face value. Looked at from a different direction, if the market price of the 7 percent bond was below its $1,000 face value, that would imply that the market is applying a discounted rate above its 7 percent coupon rate.

The mathematics get somewhat complex. As an example, if a long-term bond with a 7 percent coupon is priced to yield 8 percent, it might (depending upon its maturity) sell for about $900. Suppose you had purcahsed the bond at its original issue price of $1,000 when the corresponding market discount rate was 7 percent. Thus you would have paid the face value of $1,000 for the bond. If the appropriate market discount rate for this bond rose to 8 percent, your investment would now be underwater by $100 per bond. You would still have a bond with a face value of $1,000 and it would still pay you $35 every six months. You could hold on to your bond, collect your coupon, and would (assuming it does not default) receive the bond's face value at its maturity. In that instance, however, the sum of money that you originally invested in that bond will not be earning the current market rate of 8 percent for a bond of this risk level. Moreover, if, prior to maturity you needed to raise cash, you would have to sell the bond at a loss.

The accompanying table illustrates how different market discount rates will impact the price of bonds with differing maturity dates. We see that a twenty-year bond with a 7 percent coupon will be priced at 100 points, when discounted at 7 percent. A price of 100 points corresponds to $1,000. *Bonds are priced in points, with one point equivalent to $10.* If market interest rates on this type of bond (maturity, coupon, risk) increase to 7.5 percent, the bond's

TABLE 7.1. Market Prices for 5-, 10-, and 20-Year 7 Percent Bonds for Various Discount Rates

Discount Rate	Market Price 5-Year Bond	Market Price 10-Year Bond	Market Price 20-Year Bond
5%	108.75	115.59	125.10
6%	104.77	107.49	111.56
6.5%	102.11	103.63	105.55
7%	100.00	100.00	100.00
7.5%	97.95	96.53	94.86
8%	95.94	93.50	90.10
8.5%	93.99	90.03	85.19
9%	92.01	86.98	81.60
9.5%	90.23	84.09	77.80
10%	88.42	81.31	74.26
11%	84.92	76.10	67.91
12%	81.40	71.33	62.36

price would fall to 94.84 in points, or $948.40 in dollars. At 8 percent the market price falls to 90.10 and at 9 percent to 81.60. On the other hand, if market interest rates on bonds like this one were to fall to 6 percent, this bond's price (assuming it can't be called) would rise to 111.56. Now compare the market prices for a ten-year bond that also has a 7 percent coupon rate. It, too, would be worth its par value of 100 if discounted at 7 percent. At an 8 percent discount rate, the ten-year bond's price would be 93.56 (compared with 90.10 for the twenty-year bond). At 9 percent the prices are 86.98 versus 81.60 for the ten- and twenty-year 7 percent bonds, respectively. The price impacts of differing market interest rates on five-year bonds are even smaller. For example, the 7 percent, five-year bond will be priced at 95.94 at an 8 percent discount rate compared to 93.5 for the ten-year and 90.10 for the twenty-year bonds. Clearly, shorter-term bond market prices are less affected by changing interest rates than are the market prices of long-term bonds.

The above discussion illustrates one very basic point: *bond prices move inversely with interest rates* in the marketplace. When market interest rates rise, bond prices decline. That relationship between market interest rates and bond prices creates a major risk for bond investors. If you purchase a bond when market interest rates are relatively low and subsequently they rise, your bond's market price will go down. The longer the term of the bond, the greater the price impact of this type of risk. On the other hand, when market interest rates go down, bond prices go up. So you can benefit from a favorable move (decline) in interest rates. The potential benefit is, however, limited by the right of the issuer (if available) to call the bond early. Moreover, declining interest rates will also have the effect of reducing the income that you can earn on any coupon payments that you receive and then reinvest.

The market prices of short-term bonds are much less sensitive to interest rate moves than are those of long-term bonds.

The market-determined price of a bond is equal to the present value of its expected payment stream. The impact of the discounting process increases as the payment to be present valued is moved further into the future. For example, a payment of $100 to be received a year from now is worth $96 if discounted at 4 percent and $95 if discounted at 5 percent, a $1 difference. A $100 payment to be received twenty years from now is worth $45.61 with a 4 percent discount rate and only $37.51 when discounted at 5 percent, a difference of more than $8. In percentage terms, a 1 percent change in the discount rate (from 4% to 5%) changes the present value of a payment one year off by a little more than 1 percent. When, however, the payment is to be received in twenty years, a 1 percent change in the discount rate (from 4% to 5%) causes the present value of the payment to change by almost 18 percent. The point of the above analysis is as follows: *You are much better positioned to limit the risk inherent in a potential interest rate increase if you hold short-term rather than long-term bonds.* An interest rate rise will have a *marginal* impact on the market value of a short-term bond, but a *substantial* impact on the price of a long-term bond. The same relationship applies to short- versus long-term bond funds.

Opting for short-term bonds or bond funds does, however, have its own drawbacks. First, if interest rates decline, the lower yield's return impact will be quickly felt by a portfolio of short-term bonds. As soon as the existing bonds mature, the investor will need to reinvest the funds at the lower rates now available in the marketplace. With longer-term bonds, in contrast, the investor will (if the bonds are not called) continue to receive the higher coupon rate until the bonds mature. Second, short-term bonds often offer lower yields than longer-term bonds of similar risk. Thus, by opting for the short end of the market, you may be sacrificing something in terms of yield.

When interest rates fall, call rights may limit the profit potential of bonds, particularly long-term bonds.

Most bonds include a provision that provide the issuer with an option to repurchase the debt securities from their owners prior to maturity at a fixed price specified in the *indenture* (the contract between the borrower and lender). Just as you want to have the ability to refinance your mortgage when interest rates fall, bond issuers want to be able to refinance their debts if market interest rates fall (or if their own credit quality improves). Call provisions are designed to provide the bond issuer with that refinancing opportunity. In the absence of these *call rights,* a substantial decline in market interest rates could cause the market price of such bonds to rise much higher than their face value. The prespecified call price tends to limit that potential for appreciation. In other words, the call rights tend to put a ceiling on the bond's market price.

Most bonds are issued with an initial period of call protection (e.g., five years). During this period, the bond issuer is barred from calling its bonds. Thereafter, the bond issuer can demand that the bondholders surrender their bonds in exchange for a cash payment whose amount is specified in the bond's indenture. The amount of this payment is usually equal to the bond's face value plus a modest premium. This premium is typically equal to one additional year of coupon payments. Thus a 6 percent bond might be sold with a call provision that allows the issuer to buy it back at 106 percent of its face value.

These call rights provide the bond issuer with a mechanism for replacing high-yield bonds with lower-cost debt when market interest rates fall. Such a provision allows companies to raise debt capital in a high-interest-rate environment and yet position themselves to refinance that debt at lower coupon rates if interest rates in the marketplace fall. That is, if market rates fall, the bond issue can be called and then replaced with a lower coupon instrument.

A feature such as call rights provides an attractive option for the bond issuer. The issuer will exercise the call options only when doing so is attractive to the issuer. That same feature is potentially detrimental to the interests of the bondholder. If your callable bond is never called and does not default, you will continue to receive its coupon until its scheduled maturity date. If, however, your bond is called, you will be paid off early on your high-yield bond. You will now have cash in place of the bonds that were called before their scheduled maturity. The bonds had been yielding an attractive return. Until it is reinvested, that cash payment produces no income. If you are to continue earning a return, the cash that you now have must be put back to work. When your bond is called, market interest rates are quite likely to be lower than they were when you first bought your bonds. To illustrate this point, consider an example. Suppose you assembled a small portfolio of callable bonds yielding 8 percent when interest rates in the marketplace were relatively high. Therefore you had $100,000 invested in twenty-year, 8 percent callable bonds producing an annual income of $8,000. You were expecting to receive $8,000 a year for each of the next twenty years. What happens if market interest rates for bonds of this risk level fall to 6 percent? If your twenty-year, 8 percent bonds could not be called, they would trade for about 123 (corresponding to $1,230) when priced at a 6 percent yield to maturity. Your 8 percent callable bonds are, however, very likely to be called. You might be paid $108,000 (face plus one year's interest income) for your holdings. The extra $8,000 represents the call premium that the issuer must pay in order to repurchase the bonds. But if you can earn only 6 percent on the money, your cash income on the $108,000 would fall from $8,000 to $6,480 per year. That new sum is $1,520 less than the $8,000 that you had been earning. The issuer who called your bonds would save on debt service cost, but you would have to give up the income that you were earning on your high-yield bonds. That is how *call risk* operates. If after the bonds are called and the payoff funds are reinvested at 6 percent, market interest rates rise back up to 8 percent, that is just too bad for the bond investor. The payment stream will stay at $6,480 a year. Moreover, the market value of the bond portfolio will fall to reflect the higher level of market interest rates.

Other things being equal, the riskier the bond, the higher its promised
yield and the greater the chance that it will default.

Bonds issued by the federal government and backed by the U.S. Treasury are considered to be so safe as to have essentially no risk of default. All other types of bonds are thought of as having at least some risk of defaulting. Technically, a bond defaults whenever it fails to live up to any of the provisions in its *indenture*. The indenture is the contract that the issuer enters into with the bondholders. For most of our purposes, however, the only default that matters is one involving a failure to make coupon or principal payments when they are due. Such a failure is a serious matter. Unlike a failure to pay a dividend to shareholders, a failure to pay creditors the coupon and/or principal payments as specified in the indenture usually leads to a bankruptcy filing on the part of the debtor (the bond issuer). In some instances, the issuer may cure the default or undertake an out-of-bankruptcy *workout* settlement with its creditors. In a workout, creditors make measured concessions to the borrower in an attempt to preserve value for the benefit of the lenders. A successful workout will avoid the expense of bankruptcy. Because participation by individual creditors must be voluntary (per the Trust Indenture Act of 1940), out-of-bankruptcy workouts are difficult to accomplish. Each creditor is likely to prefer to hang back and hope that the other creditors are willing to make the requested concessions. In other words, everyone is hoping for a free ride.

Clearly, bond issuers would prefer not to be put into bankruptcy. The managers of the bond issuer (e.g., firm) don't want their employer to be placed in bankruptcy, so their creditors and the bankruptcy court are looking over their shoulders and second-guessing their every move. So the bond issuer generally makes its scheduled debt payments as long as it is in a position to do so. And yet sometimes the resources needed to service these debts are simply unavailable. Once the debtor runs out of cash, it has no choice but to stop paying its creditors. Such a payment default is bad news for the bondholders. Not only does it mean that the coupon and principal payments stop, it is also almost always accompanied by a bankruptcy filing and a large decline in the market value of the bonds.

The bond market is well aware that a bankruptcy proceeding tends to be a very expensive process. The cost of administering a company while in bankruptcy consumes a significant amount of value that would otherwise be available to distribute to the creditors. So when a bond issuer defaults, its asset base is already inadequate to cover its liabilities. Then the bankruptcy process further diminishes the bond issuer's asset values.

A bond issuer who defaults on a payment is almost certain to be forced into bankruptcy. The bondholders then become claimants in the bankruptcy proceeding. The legal procedings involved in a bankruptcy case typically take about two years to play out. During that two-year time period the bond-holders generally do not receive any cash payments. When the proceedings are completed, the creditors are awarded a distribution based on two factors: (1) the resources available from the issuer (relative to the amount of debt outstanding) and (2) The priority of their claim. Holders of defaulted bonds could receive a distribution from the bankrupt estate equal to anything from a full recovery of the creditor's claim (almost always limited to the face value of the claim as of the date of the bankruptcy filing with no accrual of interest during the period of the bankruptcy) to nothing at all. Payouts in corporate bankruptcies tend to be in the range of 40 to 60 percent of the face value of the claim, but are frequently above or below this range. Payments may be in the form of cash and/or securities. Often the consideration that is distributed to creditors in payment for their claims is in the form of shares of stock in the newly reorganized company.

Default risk is a serious concern for bond investors, particularly those who invest in high-risk (e.g., junk) bonds. Accordingly, bond investors need to understand and assess the risks associated with the bonds that they consider investing in.

Notwithstanding their higher risk, a diversified portfolio of high-risk, high-yield (junk) bonds tends to produce attractive returns, most of the time.

The market tends to compensate investors who are willing to accept high risk. It does so by providing them with relatively high expected returns. Low-quality, high-risk bonds have a significant chance of defaulting. They must be priced such that the bonds offer a high enough promised return to com-pensate for their high default risk. Put another way, the number of willing buyers will be sufficient to absorb the available supply of high-risk bonds only if the anticipated return is large enough to offset the negative impact of the high risk. Even after the typical loss from default is subtracted from the high level of promised returns, the net yield on junk bonds still tends to remain attractive. Thus, *after subtracting losses from defaults, a junk bond portfolio's net return is generally higher than the net return on portfolios of lower-risk bonds.*

While the average return on diversified portfolios of junk bonds tends to be relatively attractive (to compensate investors for the high risk), the return has also tended to be quite variable. That is, the market for high-risk bonds can be and often is quite volatile. When investors' confidence in the econ-omy's future is increasing, junk bond prices tend to rise, thereby producing attractive performance for junk bond portfolios. When, however, the economic outlook is poor and declining, weak firms are more likely to fail. When weak firms are at a greater risk of failing, junk bond prices tend to fall, often by substantial amounts. Worse still, default rates tend to rise, further reducing portfolio values. This fluctuation in junk bond prices can lead to very volatile returns for portfolios of such bonds. Even well-diversified portfolios of such bonds tend to produce not only high but also very volatile returns. Thus, for any given holding period, the returns on junk bond portfolios can be well above or well below the long-term averages.

Diversification is every bit as important with bond portfolios as with stock portfolios, particularly for portfolios of junk bonds.

Bond investors are exposed to several different types of risk. When market interest rates rise, bond prices decline. That effect has an impact on the entire market for bonds. Individual bond values are also adversely affected by a decline in the issuer's credit quality. Such a decline may involve a default but most of the time it does not. Sometimes an investment-grade bond is downgraded to junk bond status. What had been thought of as a strong issuer becomes viewed by the investment community as considerably weaker. For example, AT&T's stocks and bonds were once considered to be very safe investments. Its stock was considered to be a blue chip and its bonds were rated AAA (the highest possible risk rating). In 2004 its bonds were downgraded to junk bond status (BB).

A downgrade in a bond's credit rating does not mean that the issuer's bankruptcy is inevitable. The issuer may very well avoid default even though the credit quality has fallen and the risk of default has risen. Thus, payments of coupon and principal will continue, at least initially, even though the market now views the bond as having a greater risk of default than when it was rated investment-grade. When such a downgrade occurs, the bonds' price and yield will adjust to its lower credit quality. The downgraded bond will, however, still maintain a substantial value. Thus a bond that was priced at close to par ($1,000 face value) when considered investment-grade, might fall by, say, 20 percent (to around $800 a bond) if downgraded to junk bond status. The downgraded bond will remain obligated to pay its same coupon and principal at maturity regardless of its rating. The investment would, however, have suffered a loss in market value as a result of the decline in the bond's credit quality. That loss (on paper) would turn into a realized loss if the bondholder had to sell or if the bond subsequently defaulted.

Bonds may, on occasion, be upgraded. A company may have originally issued high-yield junk bonds when it was a relatively weak credit. Later it may have appreciably increased its revenues and profitability and thereby enhanced its credit quality. If its credit quality rises sufficiently, its bonds may be upgraded from junk to investment-grade (or from lower investment-grade to higher investment-grade, etc.). Generally, however, far more bonds are downgraded than upgraded. Moreover, when a company does succeed in enhancing its credit quality, it may also choose to call in its old bonds. By calling these high-yield bonds, the now stronger firm can refinance its outstanding debt at lower interest rates.

So we see that individual bond values may go up or down as their investment qualities change over time. Careful credit analysis of the issuer may help you avoid some negatives (e.g., bond downgrades) in your bond portfolio. Most such changes, however, are the result of unexpected developments. A bond portfolio consisting of only one or a few bonds is particularly vulnerable to isolated events having an adverse impact on one or more of those few bond issues. A bond portfolio containing similar amounts of eight to ten or more different bond issues should be sufficiently diversified to spread the risks reasonably well. As a result of that diversification, isolated events are much less likely to have a major impact on portfolio performance. Thus we see that diversification is an important device for spreading the risks inherent in a bond portfolio.

When one company acquires another company, the target company's bonds are often downgraded. Be cautious with the bonds of potential takeover candidates.

When one company acquires another company, it frequently uses debt to finance part, or in some instances, all of the purchase of the target company's shares. The assets of the target company are used to collateralize the new debt. The target company's existing bonds are usually also left in place. The acquisition process is, however, very likely to increase the combined firm's leverage. Such acquisitions are called *leveraged buyouts* or *LBOs*. As a result of the LBO's increased leverage, the credit quality of the bond issuer generally declines. This lower credit quality affects the value of not only the bonds issued to finance the acquisition but also of the bonds of the target company that were already outstanding before the takeover. Thus the shareholders of the target company may receive a nice premium for their shares while the company's bondholders are made worse off. Accordingly, bond investors need to be cautious about investing in bonds of companies that are potential takeover candidates. Identifying potential takeover candidates is discussed elsewhere in this book.

Agency bonds, FDIC-insured CDs, and collateralized mortgage obligations (CMOs) holding government guaranteed mortgages represent an attractive alternative to U.S. Treasury bonds.

The market views the bonds issued by the U.S. Treasury to be the safest and most secure bonds available. Such bonds are backed up by the *full faith and credit* of the United States government. Given the taxing and borrowing capacity of the U.S. government, coupled with the power of the Federal Reserve to manage the money supply through its open market operations (trading in Treasury bills), nothing short of a revolutionary overthrow of the government, a U.S. loss in a nuclear war, or a successful invasion from outer space is thought at all likely to lead to a default of Treasury debt obligations. Clearly, Treasury bonds are extremely safe. They are viewed by the marketplace as being much safer than the safest corporate or municipal bond. The latter two bond types are known to default on occasion. Even the highest-quality corporate and municipal bonds are viewed as having some risk of default. Thus, investors who wish to own the ultimate in safe bonds should buy U.S. Treasury issues.

In addition to Treasury issues (called "governments"), three other types of debt instruments are, in many cases, almost as devoid of default risk as governments. Agency securities (called *agencies*) are debt instruments issued by U.S. government agencies such as the Government National Mortgage Association (GNMA). The bonds issued by these agencies are, in some cases, backed by the same full faith and credit of the U.S. Treasury as governments. For most of the other agency issues, the market assumes the existence of an implied backing by the Treasury. Therefore, both their past history (devoid of defaults) and their association with the federal government imply that these agency debt issues are very safe.

A second category of extremely safe debt issue are FDIC (Federal Deposit Insurance Corporation) insured certificates of deposits (CDs) sold by banks and other government-guaranteed depository institutions. The FDIC insurance is, however, limited to $100,000 per depositor, per issuing institution. The FDIC collects insurance premiums from member banks. In most years these insurance premiums far exceed the FDIC's costs of operations. The FDIC has utilized the excess from these payments to build and maintain a substantial reserve fund. This reserve fund is available and, when necessary, to be used to cover what would have been the losses of insured depositors of failed banks. The FDIC can also borrow funds from the U.S. Treasury if need be to perform its insurance functions. Finally, Congress demonstrated in the S&L crisis of the 1980s a willingness to bail out the financial system with additional funds when necessary.

FDIC insurance has a flawless record of protecting insured deposits. Since its formation in the 1930s, no one has ever lost money in an FDIC-insured account. Thus FDIC insurance makes a debt issue very safe. The $100,000 per institution, per depositor limit on FDIC insurance is a relevant constraint when substantial sums of money are involved. One can, however, assemble a large portfolio of insured CDs by purchasing one $100,000 CD from each of a number of issuing banks. For example, a portfolio of fifty $100,000 CDs issued by fifty different banks adds up to $5 million of fully FDIC-insured funds.

The third category of very safe debt instruments consists of collateralized mortgage obligations (CMOs), which contain only government-guaranteed mortgages. Both the Federal Housing Administration (FHA) and the Department of Veterans' Affairs (VA) provide federal government guarantees to qualified borrowers seeking mortgages. Such FHA and VA-guaranteed mortgages have a number of layers of protection: First, the (creditworthy) borrower's ability to service the mortgages, then the (appraised) collateral value of the mortgaged property, and finally the government guarantee all provide protection to the CMO investor. CMOs are pools of mortgages that are assembled and sold to investors. These CMO investors receive their pro rata share of the mortgage pools' cash flows, minus a small sum deducted for administrative expenses.

Notwithstanding their safety and relatively high yields, mortgage pool investments do have one significant disadvantage. With a bond, the payment stream (dates and amounts of coupon and principal payments) is precisely defined in the indenture. Barring a default or early call, a bond investor knows exactly what the payment stream is to be. While the payment streams of individual mortgages are also specified with precision, individual mortgages are often paid off early. Homeowners are particularly likely to prepay their current mortgages in periods of falling interest rates. Thus the actual payment stream on a portfolio of mortgages is much less certain than that of an otherwise similar portfolio of bonds.

Very Safe Types of Bonds and Depositor Accounts

U.S. Treasury Issues (governments): Treasury bills, notes, and bonds are backed by the full faith and credit of the U.S. government. In light of the government's power to tax and the Fed's control over the financial system, these debt instruments are considered as safe as possible.

U.S. Agency Securities: Agencies are set up by the U.S. government. Most agencies were established for a special purpose by an act of Congress. Many of these agencies are allowed to borrow money (issue bonds) in their own name. Their securities may or may not be backed by the full faith and credit of the U.S. government. The U.S. government is unlikely, however, to allow any of its agencies to fail. Accordingly, the risk of a default on such issues is remote.

FDIC-Insured CDs and other types of Depositor Accounts: Banks and thrift institutions issue debt instruments (CDs) and offer accounts (e.g., passbook savings accounts) with FDIC insurance covering the first $100,000 per investor, per issuing institution. The government-backed FDIC insurance makes these types of instruments extremely safe from default losses.

Government-Guaranteed Collateralized Mortgage Obligations: CMOs contain pools of real estate mortgages. Most CMOs are very safe investments because of the quality of their collateral. CMOs that contain only government-guaranteed (VA & FHA) mortgages are particularly safe.

The market views these three types of non-Treasury debt instruments to be neither as safe nor as liquid as governments. Accordingly, their yields tend to be significantly higher than otherwise similar governments. That is, the interplay of supply and demand results in a market price that corresponds to a somewhat higher yield for these types of government-guaranteed or government-related instruments than is the market-established yield established for otherwise-equivalent governments. These three government-associated debt instruments (agencies, FDIC-insured CDs, and government-guaranteed mortgage pools) are, nonetheless, still very safe. Thus, one who is willing to tolerate a *di minimus* amount of additional default risk should take a close look at them as a substitute for governments.

Because of their low risk, all of the above mentioned types of debt instruments offer somewhat lower yields than otherwise similar but higher-risk debt instruments such as corporates. Compared to Treasury issues, however the other types (CDs, agencies, and particularly CMOs) tend to offer somewhat higher yields.

8

Bankruptcy Investing

W hile U.S. government-guaranteed bonds and high-quality uninsured corporate bonds offer a substantial degree of risk protection, the trade-off is in the form of lower promised yields. At the other end of the spectrum are the bonds of companies that have already declared bankruptcy. Clearly, such bonds contain high levels of risk. Both the timing and amount of any recoveries on defaulted bonds are typically very uncertain. Accordingly, defaulted bonds need to be priced at levels that will offer relatively high potential returns if they are to attract enough investor interest to absorb the available supply. Assembling and managing a portfolio of such bonds constitutes one of a number of specialized areas of investing.

One may invest in bankruptcies by purchasing claims on a firm that has failed and filed for bankruptcy under either Chapter 7 (liquidation) or 11 (reorganization). Most such investing is in the defaulted bonds (secured, senior, or subordinated) of the *debtor* (the firm that declares bankruptcy). Trading does, however, take place in other instruments including defaulted bank loans, trade claims, and damage claims as well as the common and preferred stock of the debtor. Investors in such instruments are generally betting that the market is more pessimistic on the recovery prospects for the failed firm than is warranted by the facts. Those wishing to read a more in-depth treatment should obtain a copy of *Bankruptcy Investing*, by Ben Branch and Hugh Ray (Beard, 2002).

THE HISTORY OF BANKRUPTCY INVESTING

Early in the 1980s a few savvy investors appeared to have found a surefire way to make money. As large public companies started to reorganize successfully in Chapter 11 (the current revised Bankruptcy Code had become effective in 1979), many bankruptcy investors realized that one could hardly lose by purchasing the stock of a newly reorganized company emerging from Chapter 11. Why was this?

First, as of 1979, Chapter 11 became much more "user friendly" and popular. The Bankruptcy Code completely reworked the way large corporations rebuilt their capital structures. The old Chapter XI and the old Chapter X each had serious legal failings that tended to prevent either one from being utilized as an effective tool to correct the capital structure of a publicly held firm that failed. Liquidations that tended to recover relatively little value for the claimants were the usual result. Often, greater value can be preserved by reorganizing the bankrupt firm and thereby retaining its value as a going concern. These early bankruptcy investors realized that, to become viable, many firms simply needed a more realistic capital structure. Creating this more realistic structure usually meant that much or perhaps all of the recognized firm's old debt was converted into equity and that its old equity was largely or totally wiped out. Such a shift in the capital structure allowed control to be transferred to the true economic owners (old debt-holders). A fundamentally strong business with too much debt could equitize its liabilities. Along with favorable tax treatments concerning net operating loss carry forwards (now severely limited), a great investment opportunity usually existed in the new balance sheet of the reorganized firm.

Second, most of the creditors who received the new postreorganization stock were not traditional equity-holders. They were either trade vendors who were receiving stock in lieu of their trade claims, or bondholders who were receiving stock in lieu of their debt holdings. Only rarely did such creditors have any interest in becoming stockholders in the company that had defaulted on their debt. As might be expected, these former creditors promptly dumped their new shares in the reorganized debtor on to an unreceptive market. This rush for the exit caused a downward pressure that the successful bankruptcy investors spotted, jumped on, and rode up as the fortunes of the newly reorganized firm became apparent. Unfortunately, bankruptcy investing is no longer so simple.

Bankruptcy investing is just the latest iteration in the history of distressed debt investing. The process started with Revolutionary War bonds in the 1780s and continued into the following century with railroad bonds; next came the 1929 Crash, followed by substantial investment opportunity, the REITs, LBO junk bonds, and the FDIC crises of the eighties and nineties. The late 1990s brought us Japan's difficulties and problems in the emerging markets. All of these situations presented bankruptcy investing opportunities.

Today a number of trading desks have sophistication in the area. Among them are Cargill, CS First Boston, Goldman Sachs, Lehman Brothers, Merrill Lynch, and Morgan Stanley.

WHERE ARE WE NOW?

Competition among distressed investors has become more and more intense. Not infrequently too many bankruptcy investors are chasing too few bankrupt situations. Prices tend to be bid up to full value or even higher. The prices of defaulted bonds are, however, often lower in the early, uncertain stages of a bankruptcy. Accordingly, a trend toward earlier investments in bankrupt companies has developed. This early investment in ongoing bankruptcy cases (when values are much less certain) has increased the risk of losses. It has also substantially increased demands on the savvy bankruptcy investor. Such an investor needs quickly to ascertain the likelihood of success or failure for the bankrupt firm, and accurately, in order to predict the consideration that will be received by each of the different classes of debt-holders as part of the plan of reorganization.

Those who wish to invest in the early stages of a bankruptcy need rapidly to ascertain the following: (1) the chances of the bankrupt firm's success with its underlying business model and a realistic capital structure; and (2) an assessment of what that capital structure will be and how new value will flow to each of the current classes of creditors.

The first assessment is relatively straightforward. Would the firm be profitable if it had little or no debt to service? The second assessment requires not only a firm grasp of economics, but also of the political and legal processes that pervade the Chapter 11 process. Having defined the topic, I shall now provide a series of rules designed to assist one who would like to participate in the bankruptcy investing market.

Avoid the stocks of bankrupt companies. If you want to bet on a turnaround, buy their bonds (not their stock).

A company declares or is forced into bankruptcy because it is unable to pay its bills as they come due and/or because the monetary value of its liabilities is greater than that of its assets. Under bankruptcy law, creditors' claims have priority over claims of shareholders'. According to the *absolute priority of claims principle,* all valid creditor claims are to be paid in full before the equity-holders receive anything. This principle is applied absolutely in Chapter 7 bankruptcy cases where the firm is liquidated. It also guides allocation of value in Chapter 11 cases where the firm is reorganized.

While saying "equity comes out last" seems trite, this maxim guides the process in terms of who gets what. Distributions trickle up from there. Some nominal payout to prepetition equity is not uncommon. Generally, however, these holders will receive only a *di minimus* (5% or less of the stock in the company coming out of bankruptcy) interest in the reorganized debtor. This modest allocation may be assigned to the old (prebankruptcy filing) share-holders primarily in order to speed the reorganization process along. This departure from the absolute priority principle is only one of many legal variances that exist in the Chapter 11 process. That process involves a great deal of give-and-take and consensus-building designed to move the process along speedily.

A bankrupt company almost always finds itself with an unmanageable debt burden. The face values of its outstanding liabilities substantially exceed the market value of its remaining assets. A firm whose assets could be sold for a greater amount than it owes to its creditors could probably have avoided a bankruptcy filing in the first place. Such a firm should be able to liquidate some of its assets and use the proceeds to reduce its debts by enough to regain its financial health. Alternatively, the firm could be sold as a unit. The proceeds could then be used first to pay off the creditors, with any excess being distributed to the shareholders. Thus, firms that are forced to declare bankruptcy are almost always unable to raise enough money from asset sales to pay their creditors in full. As a result, once the bankrupt firm's remaining value is distributed to satisfy (usually only partially) the creditors' claim, nothing is likely to be left for the old shareholders. True, the company itself often survives, but usually in a slimmed-down form with a new, less debt-heavy capital structure. When the reorganized firm does survive and emerge from bankruptcy, it does so with new shareholders composed largely or exclusively of those who had been its creditors. Bondholders and other creditors end up owning most or all of the stock of the recognized company. Usually the distribution does not even fully cover the creditor claims, to say nothing of having something left over for the shareholders.

Unsophisticated investors may sometimes take a look at a bankrupt company whose stock had traded at, say, $80 a share, and was now down to $0.25, and say to themselves, "How much lower can it go? If only it went up to fifty cents, I would double my money." They reason that the company, although bankrupt, is likely to survive, and if it does, certainly the business will retain some value. These underinformed investors don't realize that most if not all of that value will be distributed to the creditors. Unfortunately for these newly minted shareholders, the price of this bankrupt company's stock is far more likely to go to zero than to double. For some research on this question, see "Penny Stocks of Bankrupt Firms, Are They Really a Bargain," Ben Branch and Philip Russel, in *Business Quest*, 2001, www.westga.edu/~bquest/2001/penny .htm. This Branch/Russel study found that the vast majority of bankrupt companies' stocks either became worthless (93 out of 154) or declined in value (44 out of 154) over the course of the bankruptcy proceeding. Less than 10 percent (14 of 154) gained value. For every dollar invested in a bankrupt company's stock, the investors recovered an average of 30¢ and lost 70¢. Even lottery tickets have a higher payout (around 50%).

While the stock of bankrupt companies is rarely an attractive investment, the bonds of such companies may be. Whatever value of the bankrupt company that remains tends to be awarded to the creditors (after the lawyers and the tax collectors get their pound of flesh). The question then becomes: How much value is left relative to the price that the market is putting on the debt? Any generalizations here are uncertain at best. This much, however, seems safe to say: *The bonds of bankrupt companies are much more likely to emerge from the bankruptcy proceeding with some value than are the stocks.* Indeed, most of the time, the bonds of a bankrupt firm will produce a higher percentage return (with a lot less risk) than does the stock. *The bonds of bankrupt companies may or may not be an attractive investment, but they are almost always a better investment than the bankrupt company's stock.* If you want to bet on the turnaround of a company that has declared bankruptcy, you should buy its bonds, not its stock. Normally, high-risk investments tend to produce high returns. The performance of the stocks of bankrupt companies is an exception to this general tendency. By no means do all high-risk investments pay off, even on the average.

In this regard, many sophisticated vulture investors like to assemble a hedge position involving a combination short position in the stock of a troubled (but not yet bankrupt) company coupled with a long position in its bonds. If the company does continue downhill, the price of its stock is likely to drop by a much larger percentage than do its bonds. Indeed, the stock's market price may decline to zero while the bonds retain substantial value. If the company somehow stays out of bankruptcy, the bonds will eventually pay off (pay all principal and interest as due) while the stock may or may not do as well. An investment based on a careful computation of the related values can, in some cases, produce what approaches a win/win investment when pricing anomalies appear. That is, on occasion the bonds' price may rise while the bankrupt company's stock price declines all the way to zero. Thus both parts of the hedged position show a profit.

Understand the absolute priority of claims principle and how it applies.

Under the so-called *absolute priority rule* in bankruptcy, the assets of the debtor are liquidated and the senior-most claims are to be paid in full (if possible). What is left after the senior creditors are paid goes to the next level of claimants under the intercreditor pecking order. This process continues from the top of the capital structure down through the various levels of priority until the bankrupt estate's funds are exhausted. The claimant class on the bubble is paid pro rata. Nothing is distributed to the lower classes of claimants unless the higher class is paid in full. This principle applies almost absolutely in Chapter 7 cases. Chapter 7 cases, one of two types of bankruptcy cases, are liquidations with an independent trustee selected to manage the liquidation. Once all the assets are sold, the proceeds are distributed to the claimants in the form of cash.

Order of Priority in Bankruptcy

1. *Priority and Administrative Claims:* Taxes, legal and accounting fees, debtor in possession (DIP) financing, back wages, trustee fees (separate priorities attach to each of these categories, but in most cases they are all paid in full in cash)
2. *Secured Claims:* Up to the value of the collateral, then the remainder if any, becomes a senior claim
3. *Senior Unsecured Claims:* Relative to any subordinated claim
4. *General Claims:* Such as those of trade creditors (on the same level as senior claims, but are not senior to subordinated claims)
5. *Subordinated Claims:* Relative to any senior claim; may have several layers
6. *Preferred Shareholder Claims:* Rarely does the distribution reach this level
7. *Common Shareholder Claims:* Payout here is even rarer

In Chapter 11 cases, absolute priority, while the law, is only a guide in practice. Under the so-called *best interest of creditors* test, each creditor class must be allocated at least as much value as the class would receive in a liquidation. In a successful Chapter 11 reorganization, the firm's assets are not sold off and thereby reduced to cash. The firm is considered to be worth more as a going concern than it would be through the sale of its assets. This failure to reduce the bankrupt firms' value to cash opens a Pandora's box in regard to who gets how much of a distribution. The value of a cash distribution is easy to evaluate: Cash is cash. But the value of a package of to-be-issued securities (especially equity securities) in a reorganized firm coming out of bankruptcy is not so easy to place a value on. When a bankrupt firm is reorganized, a set of securities (debt and equity) reflecting claims on the company emerging from bankruptcy are distributed to the claimants. These securities have not yet been priced by the market. Accordingly, estimating their value is an uncertain process. How much stock (or other securities) of undetermined market value needs to be distributed to a given class of creditors to satisfy their claims cannot be established until the new stock begins to trade. That trading usually does not begin until the securities are distributed and the reorganized firm emerges from bankruptcy. Often the market value assumptions made in the court-approved plan of reorganization turn out to be very wide of the mark. A low estimate for the total value for the reorganized firm can create a substantial investment opportunity for the savvy bankruptcy investor. Such an investor will realize that the postreorganization securities to be distributed to the claimants are based on an assumption that the reorganized debtor is valued at much less than it actually turns out to be worth. How could such a misvaluation occur? Bankruptcy cases are, by their nature, a very political process, with lawyers representing several distinct groups of claimants. Each of these creditor groups has an agenda. In many reorganization cases, the more senior classes of debt-holders will seek to persuade the court to adopt a relatively low valuation for the bankrupt company. If the seniors' efforts are successful, such an undervaluation is likely to result in little or no distribution to the junior classes of debt (e.g., subordinated bondholders). The senior bondholders will thereby capture a greater percentage of the reorganized firm's value than they would be entitled to under a more realistic valuation. The junior bondholders will, on their part, seek to establish a higher valuation and, if successful, capture a larger share of the reorganized firm's value than they would if the estimated value was lower.

How are these valuation estimates generated? The bankruptcy court must approve the plan of reorganization if it is to go forward. As part of its approval process, the court must make a factual determination regarding valuations. The goal of this process is supposed to be to establish a fair benchmark valuation estimate for the enterprise. If, for example, the reorganized firm is estimated to be worth $100,000,000 coming out of bankruptcy and it issues 10,000,000 shares (and has no debt), the plan can treat each share as being worth $10. Under these circumstances, a claim of $100,000 could be satisfied in full with an award of 10,000 shares. If, however, the enterprise was estimated to be worth only $50,000,000 and issued 10,000,000 shares, each share would be projected to have a value of $5. Twice as many $5 shares would be required to provide a full recovery on a $100,000 claim as would he needed if the share value was projected to be $10. Establishing an estimated valuation for the company is a fact question with dueling experts on valuation issues. By the time a case is set for reorganization, adequate data are generally available in the marketplace to make an intelligent determination. Sometimes, however, the results have been skewed during the reorganization process. All of these situations create investment opportunities.

Successful bankruptcy investing requires a better than average knowledge of valuation techniques and legal niceties. Valuation's interaction with bankruptcy law is the often major driver in Chapter 11 cases. These subjects can be mastered by an individual investor, but the initial time and the cost in the form of investment losses that it takes to "spool up" helps explain why bankruptcy investing has historically been the province of institutional investors. Moreover, the creation of bankruptcy investing opportunities is a very uneven process. When the economy is strong, few firms fail. When it is weak, many do. As a result, expertise in bankruptcy investing is a skill in high demand in some market environments, but not so high in others.

Be mindful of the political nature of the Chapter 11 process.
Invest accordingly.

Drafting a reorganization plan and obtaining approval from the creditors and court always requires some give-and-take by the parties. Whatever reorganization plan emerges from the Chapter 11 process reflects the interplay of a group of varied parties' interests. The process is inherently political. The relevant players to this process include:

The Bankruptcy Judge: He or she alone among the various participants does not have a financial interest in the outcome. The judge does, however, play a very important role in deciding how much latitude to give to the debtor relative to the creditor, and how fast to push the process along.

The Debtor: The prebankruptcy managers of the now-bankrupt firm often remain in place through the bankruptcy/reorganization and, possibly, once it emerges from bankruptcy. In many cases, new management will eventually be brought in. Whether under new or old management, the debtor will have a lot to say about any reorganization plan as well as what is done with the firm's assets during the period in bankruptcy. At least for the first 180 days (and this period of exclusivity may be, and often is, extended), only the debtor can propose a reorganization plan. That plan is, however, subject to creditor approval. Each class of creditors must vote by majority of number and two-thirds of dollar value to approve the plan. For a reorganization plan to be implemented, the senior creditors must give their approval. If junior creditors reject the plan, the bankruptcy court may, nonetheless, approve it over their objections (cramdown).

The debtor's managers will be interested in preserving their jobs, protecting their reputations, and avoiding being targets of lawsuits from angry claimants. They will want to assist in the process of assembling a viable enterprise to emerge from bankruptcy, and they will want to pursue and/or create value for the claimants. The more selfish objective of protecting their own financial position is, however, likely to play an important role in their decisions. Often in an attempt to preserve some value for their own equity holdings (stock) and jobs, they have waited for too long to file Chapter 11. They may well have chosen to ignore advice and facts that clearly demonstrated their need to seek court protection. By the time they are forced to file, a great deal of the enterprise's value is likely to have eroded away. At least some of that value might have been preserved by court protection, had the firm filed bankruptcy sooner.

The creditors, as a group, are focused almost exclusively on maximizing the recovery value of their investment. Creditors, however, are not a homogeneous group. They are often divided into several separate categories with differing priorities and interests. Specifically:

- *DIP (Debtor in Possession) financing lenders* head up this group as secured claimants who are usually paid before any value goes to prebankruptcy filing claimants.
- *Tax claims* filed by IRS, state, and local governments have high priority. These claims are usually paid off in cash even when the debtor reorganizes in a Chapter 11.
- *Administrative claims* from lawyers and other professionals are also a priority and paid in cash.
- The *claims of the Pension Benefit Guaranty Corporation (PBGC)* are also high-priority and usually satisfied with cash.

- *Bank lenders* will generally have secured claims. As such, they are in a strong position to maximize their recovery.
- *Bondholders* may have secured, but more typically, have either senior unsecured or subordinated claims. The larger bondholders, who may be either senior or subordinated claimants, generally pursue a reorganization plan structure that will enhance their recovery.
- *Trade creditors* round out the list of major constituents in most cases. If represented by a union, the employee claimants may also have an important voice.

Each of the above-mentioned creditor groups has its own agenda and separate interests. A reorganization plan allocates differing amounts of value to different categories of creditors. Accordingly, the creditor classes act together to maximize the size of the pie but are often in conflict over how to divide it up.

Understanding how these creditor groups interrelate is an important key to any successful bankruptcy investing program. One useful way to grasp how these cases sort out is to study some of the reorganization plans for major Chapter 11s. Copies of these plans are available online at the websites of many of the bankruptcy courts around the country. For example, those for the Southern District of Texas can be accessed at http//ccF.txb.uscourts.sav. You will need to obtain an ID number from the court in order to access the website, but this is free and easy to do.

After reading a few reorganization plans, take a look at several of the official disclosure statements that accompany the plans. Reading these plans and disclosure statements should provide you with a feel for how the process works.

Much of the conflict in the reorganization process involves estimating the value of the emerging firm.

Placing a fair and realistic value on the reorganized firm and its securities as it emerges from bankruptcy is an inherently uncertain and often contentious process. To estimate the enterprise's value properly, you need to project the emerging firm's income and growth potential as well as the risks attached thereto. Then you need to allocate the firm's estimated value onto the securities (debt, equity) to be issued and distributed to the claimants. Only then will you be able to place a meaningful value on the package of securities scheduled to be distributed to the various claimants.

Estimated values can be derived from an analysis of cash flows, industry comparables, market multiples, and liquidation values. In addition, a quick assessment needs to be made concerning the secured creditors' rights in bankruptcy. This assessment will require a horseback analysis of the off balance sheet liabilities, the collateral values, and the liquidation priorities as well as the practicalities of enforcing the rights of the secured creditors. For example, how would you foreclose on a satellite? An assessment also needs to be made of what guarantees might be outstanding. How strong are the guarantees? How creditworthy is the guarantor?

Different groups of claimants have differing interests in determining how large or small an estimated value is to be placed on the reorganized firm. By its very nature a bankruptcy filing results when an enterprise's value is expected to be less than its creditors' claims. Reorganizing a firm that has had to file for bankruptcy rarely changes the reality that creditor claims exceed the enterpriser's value. In other words, in a bankruptcy the value available to satisfy the creditors' claims is almost always too small to pay off those claims in full. Indeed, the cost of the bankruptcy process itself (legal and other professional fees, lost business due to disruptions, etc.) is likely to reduce the firm's value further. At least some (and perhaps all) of the bankrupt firm's creditors are very likely to suffer losses. Each group understands that the estimated value of the reorganized enterprise, whatever it may be, will be used for the purpose of determining how the reorganized firm's value is to be distributed to the various categories of claimants. The percentage of value allocated to the more senior creditors varies inversely with the emerging firm's projected value relative to the size of their claim.

Suppose, for example, that senior creditors have claims of $40 million, and the reorganized firm is estimated to be worth $50 million when it comes out of bankruptcy (assume that it has paid all its administrative and priority claims before coming out). The senior claims are satisfied first and then junior claimants are assigned what is left. With these numbers, the senior creditors might be awarded about 80 percent of the firm's value ($40/$50 = 80%). A distribution of this amount to the seniors would leave 20 percent of the firm's value for the more junior claimants. If, in contrast, the reorganized firm is estimated to be worth $60 million, the seniors' share would fall to about 67 percent ($40/$60 = 67%) and the juniors' would rise to about 33 percent. Frequently the valuation process is sufficiently uncertain that one could reasonably estimate the value of an emerging company at $50 million or $60 million. At the point in time when the court is determining whether to accept an estimated value for the firm of $50 million, $60 million, or some other amount, the security market has not had an opportunity to establish a true market price through the interplay of supply and demand. The market-determined valuations will not emerge until after the reorganized firm comes out of bankruptcy and its securities start trading. By that time, however, the firm's securities will already have been distributed to the claimants. Clearly, the value estimate that the court accepts and uses in the reorganization plan will play a large role in determining how much of the total pie goes to each class of claimants.

Sometimes these valuation issues are settled within the creditor's committee. At other times the judge must sort things out. Frequently the junior and senior creditors will each hire their own separate experts to argue for their preferred valuation estimates. Because value estimates involve substantial subjectivity, different experts can come up with and seek to justify the accuracy of very different numbers.

Learn the identities and agendas of the players in a bankruptcy.

Event dynamics are an important part of assessing bankruptcy investment opportunities. Timing is crucial. An investment will normally require an evaluation of such matters as which creditors hold strategic blocking positions in terms of voting rights and what unresolved regulatory issues might be outstanding.

Successful bankruptcy investing often involves playing the angles for maximum advantage. Given the political nature of the process coupled with all the other uncertainties, the value to be distributed to any particular claimant class will depend greatly upon how things develop over time. Knowing who the players are and how they are motivated can be very helpful information to be used in analyzing how the reorganization plan will be constructed and how fast it will proceed. Pursuant to this issue, consider the following list of players and their agendas.

THE JUDGE AND COURT

Does the *bankruptcy court judge* have a reputation for being debtor-friendly? Such an orientation would not be favorable to the creditors. A debtor-friendly judge is likely to allow the bankrupt firm's managers a substantial amount of latitude. The use of that latitude may lead to the dissipation of a significant amount of the firm's assets. Recall that the debtors' and creditors' interests are not necessarily aligned.

Does the court have a crowded docket and does the judge have a reputation for moving slowly? The time spent in bankruptcy is costly. The slower the process, the worse things are for the creditors. The expenses incurred in the form of professional fees tend to increase with the length of time the case takes. If more time is available, more tasks will be undertaken and more fees will be charged. Furthermore, the sooner creditors receive their recovery, the greater its value to them.

Are *banks* major participants? If so, their presence in this case could be either favorable or unfavorable for the other (e.g., bondholder) creditors. Banks are usually experienced and motivated to get the job done. They will push to recover as much of their money as they can, but they are usually realistic about what is possible. Most banks have a good sense of when to cut their losses and move on. If banks are creditors in the case, their presence will be felt by the other creditors. Usually, banks will hold senior secured claims, which gives them considerable leverage in the bankruptcy process.

Are *institutional investors* major players? Mutual funds, insurance companies, and other institutional investors are also experienced and motivated much like the banks. Having them on the creditors' committee is usually a plus, particularly if your claims are *para pasu* (at the same priority level) with theirs.

Vulture investors are also usually well equipped to navigate the ins and outs of bankruptcy proceedings. They do, however, come in a variety of flavors. Often, the vultures represent themselves in the process. Some vultures (with their own money at stake) are not at all afraid to play a game of *chicken, skunk at the picnic, or monkey with a gun* (see below) in an attempt to improve their recovery for themselves. They may have purchased a position for pennies on the dollar. As such many believe that they have little to lose by being very aggressive. Accordingly, they may sometimes appear to act irrationally and hold out for unreasonable recoveries.

All of these games involve the risk that the game-playing can have an adverse impact on everyone involved in the case. The larger the positions of the ones playing the game, the greater the risk.

The bankrupt firm's mid and lower-level employees (past and present) tend to have the court's ear, especially when they are represented by a union. Their claims are frequently disputed as they may relate back to written or verbal contracts and understandings that can be subject to varying interpretations. The equities of the situation often incline the court to be sympathetic to the firm's employees. Through no fault of their own, these current or former employees have already lost a great deal (perhaps their jobs, money in their 401Ks, etc.) as a result of the bankruptcy. Higher-level employees and former employees whose actions may have played a role in the firm's failure are likely to appear less sympathetic to the judge.

Government agencies such as the PBGC, IRS, FDIC (Pension Benefit Guaranty Corporation, Internal Revenue Service, Federal Deposit Insurance Corporation) are often claimants in bankruptcy cases. Unless they appear

---

Games Played by Aggressive Creditors

Chicken: Two groups of creditors threaten each other (e.g., banks versus bondholders) with legal action (e.g., convert a Chapter 11 case to Chapter 7, or oppose the proposed reorganization plan) unless it is structured in a way that is more favorable to their position. Each side threatens action until one side blinks or the threats are carried out by both sides.

Skunk at the Picnic: One particularly aggressive claimant refuses to go along with the deal worked out by all of the other creditor groups unless he or she is given some sort of special consideration.

Monkey with a Gun: One aggressive claimant convinces (or attempts to convince) the other parties to the negotiation that he or she is so irrational that unless they go along with his or her demands, the aggressive claimant is likely to do something that is destructive to everyone's interest.

too arrogant, the courts tend to give careful consideration and some degree of deference to these fellow government employees who represent such agencies.

Companies find themselves forced into bankruptcy for a variety of reasons. Understanding the history and underlying causes of the company's insolvency and descent into bankruptcy can be quite helpful in assessing the chances for a successful investment. For example, the asbestos liability cases and the Texaco situations are totally different from the excessive leverage situations like Federated Department Stores, Macy's, and the like. Firms with deteriorating operations have fundamental problems that tend to be very difficult to address: Boston Chicken and Fruit of the Loom are examples. Going through Chapter 11 bankruptcy and coming out as a reorganized enterprise cannot by itself cure a basic problem with the emerging company's business plan.

The most straightforward bankruptcy cases to analyze are those in which a basically healthy company is leveraged to the point where it cannot service its debt. Such a situation is relatively easy to fix by simply reducing the over-leveraged firm's debt level. Similarly, a company that has been hit with a raft of damage claims (e.g., asbestos) but is otherwise healthy can generally be repaired by isolating the claims and assigning a portion of the firm's value to the claimants. Situations in which the firm itself has deep-seated fundamental difficulties (e.g., obsolete technology) are much more problematic. For example, some firms may be operating in declining industries (video rental) or facing serious foreign competition (steel, textiles). No amount of capital restructuring is likely to deal effectively with their long-term problems. In the middle are those firms that have a basically viable business, but have been poorly managed. New management may or may not succeed in overcoming the problems. Clearly, one needs to assess the underlying causes for the bankruptcy. Some problems are relatively easy to deal with. Others are more difficult, and still others are essentially impossible to repair.

Obtain copies of and analyze the prebankruptcy filing financials and the schedules filed in the bankruptcy case. But do not accept these numbers at their face values.

Firms that file for bankruptcy have generally been fighting a losing battle for months (or in some cases years). During the course of that battle, they have almost always been trying to put a positive spin on a negative reality. Whatever financial numbers were released in their public reports (quarterly and annual) prior to the bankruptcy filing are almost certain to reflect much wishful thinking, if not outright fraud. Don't ever make the mistake of relying on the values contained in those statements. The firm has been resisting recognizing and reporting realistic accounts of underlying values in an attempt to avoid, or at least to put off, the inevitable. Basic maintenance has been deferred to conserve cash. Some assets have been sold at fire sale prices

TABLE 8.1. Selected Bond Recoveries in Chapter 11

Debtor	Percent of Par Price on Filing	Year	Percent of Par Price on Reorganization	Number of Months in Chapter 11
Carter Hawley Hale	17.9%	1991	39%	15
Federated Dept. Stores	51%	1990	98%	24
Flagstar Corp. (Denny's)	98.5%	1997	110.7%	8
Public Service of New Hampshire	30.4%	1988	99.1%	28
Southland Corp (7-Eleven)	38%	1990	91.5%	3
USG Corp.	67%	1993	93%	27

in order to raise more cash. The company has continued to bleed profusely as it moved from the last prefiling reporting date to the point of a bankruptcy filing. Thus, the company's true financial picture is almost always worse than the numbers shown in the last financial report that it filed before the company went into bankruptcy.

Table 8.1 contains some examples of defaulted bonds and their Chapter 11 prices at inception, their prices on emergence, and the number of months that it took them to emerge.

These recoveries are not representative. Over half of the companies that file for bankruptcy yield lower recoveries than their market value levels just before (but not just after) they went into Chapter 11. These statistical data do, however, provide support for the theory that the flow of information is inefficient.

Moreover, the bankruptcy process is itself almost certain to be quite costly. The lawyers and other professionals (accountants, actuaries, appraisers, auctioneers, brokers, investment bankers, etc.) all charge fees of hundreds of dollars an hour for their services. They can quickly rack up many billable hours. Furthermore, the ongoing businesses tend to lose value throughout the bankruptcy process as customers and key employees fall away. Thus any attempt to place a value on the business should place a high discount on the numbers in its prefiling financials.

Intangible assets reported on the bankrupt firm's balance sheet usually have little or no actual value.

In evaluating the potential to recover value from a bankrupt enterprise, one place to start is with the firm's last prebankruptcy balance sheet. That balance sheet will contain a number of different categories. One category of assets that should generally be assigned very little value is the now bankrupt firm's intangible assets. Assets on the balance sheet such as goodwill, franchise value, deferred tax credits, and so on may have some value to a healthy, going concern. They have little or no value in a liquidation and may have relatively little value in a reorganization.

The point is particularly relevant in the post-2000 era, when many of the more recent bankruptcies are of high-tech, dot.com, telecom-type enterprises. In a bankruptcy situation, "assets" such as software under development, fiber-optic cable rights, domain names, and the like tend to have much less value relative to their cost than do hard assets such as those made of bricks and mortar.

Notwithstanding all of the above, the market often undervalues distressed and default securities.

The securities market hates uncertainty. And yet the outcome from a bankruptcy proceeding is full of uncertainties. As a result, the bonds of bankrupt and near-bankrupt firms are usually very depressed and frequently even more depressed than the situation warrants.

Each bankruptcy situation is different. An uninformed, random investment in defaulted securities is likely to produce uneven results. On the other hand, one who carefully analyzes the available information for distressed and defaulted securities and then assembles a well-diversified portfolio of those securities that the investor's analysis suggests are undervalued may thereby achieve an attractive return.

Do not overlook potential causes of action as possible sources of recovery.

Sometimes much of the potential recovery for the bankrupt firm's creditors can be derived from its *causes of action*. Causes of action are fact patterns that may give rise to a claim for damages from the cause of action's owner. The bankrupt firm may be able to pursue various types of claims against former officers and directors, auditors, and other professionals and related firms, those who did business with the debtor shortly before it failed. If the pursuit of these claims is successful, they may result in substantial recoveries for the bankrupt estate and its creditors.

One category of such claims involves what are called *fraudulent conveyances*. A fraudulent conveyance is a transaction that has the effect of "hindering, delaying or defrauding" the collection of the debts by the debtor's creditors. Suppose the debtor and a third party entered into a transaction that was detrimental to the debtor at a time when the debtor was insolvent. If substantial value that would otherwise have been available to the debtor's creditors was dissipated, the transaction would constitute a fraudulent conveyance. The debtor would be entitled to avoid (reverse) that transaction and thereby recover the amount of value that was lost. If, for example, a debtor sold a subsidiary to a third party at a price well below its true market value at a time when the debtor was already insolvent, the debtor would be entitled to recover the lost value from the buyer.

Preferences constitute a second category of claims that are frequently a source of recoveries for the bankrupt estate and its creditors. Preferences may arise when the debtor repays some of its debts shortly before it files for bankruptcy. Suppose that just prior to the bankruptcy filing, the debtors paid off one or a few of its debts to a favored creditor or group of creditors. Such a prefiling payoff would be made at the expense of the other creditors' interests. The favored creditor gets paid in full while the others are left to collect (usually only partially) from a depleted estate. Any creditor that was preferred in this way is said to have received a preference. If, for example, the manager of a firm that was about to declare bankruptcy paid off its debts to a few favored creditors just before the debtor filed for bankruptcy, these payments would be subject to a preference action. The recipient of the preference may be required to repay the payment money to the bankrupt estate. Once the preference money was repaid, the creditor would get in line for recovery with the other creditors. Usually, the bankrupt estate's recoveries from preferences are modest.

Various types of misbehavior by the former managers or directors, including gross negligence, fraud, or acting to the firm's detriment because of a conflict of interest, give rise to a third category of claims. Similar issues can arise with professionals (e.g., auditors). Often the true defendant in those matters is the insurance company providing coverage. They are the ones who will pay the claim up to the limits of coverage.

A dollar in the form of a claim is almost always worth substantially less than a dollar of cash (a bird in the hand versus a bird in the bush). Recoveries on claims require success in a variety of areas, not the least of which is collectibility. Winning a judgment may be only the first step in the recovery process. Moreover, the cost of pursuing claims is often substantial. If the recovery effort is unsuccessful, the distribution pot will be further diluted by the costs of the effort. Still, these types of potential recoveries should not be overlooked. Sometimes such claims are the only potential upside value that remains in the bankrupt estate. Also, be aware that the anticipated litigation costs of pursuing certain claims may be so large as to prevent such claims from being pursued.

The market for distressed and defaulted securities is volatile. Don't invest unless you can tolerate its fluctuations.

The supply of distressed and defaulted securities depends upon the misfortunes of the issuing companies. The more companies that fail, the more defaulted securities enter the market. Such calamities depend, to a large degree, upon the state of the economy. When the economy is strong and the securities market robust, relatively few companies get into trouble and rather little new product is created. At such times, those investors who specialize in distressed and defaulted debt instruments are all seeking to acquire similar resources. Too much money is chasing too little product. Such an imbalance can lead to inflated prices for distressed and defaulted securities.

At other times, the market is overwhelmed with supply. In the early 2000s, many companies found themselves in financial difficulty first because of an unsustainable boom that allowed half-baked ideas to raise money for ventures destined to fail and then because the unsustainable boom turned into a recession. Many of these companies had relied on the capital markets to provide them with an endless supply of cash. When the market turned off the spigot, they had nowhere else to turn. They failed in droves. The bond market was soon flooded with distressed and defaulted products. Such down cycles never last forever. Eventually the economy began to recover and the supply of problem debt securities started to decline.

The demand for distressed and defaulted debt instruments rarely keeps pace with the fluctuations in supply. A hardy band of vulture investors stays in the market through thick and thin. Others come and go as circumstances change. The variations in demand are, however, small compared to the volatility of supply. When new supply overwhelms the demand from those who like to participate in this market, the new product tends to remain in the hands of others, particularly its original owners. That is, the holders of investment-grade and high-yield debt instruments find that their portfolios are accumulating an unwanted percentage of downgraded-to-distressed-and-defaulted-level debt instruments. Banks experience a similar phenomenon with their distressed and defaulted loans. Some of these investors hold on to the downgraded paper and try to salvage what they can. Many others try to sell their holdings into an unreceptive market. A very depressed market for distressed and defaulted debt securities is the result. A large supply of such debt instruments may create an attractive opportunity to buy, but not such a great time for those who are already holding a portfolio full of such investments. If you can hold your positions long enough for a turnaround to occur, you may have found your market. If you need the cash, you may well be in serious trouble.

Many holders of bankrupt companies' indebtedness become distressed and defaulted debt-holders by default. A number of these investors have no choice in the matter. They cannot hold for security. They must sell. For example, many banks and insurance companies are forced by preestablished loan ratios and capital reserves to unload any debt holdings that they have in a bankrupt firm. Likewise, certain pension funds and managed accounts are prohibited by their charter from holding any bankrupt indebtedness. Similarly, high-yield mutual funds simply can't tolerate the elimination of the high-yield coupon and must unload. They need to redeploy their funds into earning assets.

Non–investment grade bank lending quadrupled from $150 billion in 1993 to $626 billion in 1999. This growth continued into the 2000s. High-yield bond issues tripled to $650 billion in the seven years preceding 1999. By the end of 2004 the total had risen to $952 billion. The May 2005 downgrading of

GM and Ford added $450 billion to the total. Starting in 1999, the default rates on high-yield bonds also tripled. Post-2000, telecom, energy, and airlines lead the list of distressed debt opportunities. As more and more bonds default, more and more bankruptcy-investing opportunities await. Rest assured that while the rate of bankruptcy filings will ebb and flow (indeed, default rates fell to a very low level in 2004–5), bankruptcies and bankrupt securities will always be with us.

Takeovers and Risk Arbitrage

Bankruptcy investors seek to take advantage of the opportunities created by what they believe to be too much pessimism in the corner of the marketplace where they operate. Other types of investors rely on the market's optimism. One such specialized area of investing called *risk arbitrage* involves trading in the securities of firms that are the targets of takeover offers. Risk arbitragers take positions in the stocks of firms that are potential or actual takeover targets. They may also trade in the stocks of the would-be-acquires. Buying and selling stocks of companies involved in takeover attempts can be quite profitable but does involve significant risk. As always, you should be selective.

The stocks of actual and potential takeover targets
are often attractive investments.

A company seeking to acquire another company usually does so by making an offer for the target company's stock. That offer price is almost always substantially above the stock's current market level. Such a premium price is needed in order to entice the existing shareholders to accept the offer. If the current shareholders had wanted to sell their holdings at pre-offer levels, they would already be out of the stock. Typically a premium of 20 to 30 percent or so above the pre-offer market price of the target company's stock is sufficient to capture the existing shareholders' attention. If you happen to buy stock in a company just before it becomes a takeover target, you may soon be able to liquidate your position at a very attractive short-term gain. If you have held the position for a longer time, you may or may not (depending upon what you paid for it) be able to sell out at a profit. The offer will, however, at least be above what had been the pre-offer market price.

Sometimes you will find that a stock that you own is subject to a takeover offer. You happen to be in the right place at the right time. You may have identified this stock as a takeover candidate through your superior investment selection skills. Often, however, you are just lucky. Identifying companies that are likely to be subject to takeover offers is difficult. If you receive advanced nonpublic warnings of such offers, you cannot legally trade on that information. If you trade anyway, you are guilty of *insider trading*. You could end up in prison. Investing involves risks, but that is one risk that you certainly don't want to take.

Various characteristics of the potential target firm may help you identify likely takeover candidates.

The legal way to try to profit from takeovers before they are announced begins with an attempt to identify the targets from publicly available information. Then, you would take a position in those firms that look likely to attract a takeover offer and wait for the offer to emerge. Successfully predicting which firms will receive takeover offers is not an easy thing to do. Nonetheless, some general guidelines can be noted. Companies are more likely to be takeover candidates if they:

- Hold a lot of cash
- Have a strongly positive cash flow
- Operate in industries experiencing prior takeover activity
- Have large (e.g., founding) stockholders with a reason to sell
- Are asset-rich with holdings that can easily be sold at attractive prices
- Have managers who are buying and holding stock in their employer
- Have been the subject of prior takeover attempts
- Have relatively little debt but considerable capacity to take on additional debt

Most of these criteria describe characteristics of firms that acquirers would like to own. Note, however, that many companies that appear to be attractive as takeover candidates nonetheless remain independent. Others may be taken over eventually but not until much time has passed. Sometimes a firm is rumored to be a takeover target, causing its price to be bid up. Once the market realizes that a takeover offer is not imminent, the firm's stock price is likely to drop. Often the price of the erstwhile target declines back to the stock's prior (pretakeover rumor) level. Clearly, betting on potential takeovers is an uncertain process. You should not take a position in a company just because you think it is a potential takeover candidate. *Only buy the stock of a takeover prospect if you like the firm's potential as a stand-alone company.* If it receives a takeover offer, that is icing on the cake. If not, you still have ended up owning a stock whose prospects you find attractive.

Risk arbitrage, while practiced by large, sophisticated investors, can also be undertaken by smaller investors. Such activity can be quite profitable.

Risk arbitrage is a trading strategy designed to take advantage of the gap between the value of a takeover offer and the market price of the target. When a would-be acquirer offers to purchase a target company (almost always at a premium price relative to the pre-offer market price level), the market price of the target generally moves up. Immediately after the offer is announced, the target stock's price generally moves above its previous price range but remains below the value of the consideration offered by the would-be acquirer. If, for example, the would-be acquirer offers $30 for a stock that had been trading at $24 (a 25% premium), the target stock's price might initially increase to $27. The market price typically remains some distance below the offer level at the time of the announcement largely because of uncertainty over whether the takeover attempt will succeed. This discount ($30 − $27 = $3, or 10% of the $30 offer price) presents the risk arbitrager with an opportunity to profit from the disparity. Assuming the takeover ultimately occurs as planned, the profit potential is substantial. The danger of risk arbitrage investing arises largely from the possibility that the proposed deal will collapse. If the offer is withdrawn or successfully rebuffed by the target's management, the target's stock price may fall back to about its pre-offer level. In the above example, the risk arbitrager would earn a profit of $3 per share if the deal went through, but could lose $3 ($27 − $24 = $3) if the takeover effort failed.

Sometimes another bidder enters the picture and offers a still higher amount for the target. A bidding war may ensue. The original bidder may raise its offer to top that of the new bidder. The risk arbitrager may do very well when a bidding war erupts, even if the original bidder loses out. At other times, the takeover attempt fails because the target company's management successfully fights off the potential acquirer. In still other cases the party making the offer undertakes extensive due diligence and then decides to withdraw the offer. When an offer fails or is withdrawn for whatever reason, the target stock's price often falls back, causing the risk arbitrager to incur losses on the transaction.

Sometimes a takeover offer is followed by a rise in the price of the target's shares that takes the price above the offer level. Such a price move is almost always an indication that the market expects a higher offer to emerge. This expectation will be confirmed either when a new offer does emerge, or be proven wrong when no such offer appears. Uncertainty over whose offer may succeed compounds the difficulty of hedging the position. You don't want to end up with a short position in the would-be acquirer's stock if the bidder's offer is rejected. The would-be acquirer's stock price tends to drop when the takeover offer is announced and rise if the offer is withdrawn.

Understand the structure of the three types of takeover offers; each requires a different risk arbitrage strategy.

Takeover offers are generally made in one of three ways. In the simplest type of offer, the would-be acquirer proposes to pay a specific amount of cash for each target share. With such a *cash offer*, you can easily calculate the profit potential. If $25 a share is offered and the target company's stock is trading for $22, the potential gain is $3 a share (less commissions, plus any dividends to be paid by the target). If the merger takes six months to complete, a $3 gain on a $22 investment works out to an annualized return of about 27 percent. An annualized return of 27 percent is about three times the average annual return on the market.

The second type of offer involves a fixed ratio exchange of shares (a *stock offer*). The bidder offers to pay for the target shares with shares of the acquirer's own company. Thus the company making the offer will use its own shares as takeover currency. These additional shares will be issued at the time of the exchange, thereby increasing the total number of acquirer shares outstanding. Increasing the number of shares outstanding dilutes the ownership positions of the pre-merger shareholders. In other words, the target shareholders are offered part of the acquirer's company in exchange for their shares in the target. Of course, the acquisition will increase the size of the company. As a result, the pre-acquisition shareholders will own a smaller share of a larger company. For the acquiring company's shareholders to gain from the transaction, the total market value of the combined company must rise by more than the increase in the number of shares outstanding. In other words, the acquirer's shareholders will benefit if the post-acquisition stock price rises above the pre-offer level.

Suppose the would-be acquirer offers 0.5 of its shares for every share of the target. If the acquirer's stock is trading at $60 a share, half a share of stock is worth $30. If the target stock sells at $25, the offer represents a potential $5 gain on a share of target stock. But the target stock will be exchanged for acquirer stock only if and when the merger is consummated. The acquirer stock that sold for $60 when the offer was extended could be trading at a rather different price level when the actual exchange of shares occurs. Consider the impact of the acquirer's stock declining to $50 by the time of the exchange. At that level, the value of the target's consideration (half of an acquirer share) would fall to $25, wiping out any profit for one who paid $25 for the stock. If you had bought the target's stock at $25 and the acquirer's stock price falls even lower, you would lose money. That is, you would lose money on the transaction unless you had hedged your position. Read on.

Risk arbitragers generally prefer to take a position in the transaction around the time that the offer is announced (when the spread between the target stock price and offered consideration tends to be wide) and then liquidate their position around the time of the exchange (when the spread has been eliminated). In other words, they would like to extract their profits and move on to other investment opportunities as quickly as they can. But can they be sure of earning a profit even if the merger takes place at the announced terms? Clearly, risk arbitragers don't know, at the time of the offer, what the price of the would-be acquirer's stock will be at the time that the target shares are to be exchanged for acquirer shares. If the risk arbitrager just buys the target stock and waits for the exchange, his or her projected profits could decline and perhaps disappear, with a fall in the acquirer's stock price. To deal with this type of exposure, risk arbitragers usually seek to hedge their positions. They do so by implementing an offsetting short sale of the acquirer's stock. Typically, they sell the acquirer's shares short in the same ratio to the target shares as the ratio embedded in the exchange offer. In the above example, the fully hedged position would reflect the sale of one share of the acquirer's stock short for every two shares of the target's stock purchased. This hedging strategy is designed to lock in a gain on the transaction. As long as the merger takes place at the announced terms, the gross (ignoring commissions, etc.) gain will equal the difference between what was paid for target shares and the proceeds of the acquirer share's short sale. In the above example, you could sell 100 shares of the acquirer's stock short at 60 and receive $6,000. You could simultaneously purchase 200 target shares at 25 for $5,000. If and when the target stock is exchanged for acquirer shares, the number of just-received acquirer shares will be exactly enough to cover (offset) the short position. The risk arbitrager would come out ahead by $1,000 ($6,000 − $5,000) regardless of what happened to the acquirer's stock price. If the initial transaction involved 200 acquirer shares and 400 target shares, the profit would be $2,000. The potential gain would rise proportionally with the size of the initial position. Commissions and financing costs would reduce the gains somewhat.

The third type of takeover offer also uses the acquirers' stock as takeover currency, but the exchange ratio is not fixed at the time the offer is announced. So-called *collar offers* involve an exchange ratio of acquirer-for-target shares that is determined by a formula. Rather than being fixed at the time of the offer, the exchange ratio in a collar offer is a function of the price of the acquirer's shares at or about the time the deal closes. The price applied to the formula is usually an average of the closing prices over some time period (e.g., the last ten trading days) preceding a predetermined date. The typical collar offer includes a maximum and minimum ratio and an equation that varies the exchange ratio inversely with the market price of the acquirer's shares. As a result, the value of the consideration offered to the target shareholders tends (compared to a fixed exchange rate offer) to be more nearly stable as the price of the acquirer's stock price fluctuates. If the acquirer's stock price declines (increases), the increase

---

Three Types of Takeover Offers

Cash Offer: Target shareholders are offered a specified amount of cash for their stock.

Stock Offer: Target shareholders are offered a specified ratio of acquirer shares for their stock.

Collar Offer: Target shareholders are offered a variable amount to acquirer shares for their stock. The actual exchange ratio is determined by a formula that is a function of the average price of the acquirer's shares over a prespecified period of time prior to the merger's consummation.

(decline) in the ratio will tend to offset the impact on the value of the consideration. Often the formula will have a range over which the ratio is unchanged. For example, a collar offer could be structured so that the exchange ratio is one-to-one if the acquirer's stock price is between $50 and $55 on the predetermined date. If the price falls below $50, the ratio increases, and if the price for the acquirer's stock rises above $55, the ratio decreases.

Risk arbitrage hedging with collar offers is more tricky than for offers where the exchange ratio is fixed. With a collar offer you don't know what the actual exchange ratio will be until the deal is finalized and the ratio is set. So you won't know the exact ratio to use in setting up your hedge. You will, however, know the exact structure of formula that is to be used to determine the ratio. You will also know the acquirer's current stock price as of the time the offer is announced. Thus you will know how the formula would be applied to determine the ratio if the acquirer's stock price stays at the current level. But, of course, stock prices fluctuate. The acquirer's stock price is very likely to be at a different level (from the current level) when the formula is applied. Thus you will not know what the actual ratio will be until the formula is applied and the ratio is set. You will, therefore, not know exactly how much acquirer stock to sell short in order to set up a complete hedge until the game is virtually over. The spread between the target's stock price and the value of the consideration offered tends to narrow as time passes and uncertainty over the deal's likelihood of completion declines. Risk arbitragers prefer to set up their positions early in an effort to capture the maximum amount of spread.

Several approaches might be employed to determine the exchange ratio to use in constructing a hedge for a collar offer. They all incur some risk of leaving the investor either over or underhedged:

- Use the current acquirer stock price to compute the expected exchange ratio
- Use the minimum ratio value in the formula
- Adjust your hedge as the acquirer's stock price fluctuates

Utilizing the acquirer's current stock price to estimate and forecast the ratio (plugging the current stock price into the formula) has the obvious disadvantage of not necessarily reflecting the actual stock price to be used with the formula at the point when it is actually applied. If the acquirer's stock price rises, the ratio will fall, and the risk arbitrager will have sold too many of the acquirer's shares short. Being short too many shares of a stock whose price has risen will reduce the risk arbitragers' profits. A large rise in the acquirer's stock price could turn what appeared to be a profitable initial position into a loss. This risk should not be overemphasized, however. Usually the acquirer's stock price does not rise, or does not rise much, when a takeover is under way. Still, the risk arbitrager would prefer to avoid or at least limit this exposure.

A strategy of adjusting the ratio of long-to-short positions as the price of the acquirer's stock fluctuates has its own problems. If, after the hedge is established, the acquirer's stock price rises, the risk arbitrager would act to reduce the number of shares sold short. If the price falls, the short position would need to be increased. A fluctuating price level for the acquirer's stock (that both rises and falls over the merger attempt period) could result in a great deal of trading and associated transaction costs. Moreover, adjusting your hedge over time may put you into the appropriate ratio by the end of the merger period, but you will not be sure of the size of your gain (or even if you will have a gain).

The simplest and perhaps most attractive approach for undertaking risk arbitrage on collar offers is to base the hedge on the minimum value for the ratio. With this strategy, the risk arbitrager would sell the acquirer shares short in the ratio that would be called for if the minimum value of the exchange ratio applies. If you set up your hedge with a low value for the ratio and then the acquirer's stock price falls, causing the ratio to rise, your profits will increase. Thus the risk that you are exposed to is the risk that your profit will be greater than expected. Clearly, that type of risk is advantageous to the investor. So, just as long as the takeover is successful, all of the profit variability is on the upside. Setting up a hedge based on the minimum exchange ratio will result in your receiving at least as many and perhaps more of the acquirer's shares as you need to cover your short position. Any extra shares that result from the exchange ratio being above the minimum can be sold for additional cash and thereby add to your profit. If your position shows a profit at the lowest ratio value, your profit will only increase if the ratio turns out to be higher. That is not a bad result at all. So if you can structure a risk arbitrage position that is profitable at the minimum exchange ratio, all of the variability in profits from a change in the ratio is on the upside. The following box illustrates how a collar offer might be structured.

In words, the hypothetical formula outlined in the box (next page) begins with a base ratio of 0.7 acquirer shares for each target share. That ratio applies as long as the acquirer's average stock price over the pricing period is between 25 and 30. If the acquirer's average stock price falls below 20 (rises above 35), the exchange ratio is set at 0.8 (0.6). Between 20 and 25 the ratio varies from 0.8 and 0.7, and between 30 and 35 the ratio varies between 0.7 and 0.6.

A Hypothetical Collar Offer

Formula: $E = 0.7 + V$

For A between 25 and 30,	$V = 0$
For A below 20,	$E = 0.8$
For A less than 25,	$V = .02\,(25 - A)$
For A above 30	$V = -.02\,(30 - A)$
For A above 35	$E = 0.6$

Where: E = Exchange ratio of acquirer shares per target share
A = Acquirer average closing price for the ten days prior to the consummation date

Maximum	$V = 0.8$	(A below 20)
Minimum	$V = 0.6$	(A above 35)

Suppose $A = 23$
$E = 0.7 + 0.02(2) = 0.74$
Value of offer $= .74 \times 23 = 17.02$

Now suppose $A = 32$
$E = 0.7 - 0.02(2) = .66$
Value of offer $= .66 \times 32 = 21.12$

Consider an example based on the formula in the preceding box. At the time that the offer is announced, the acquirer's stock is priced at 27 and the target at 16. The would-be acquirer is offering between 0.6 and 0.8 of its own shares for every share of the target. If you used the then-current price to calculate the ratio, you would sell 0.7 shares of the acquirer for each share of the target. If the acquirer's stock price remained in the range between 25 and 30 at the offer's expiration, the ratio of 0.7 would apply. Under that scenario your result would be as follows: For every one share of the target you purchase for $16, you would sell 0.7 shares of the acquirer short, thereby receiving $18.9 ($0.7 \times 27$) from the short sale. If the ratio turned out to be 0.7, your position would show a gain of $2.9 per share of target stock purchased. Undertake this transaction for a thousand target shares and your corresponding projected gain becomes $2,900. Using this ratio to establish the hedging position exposes the arbitrager to the possibility that the acquirer's stock price could rise above 30 at the point where the formula was applied. If that happened, the final ratio would be lower than 0.7. You would have sold more shares short than you would receive in the exchange. If, for example the acquirer's stock price rose to 35, the exchange ratio would fall to 0.6 and you would be short 0.1 acquirer share too much for every target share that you hedged. To cover that short you would have to buy acquirer shares at $35 for a cost of $3.5 per target share hedged ($0.1 \times \$35 = \$3.5$). That would more than wipe out your projected profit of $2.7 per target share. If, in contrast, you sold only 0.6 acquirer shares short for each target share bought (the minimum ratio value), you would be sure of receiving at least as many shares in the exchange as were required to cover your short position. With this strategy, you would be assured of receiving 0.6 shares of the acquirer to replace those that you sold short at 27, for a total value of $16.2 per target share purchased. You bought the target shares for $16, so you begin with a minimum profit of $0.2 per share (or $200 on a thousand shares). If the acquirer shares are trading at 27 when the formula is applied, you receive an additional 0.1 share of the acquirer's stock for each target share exchanged. You would be able to sell this 0.1 share for $2.7. Under this scenario you would earn the same profit as if you had initially sold the full 0.7 shares short ($0.2 + $2.7 = $2.9 per share). Suppose, however, that the stock price falls to 20. Under this scenario the ratio becomes:

$$0.7 + .02\,(25 - 20) = E$$
$$0.7 + .02\,(5) = E$$
$$0.7 + .1 = 0.8$$

Now you are paid 0.8 shares of the acquirer's stock, but you are short only 0.6. The extra 0.2 shares can be sold for $(0.2)(20) = \$4$ each. As a result your

---

Hypothetical Collar Offer Results

Acquire Stock Price @ time of offer   27
Target Stock Price @ time of offer   16
Exchange ratio if current acquirer stock price
is also the price when the formula is applied: 0.7

Buy one target share   @   16
Short 0.7 acquirer shares   @   27 $0.7 \times 27 = 18.9$
Gain $18.9 - 16 = 2.9$

Minimum Exchange Ratio   =   0.6
Buy one target share   @   16
Short 0.7 acquirer share   @   27
                                     $.6 \times 27 = 16.2$

Minimum Gain (per share) $16.2 - 16 = 0.2$
Additional Gain if acquirer stock is 27 when formula applied: Ratio is 0.7.
Derive additional 0.1 shares of acquirer $(0.7 - 0.6 = 0.1)$
                          $0.1 \times 27 = 2.7$
Additional Gain if acquirer stock is 20 when the formula is applied:
Ratio rises to 0.8;
Receive additional 0.2 shares
                          $(0.8 - 0.6 = 0.2)$
                          $0.2 \times 20 = 4.0$
Additional gain (per share) = $4 per target share

profit rose to $4.2 per target share (or $4,200 on a thousand shares). Thus we see that with this minimum ratio hedging strategy, all the price fluctuation risk is on the upside.

The likelihood of takeover success can be forecast with better-than-random accuracy.

Setting up the hedge for fixed and collar exchange offers involves some expertise and some difficulty. The largest risk component for a risk arbitrage strategy, however, arises from uncertainty over whether or not the takeover offer will be accepted and result in a merger with the would-be acquirer. If the offer fails, the target stock's price usually falls and the acquirer's stock price frequently rises. Thus a long-target, short-acquirer hedge will typically show significant losses if the takeover offer is unsuccessful. Accordingly, an important determinant of risk arbitrage success is the investor's ability to identify which offers will succeed and which will not.

About 90 percent of announced takeover offers succeed. The losses for risk arbitragers are almost exclusively concentrated in the 10 percent that do not succeed. The losses on those failed takeover offers, however, tend to be large compared to the gains on the offers that result in a merger. Avoiding or at least minimizing these losses is clearly important to the risk arbitragers.

Certain characteristics influence whether or not a takeover offer will succeed. One factor that has a major impact on the probability of success in the takeover attempt is the reaction of the target's senior managers and board of directors. In offers where the board and managers of the target support the offer and recommend that the shareholders approve, such friendly takeover offers are generally the result of direct negotiations between the two sets of managers. They are much more likely to succeed than (hostile) bids, where the target's managers and directors resist the offer. According to one recent study, about 90 percent of takeover offers are friendly, and 94 percent of these are successful. Of the 10 percent of takeover offers that are hostile, only about 31 percent are successful. Clearly, betting on a friendly merger to take place is much safer than betting on a takeover attempt that is not supported by the target or its management. On the other hand, hostile takeovers are likely to have the most attractive (largest) spreads. Moreover, the target in a hostile takeover attempt often takes value-enhancing measures that cause its stock price to rise even if the takeover effort fails.

A second factor likely to impact the probability of takeover success is the relative size of the acquirer and target. When the acquirer is much larger than the target, the offer is considerably more likely to succeed than when the target is close to the same size as the acquirer. When the target is actually larger than the would-be acquirer (minnow swallowing a whale), the takeover effort is especially uncertain of success.

> **Characteristics of Takeover Offers Likely To Succeed**
>
> Friendly offer favored by target management
> Large acquirer relative to target
> Cash offer or, if stock, collar offer
> No antitrust problems

Cash offers are more likely to succeed than are stock offers (fixed or collar). Cash offers also have the advantage of not needing to be hedged with a short position in the acquirer's stock. Collar offers tend to be more likely to succeed than do fixed exchange ratio offers.

The likelihood of governmental opposition on antitrust grounds is another factor to consider in assessing whether or not a takeover offer will succeed. If the acquirer and target are direct competitors and if the combined entity would have a large market share, the government is likely to object to the proposed takeover on antitrust (Clayton or Sherman Act) grounds. The acquirer may sometimes be able to negotiate a compromise with the antitrust authority (Justice Department or Federal Trade Commission). If not, the government can almost always block the takeover attempt. The government is so likely to prevail if the matter goes to court that few would-be acquirers ever try to win an antitrust case against the government.

The stock of the companies making takeover offers tends not to rise and may decline, both during and after the takeover attempt, particularly if the takeover effort succeeds.

In order for a takeover attempt to succeed, the would-be acquirer needs to offer a substantial premium over the pre-offer price level of the target's shares. To earn back this premium, the acquirer must be able to integrate the acquisition into the combined company in a way that creates substantial cost savings and/or profitable revenue increases. Numerous studies have found that, for a large percentage of acquisitions, the anticipated synergies do not materialize in the magnitudes needed to offset the premium paid. As a result, many acquisitions turn out not to enhance value for the existing (pretakeover) shareholders. The expanded firm will usually be worth more as a result of the acquisitions, but that added value is offset by the dilution (increased shares outstanding or increased debt) incurred to pay for the acquisition. In other words, $2 + 2 = 4$, not $2 + 2 = 5$. The shareholders of the acquiring firm often do not benefit from the acquisition.

10

Rights Offerings and Share Buybacks

U nlike mutual funds, which make a market in their own shares, closed-end fund share prices are determined by the interplay of supply and demand in the marketplace. Recall that mutual funds stand ready to buy back their shares at their net asset values (NAV). Thus mutual fund shares are forced by the funds themselves to trade at the level of their NAVs. Closed-end funds, in contrast, have a fixed number of shares outstanding. These shares must find their own price level in the marketplace. The interplay of supply and demand will determine the market price. Nothing forces that price to equal the NAV. The price could be either above or below the NAV. Indeed, closed-end funds very often trade at a discount from their net asset values (NAV). Some of the large holders of closed-end fund shares may pressure their fund's managers to convert the closed-end fund into a mutual fund. Converting a closed-end fund to a mutual fund would result in the fund being required to stand ready to buy back its shares at its NAV and thereby eliminate the discount.

Like operating companies that are organized as corporations, both mutual and closed-end funds are organized as democracies, with each share of the fund having one vote. Accordingly, fundholders possess the ultimate power to hire and fire the managers of their funds. If enough fundholders vote for a new slate of directors, they can take control of the fund. Once in control, the new board can replace the old managers with those more willing to do the fundholders' bidding. Mindful of this possibility, the existing managers of closed-end funds tend to listen to the views of their large fundholders.

While closed-end funds usually trade at a discount from their NAVs, mutual funds are structured to allow their shares to be sold back to the fund at their NAVs (less a modest redemption fee, in some cases). So, if a closed-end fund's shares trade at a 20 percent discount from its NAV, converting to an open-end mutual fund could produce an instant 20 percent gain in its market value. Closed-end fund managers would, however, generally prefer to retain the advantages of their closed-end fund status. When a closed-end fund converts to mutual fund status, it must stand ready to redeem its shares on demand. Often the newly converted mutual fund will assess a 2 percent redemption fee for the first year after its conversion to mutual fund status. The fund justifies this redemption fee as needed to compensate for the cost of liquidating that part of its portfolio required to meet the demand for redemptions. The fee also has the effect of discouraging redemptions. Once the fundholders gain the right to redeem their shares at or near the fund's NAV (a much higher price level than before the conversion), many are likely to do so. This rush-for-the-exit by fundholders could cause the fund to become much smaller very quickly. The management fees charged by the fund managers are based upon the dollar value of the fund's assets. Redeeming shares reduces the amount of money under management and thereby reduces the management fees to be earned by the fund's managers. That asset-fee relationship helps explain why closed-end mutual funds need to be pushed into converting to open-end mutual funds. Most fund managers are reluctant to take an action voluntarily that will reduce their fees, even if that action would benefit their fundholders. Some closed-end funds do eventually respond to fundholders' pressure by converting to mutual fund status. Others try to ignore the problem, hoping it will go away. Still others try to placate their fundholders by offering to buy back a percentage of the fund's outstanding shares at a price that is at or close to its NAV. A fund that agrees to undertake buybacks on a periodic basis is called an *interval fund*. The fund managers hope that these self tenders will buy out the holdings of most of the unhappy fundholders and, by reducing the supply of shares outstanding, allow the fund's share price to be bid up.

A buyback may be structured as either a onetime transaction or as a series of periodic repurchases. Usually, the fund offers to purchase between 10 to 25 percent of the outstanding shares, at 95 to 98 percent of the NAV. Subscribers are allowed to tender as many of their shares as they would like. The fund then purchases the tendered shares on a pro rata basis. Thus, if the fund offers to purchase 10 percent of its outstanding shares and half of the fundholders participate, each participant would be allowed to tender 20 percent of his or her shares.

Some investors may wish to hold on to all of their closed-end fund shares. They bought the shares because they liked the fund's prospects. Perhaps they still view its prospects favorably. Such investors may therefore decide not to exercise their right to tender. Such a decision is very likely to leave some of their money on the table. If you are such an investor, you should consider the following strategy: Participate in the tender and then repurchase an equivalent number of shares in the marketplace. Implementing such a tender-and-repurchase strategy will leave your portfolio with the same number of shares as you started with, plus some extra cash. Alternatively, you can use all of the cash from the tender to buy more shares and thereby increase your fund holdings without spending any more of your own money. Either way, you come out ahead.

Closed-end funds that tender for their own shares usually do so because their shares are trading in a price range that is appreciably below the fund's NAV. The fund's managers hope that such buying of shares will narrow the discount. Suppose the shares are selling at a 20 percent discount (which is not unusual). If the fund offers to purchase 15 percent of the outstanding shares at 98 percent of its NAV, those who participate would probably be able to tender at least 20 percent of their holdings (because not all fundholders will tender). If the fundholder can repurchase his or her shares (either shortly before or shortly after the effective date of the offer) at approximately the same 20 percent discount as the shares typically trade for, the sale-and-repurchase maneuver will achieve a gross gain of 18 percent ($98\% - 80\%$) on the 20 percent of the shares owned. That sum is equivalent to adding about 3.6 percent to the position's return ($.18 \times .20 = .036$). If the tender offer is made twice a year, the investor's return on this fund position would be increased by 7.2 percent. If the tender takes place quarterly, the increase becomes 14.4 percent. Whether the return-enhancement is 3.6, 7.2, or 14.4 percent, that added return-enhancement is in addition to whatever is the base return on the fund holdings. So if the fund itself produced an 8 percent annual return, the total return on the investor's position in the fund would be enhanced to between 11.6 percent ($8\% + 3.6\%$) and 22.2 percent ($8\% + 14.2\%$) by this tender-and-repurchase strategy. Since commissions will be incurred on the purchase, and the market price may be somewhat different between the tender and the time of the repurchases, the actual gain could be less (or more). Still, the ability to sell closed-end fund shares at 98 percent of NAV and repurchase them at a substantially lower percentage of NAV is an opportunity that should be too good to pass up. And yet, a substantial percentage of fundholders do not tender their shares when offered the chance to do so.

As previously noted, some closed-end funds, called interval funds, agree to repurchase a set percentage of their shares on a periodic basis. An interval fund might, for example, agree to purchase 10 percent of its outstanding shares each quarter. In such a situation, an investor who follows a tender-and-repurchase strategy could add substantially to his or her overall return. Note, however, that only if the market price of the underlying shares is stable or rises will the position show very much of a profit. *Don't buy an interval fund unless you like it as an investment on its own merits.* On the other hand, if you do identify an interval fund with attractive potential, the ability to implement a tender-and-repurchase strategy makes it all the more attractive. If, for example, such a fund produces an annual return of 8 percent and a tender-and-repurchase strategy adds 4 percent, the overall return becomes 12 percent $(8\% + 4\% = 12\%)$.

We see from the above discussion how a tender-and-repurchase program enhances returns for the holder of interval funds. A similar type of opportunity arises when a company engages in a *rights offering*. A company wishing to raise additional equity capital may offer to sell shares to its existing shareholders at a discount from the current market price. Such companies do so by distributing rights to their shareholders. These rights are separate securities, which, like other types of options, allow the owner to purchase shares at a prespecified price over a prespecified time period. Sometimes the rights are listed on an exchange or NASDAQ. Such rights trade in the marketplace until they expire. Thus the shareholder who does not wish to purchase additional shares should just sell his or her rights. At other times, however, the rights may be structured so that they are not transferable. Under these circumstances, shareholders may be allowed to oversubscribe to the extent that other shareholders fail to exercise their rights. This type of offer also provides the shareholder with an opportunity. Suppose the rights allow the purchase of shares at 93 percent of the market price (a typical 7% discount). A one-for-twenty rights offering would allow the investor to subscribe for an amount equal to 5 percent of their existing shares at a 7 percent discount from the market level. An investor who does not wish to increase his or her position in this particular stock can nonetheless extract some value by subscribing to the rights offering and simultaneously sell an equivalent amount of his or her existing holdings. Capturing a 7 percent discount (less trading costs) on 5 percent of one's holdings may not seem like much. Such a small profit opportunity may well not appear to be worth the trouble required to earn it. If, however, the offer includes the opportunity to oversubscribe, the investor could end up buying and reselling far more than 5 percent of his or her position. Regardless of the amount of stock potentially available for purchase in the rights offering, the opportunity to purchase stock at a 7 percent discount should not be passed up. Commissions on the resale would be a small portion of the 7 percent discount. Remember, *investing is a game of inches*.

No transaction of these sorts is without risk. These two situations, self tenders and rights offerings, represent no exception to the general rule that something can always go wrong. You should be mindful of the following:

First, selling and repurchasing the same security usually has tax consequences (if the sell side of the trade is done in a Keogh or IRA, this issue can be ignored). Even though the position is quickly restored to its original level, the trade will probably result in a taxable event. If, for example, the closed-end fund's shares are held at a gain, the initial sale will result in a tax liability even though the tendered shares are quickly replaced. If, on the other hand, the tendered shares are held at a loss, the sale back to the company will be subject to the *wash sale rule*. If the replacement shares are repurchased within thirty days of the date of the sale, the transaction is classified as a wash sale. Any loss on the transaction cannot be reported and used currently to reduce your tax liability. Under IRS rules, losses realized on a wash sale must be carried forward in the existing holdings. That is, the wash sale loss is reflected in a lower basis on the repurchased shared. Tax issues should not be ignored.

Second, prices may move adversely between the time of the initial transaction and the subsequent transaction. The investor may have tendered his or her shares at a point when the stock was depressed. By the time he or she gets around to replacing the tendered shares, the market price may have gone up (the price could of course have gone down, in which case the gain from the sale-and-repurchase would be greater). In order to minimize this risk of an adverse price movement, you should implement the offsetting trade as close as possible to the time when the tender is priced. Note, however, that a week or two may pass between the date when the purchase price is set and the time when the funds are received for the tender. Accordingly, one who wishes to replace the tendered shares soon after the purchase price is set may need an alternative source of funds to cover the time gap. The rules on payments for securities purchases do, however, provide you with a bit of leeway. Payment is not due on a stock purchase until three days after the order is executed. Accordingly, if you know when you are to receive payment for your tendered shares, you can allocate the anticipated proceeds from the tendered shares to pay for the repurchase shares as early as three days prior to that payment day.

Third, for large-size trades, the offsetting transactions may adversely impact the market price. Exercising these replacement strategies for a few hundred shares is likely to have little impact on the market. If, however, the investor needs to offset a transaction in the tens of thousands of shares, the very act of buying or selling shares could affect the market price. That is, the very act of trying to buy back (or to sell) a large block of shares may have the effect of pushing the price up (down). This impact may be mitigated by piecing the offsetting trades out over several days or a week or two. Such a piecing out approach, however, increases the risk of encountering an adverse price move before the offsetting transaction has been completed.

Notwithstanding these risks, tendering at above the market price and exercising rights at a discount (and oversubscribing when possible) are generally attractive strategies. The investor can almost always restore his or her position to its original level and come out ahead. Accordingly, I add two more rules to my list:

1. *When a fund or company engages in a self tender at above the current market price of its shares, the investor who wishes to maintain his or her holdings should nonetheless participate in the self tender. As soon as possible thereafter, the investor should make an offsetting trade (repurchase the shares that were sold) in the open market.*

2. *When a company (or fund) engages in a nontransferable rights offering at a strike price below the current market level, the investor who does not wish to add to his or her holdings should nonetheless exercise the rights and as soon as possible thereafter make an offsetting trade (sell the purchased shares) in the open market. If the rights are transferable, a rights sale is indicated.*

———— 11 ————

Investing in Real Estate

Bonds constitute one major investment alternative to the stock market. Real estate represents another. The market for real estate is huge. Indeed, the total market value of U.S. real estate exceeds the total market value of U.S. stocks and bonds. And yet, its one-of-a-kind nature makes buying and selling real estate quite a bit different from, and generally more costly than (higher transaction costs), buying and selling an equivalent dollar value of stocks. Still, the real estate market does provide investors with some interesting opportunities.

In what follows I shall offer a few general guidelines designed to help the potential real estate investor decide whether and, if so, how to become involved in this market. Note, however, that many entire books have been written on the subject of real estate investing. If you are especially interested in the topic, you may want to pursue the matter in greater depth than I can do here. My guidelines should, however, get you started.

One of the most attractive opportunities to invest in real estate is to own the place where you live.

Owning your own home (whether house, condo, mobile home, houseboat, motor home, etc.) has many benefits. Owner-occupied housing is usually an attractive investment for the investor/homeowner. It is a useful place to begin learning about investing in real estate. Home ownership has a number of significant advantages over the alternative of renting the place where you live.

First, home ownership offers valuable tax benefits. Both mortgage interest and real estate taxes are tax deductible expenses. If you itemize (and most active investors with moderate or higher incomes do), these two deductions can be used to reduce your tax liability substantially. Taxpayers are allowed to compute their taxable income by reducing their adjustable gross income in either of two ways. Specifically, they can either itemize deductions or take the standard deduction. If the taxpayer can identify a greater amount in deductible expenses by itemizing than by taking the standard deduction, itemization will lower his or her tax liability. In 2004 the standard deduction for a married couple (single person) was set at $9,700 ($4,850). A home-owner's mortgage interest and real estate taxes alone are often more than that sum. State income taxes are another major deductible expense, as are charitable contributions. So if the sum of your real estate and state income taxes, mortgage interest payments, and charitable contributions is large enough (greater than the standard deduction), you should itemize. The money that you pay in the form of mortgage interest and real estate taxes are itemized deductions that you can subtract from your gross income in the process of computing your taxable income. Once you exceed the standard deduction amount, every dollar that you pay in the form of real estate taxes and mortgage interest reduces your tax liability by $1 times your marginal tax rate. Thus a substantial percentage of the costs that you incur as a homeowner can be used as deductions to reduce your tax bill. The higher your tax bracket, the greater is the value of these deductions.

Suppose, for example, that you are in the 35 percent tax bracket. If your mortgage payment is $1,000 a month and 80 percent of this sum represents interest, your mortgage payment of $12,000 a year would consist of $9,600 in interest ($.8 \times $12,000 = $9,600$). At the 35 percent tax rate, this amount of mortgage interest payment would save you $3,360 ($.35 \times $9,600 = $3,360$) a year on your federal income taxes. Similarly, a $5,000 real estate tax bill could be used as a deduction to save you $1,750 ($.35 \times $5,000 = $1,750$) in taxes at the federal level. Thus the $17,000 ($12,000 + $5,000 = $17,000$) in combined mortgage and real estate tax payments generates a $5,110 ($3,360 + $1,750$) reduction in your tax liability. Moreover, the other 20 percent of the mortgage payments (the $2,400 per year not allocated as interest) represents a reduction in the amount that you owe on your mortgage. This amortization of your mortgage balance is a form of forced savings. Therefore the actual economic cost of the combined $17,000 payments would be offset by a total of $7,510 ($5,110 + $2,400$) in the form of tax savings and loan pay-down. In other words, the economic impact of the $17,000 in annual home ownership payments is reduced to $9,490 ($17,000 − $7,510$) as a result of the positive effect of the payments on your tax liability and debt position.

Second, real estate market values tend to rise over time. Homes held for a number of years are almost always worth much more in the marketplace than the amount that the owner originally paid for them. When you retire, you may be able to sell your home for a substantial profit. You could buy a much smaller, easier-to-manage place with part of the money. You would then have the rest of the money available to assist with living costs once your paycheck stops.

In a typical year, a $250,000 house (corresponding to a 5.5 percent $180,000 thirty-year mortgage and a payment of about $1,000 a month) might appreciate by 3 percent, or $7,500. That sum of appreciation would increase your net worth (or wealth) and thereby reduce the net cost of your housing to less than $2,000 ($9,490 − $7,500 = $1,990) a year. Moreover, the benefits would grow over time (net cost would decline) as the house appreciates and the outstanding mortgage balance is paid down. Each mortgage payment reduces the outstanding loan balance. As the outstanding balance declines, the interest charge component of the mortgage payment also declines. As a result, less and less of the mortgage payment represents interest and more and more represents repayment of loan principal. A dollar of debt reduction is always worth more to you than a one-dollar deduction on your taxable income. Even if you are in the 35 percent tax bracket, a tax deduction of one dollar is worth only 35¢ in reduced tax liability, whereas a debt reduction of one dollar is worth $1 (regardless of what tax bracket you are in). Put another way, simultaneously reducing your debt by a dollar and increasing your taxable income by a dollar would increase your net worth by $0.65 if you are in the 35 percent tax bracket. The positive impact on your net worth would be even greater if you are in a lower tax bracket. The more of your mortgage payment that is allocated to paying off the loan balance, the greater the positive impact on your financial position. Similarly, as the market value of your house increases, a given annual percentage increase in its value represents a larger and larger sum of money. For example, after five years the market value of the home that you purchased for $250,000 could have risen to $300,000, which, at a 3 percent appreciation rate, would correspond to a $9,000 value increase in year six (compared with $7,500 in the first year). Similarly, after five years of mortgage payments, the amount of annual pay-down of the mortgage balance will have risen from $2,400 a year to about $3,300. At some point in time the total financial benefits of home ownership in the form of tax deductions, loan pay-down, and market value appreciation will equal and then exceed the amounts of the mortgage and real estate tax payments. At that juncture the benefits in terms of tax shelter, debt reduction, and price appreciation would fully offset the out-of-pocket costs of maintaining your home. You will, in effect, be living in your house for free (except for normal maintenance expenses). With a rental, in contrast, the total amount paid for housing is fully used up just to pay the landlord. The renter obtains no tax benefits, no loan pay-down, and no wealth benefit from any appreciation in real estate value. And indeed, the cost of renting is likely to increase over time.

Third, with a fixed-rate mortgage you can stabilize a large part of the monthly out-of-pocket housing cost. Real estate taxes, insurance, and maintenance costs will tend to rise with the market value of your home. But the financing costs (mortgage payment) of home ownership will not increase as long as the original fixed-rate loan remains in place. This mortgage payment is by far the largest cost of home ownership. As the loan principal is amortized, the interest cost will decline and the portion of the payment used to pay down the mortgage balance will increase. Ultimately the mortgage balance will be paid down to zero. At that point your mortgage payment obligation will disappear. Your out-of-pocket housing costs will decline dramatically and you will own a valuable asset outright. As a renter, in contrast, the cost of your housing is likely never to stop increasing.

Fourth, the equity in your home (total market value less mortgage balance outstanding) provides excellent collateral against which to borrow additional funds, if and when they are needed. The easiest way to access this value is with a *home equity loan*. Alternatively, if the existing mortgage loan balance is sufficiently below the property's market value, one can refinance (take out a new, larger mortgage) and extract cash. A third option is to enter into a *reverse mortgage*. Such mortgages are structured to make a fixed monthly income payment to homeowners who are older than a certain prespecified age (e.g., sixty-five). The sums paid out plus interest on the prior payments accumulates as a debit balance. This total becomes a lien against the home's collateral value. The lender agrees to continue making the income payments as long as the borrower continues to live in the home. Once the home is sold, the lender collects the amount due out of the sales proceeds. Even if the accumulated amount exceeds the sale price of the home, the lender is committed to continue making the payments.

Fifth, if market interest rates fall, a homeowner with a fixed-rate mortgage can refinance the debt and thereby lock in a lower interest rate. You can take out cash, reduce the monthly payment, or shorten the life of the loan while keeping the monthly payment constant. If market interest rates rise, you can stick with your existing fixed-rate mortgage and be protected from the higher rates.

Sixth, because the property is yours, you can fix it up pretty much as you like. Most homeowners realize that whatever they do to their home will affect its value. Accordingly, they tend to take much better care of it than do renters.

To sum up, the rate of return on the funds invested in a home (including the value of occupancy) tends to be quite attractive. While home ownership is not suitable for everyone, it is an attractive type of investment for many. It is a particularly attractive way to start to learn about investing in real estate. Once you have a few years of home ownership experience, you may be ready to explore other types of real estate investing. But even home ownership is not for everyone. Read on.

Advantages of Home Ownership

1. *Taxes:* Mortgage interest expense and real estate taxes are deductible expenses on your income tax return.
2. *Price Appreciation:* Real estate market values tend to rise over time.
3. *Stabilize Housing Costs:* The largest part of the cost of home ownership is the mortgage payment. A fixed-rate fully amortizing mortgage stabilizes this cost.
4. *Collateral Value:* The equity in your home represents a valuable asset against which you can borrow.
5. *Refinancing Options:* If mortgage interest rates fall sufficiently, you can reduce your monthly payment or take out additional cash by refinancing
6. *Control over Property:* It's yours, you can fix it up the way you like. If you make improvements, the increased value is yours.

Do not buy a home unless you plan to live in it for at least several years and can afford to make all of the payments as they come due.

Notwithstanding all of its advantages, home ownership is not suitable for everyone. Buying a home requires money both up front (down payment, closing costs) and over time (mortgage payment, property taxes, insurance, maintenance). If you do not make the required (mortgage and other) payments as they come due, the lender will foreclose on the property, and you will lose your house and perhaps everything you have invested in it. *Never buy a more expensive house than you can afford.*

A number of costs are associated with the real estate transaction itself. When you purchase a house or any other type of living space, you will almost always need to finance most of the purchase price with a mortgage. Obtaining a mortgage is likely to be costly. You will need to hire a lawyer to undertake a title search. Various other fees and expenses (loan application fee, points, etc.) will also be incurred. If you buy or sell through an agent, a substantial brokerage fee (perhaps 6 percent of the sales price) will be assessed on the transaction. Technically the seller pays the broker's commission in the form of a deduction from the selling price. That real estate agent's fee tends, however, to be reflected in the price that the seller charges. Thus both buyers and the sellers can be said to share in the cost of the agent's commission. Moreover, when the time comes to sell your home, you will need to pay the real estate agent's fee again (assuming you use a broker). In addition, you will have to bear the cost of a move as well as the implicit cost of searching for a new home. Accordingly, the transaction costs involved in purchasing or selling real estate (house or otherwise) can add up to as much as 10 percent of the market value. Clearly, you don't want to incur these costs over and over again.

If you find yourself in a position where you must sell too soon after your purchase, all of the financial benefits of home ownership can be offset by these transaction costs.

If you end up living in a house five or ten years or more, the initial costs (real estate commission, title search, points, bank fees, etc.) of the transaction are, in effect, spread over an extended period of time. Moreover, the house's value would have had a reasonable chance to appreciate. If, however, you buy a house and then must sell it a year or so later, these transaction costs are likely to eat up any modest gain you might otherwise have achieved for the short time that you owned it (and perhaps more). Furthermore, the housing market itself has ups and downs. If you have owned your house for, say, ten years, chances are very good that you will still be able to sell it for a nice profit, even if the housing market is depressed. The appreciation in your home's market value will, in all probability, much more than offset the transaction costs. If, however, you must sell within a year or so of the initial purchase, a soft housing market can mean that you will be able to sell your home only if you are willing to accept a loss. And, in addition, you will incur transaction costs on the sale. Moreover, selling real estate takes time, sometimes a long time.

While investing in rental property can be quite profitable, active real estate·investing is much more demanding than the much more passive process of investing in securities.

Many people begin investing in real estate with a small sum of money. Utilizing this seed capital, plus a lot of sweat equity and an aggressive use of leverage, they are able to build an extensive portfolio of real estate properties over a period of time. They might begin by making a small down payment on a duplex and taking out a large mortgage loan. They can live on one side and rent out the other. The rental payments that they receive on the side that they lease out may be sufficient to cover most of their mortgage payment. They set aside the money that they save on their own housing. After a year or so, they have saved enough to buy and rent out both sides of another duplex (and, of course, take out another large mortgage). After another year or so they may have accumulated sufficient funds for still another down payment. At that point they might move up the real estate food chain. They could sell their second duplex at a substantial profit and use the net proceeds to invest in a small apartment complex or strip mall. Before long this budding entrepreneur has constructed a little real estate empire. It sounds simple. It's not.

Owning and operating a portfolio of developed real estate properties requires extensive management. As a landlord, you assume the responsibilities of a plumber, carpenter, accountant, bill collector, electrician, credit analyst, and financial officer. You may take on many other roles (e.g., amateur psychologist) as well. These tasks are time-consuming and challenging. You can do much of the property management and maintenance work yourself. Or, for a price, you can hire someone else to do the work. A great deal of the money earned by real estate investors represents compensation for the time and effort they must expend to manage their property.

In addition to being time-consuming, investing in rental real estate can also be rather risky. Most real estate investors make substantial use of leverage. They may, for example, invest 25 percent of their own money and borrow 75 percent on each property that they buy. They may borrow an even higher percentage if the lender will allow. Real estate investors almost always depend upon the rental income from their properties to cover the cost of debt service, real estate taxes, and upkeep on their property. They hope that enough money will be left over after making these payments to provide an attractive cash return on their investment. They also hope, and indeed generally count on, the rental income increasing at a faster rate than the rate of increase in the combined costs of servicing the debt and maintaining the property. Their projections generally show a tight cash flow situation initially coupled with a handsome potential profit to be derived from their properties' anticipated market value appreciation. The investments are almost always projected to work out well on paper. All too often, however, they do not perform quite so well in practice. Projections always involve assumptions. Assumptions can (and often do) turn out to be too optimistic (or sometimes too pessimistic).

Realize that the costs of maintaining rental real estate are steady, relentless, and in some cases, increasing (e.g., property taxes, costs of maintenance; have you ever known a plumber to reduce his rates?). Indeed, large unexpected costs may be incurred from time to time (for example, when a roof or furnace needs to be replaced). The rental revenues, in contrast, tend to be much more variable. Only when property is leased will rents be paid by the renter and received by the owner (and you have to be sure to collect, as renters sometimes skip out without paying). If the occupancy rate falls, so will the property's rental revenues. Moreover, the rental market will itself vary with market conditions. When the overall vacancy rate in the community is low, rental rates tend to rise, but when a substantial excess of unused space is available on the market, rental rates are likely to fall.

Many a would-be real estate mogul has been caught with too much debt on too many properties when the rental real estate market turns south. Unless he or she has the staying power (financial resources) to ride out the weak market, the budding real estate empire is likely to collapse. *If you invest in rental real estate, be cautious and conservative. Don't let yourself become overextended.*

One attractive alternative to investing in rental real estate is to buy undeveloped land.

Unlike developed properties, land ownership requires very little management. Leave it alone and let the trees grow taller. Some day you may be able to sell the timber. Eventually someone else may come along, see development potential, and offer you an attractive price for your property. The profit potential from land investment is substantial. As cities grow out and as the population increases, undeveloped land becomes economic to develop either residentially or commercially. The process proceeds haphazardly, in fits and starts, but it proceeds.

Investing in land does not take a lot of work on the part of the investor. You buy the property, pay the taxes and insurance, and wait. You may even be able to enjoy your land as a campsite, wood lot, or spot to plant a nice garden.

The disadvantages of land investing include the following: First, undeveloped land produces little or no current income. Perhaps you can sell off some timber or, if you put in the effort, sometimes more (vegetables, Christmas trees, etc.) but for the most part, undeveloped land produces no income. And yet its upkeep continues. You must pay real estate taxes and you will need to purchase some liability insurance. In addition, lenders will not advance very much loan money on land. You will have to pay most or all of the property's purchase price up front. Lenders realize that land produces little or no income and that its market price is speculative. Accordingly, most lenders will not allow you to use the land as collateral to borrow more than a small percentage of the property's market value. If you invest in land, be prepared to wait. Don't expect to receive any income on your investment until you sell.

Another attractive alternative to direct ownership of rental real estate is the Real Estate Investment Trust (REIT).

REITs are a bit like mutual funds that invest in real estate. Their ownership units trade on the market like the stocks of corporations (exchange or OTC), but unlike corporations, REITs are not liable for corporate income tax. REITs assemble portfolios of real estate–related assets. Some own developed rental properties (apartments, office buildings, shopping centers, warehouses, etc.). Others have inventories of land that they subdivide, develop, and sell as homesites. Still others own portfolios of real estate mortgages (commercial and/or residential).

By purchasing shares of a REIT, you acquire a stake in a portfolio of real estate–related assets. But you leave the management of the properties to the professionals running the company. Qualifying REITs pay no federal income tax. The special tax treatment is available only if the REITs pay out all of their net income to their shareholders. Because they must distribute all of their income each year, REITs generally pay rather attractive dividends. In addition, the properties that the REITs own tend to appreciate in the marketplace, thereby producing both growing rental income and capital gains when sold. As a result, the dividends and market prices of most REITs tend to increase over time. The dividends on most common stocks are subject to a 15 percent maximum federal tax rate. REIT dividends are, in contrast, fully taxable to the recipient as ordinary income. So if you are in the 35 percent income tax bracket, your REIT dividend will be taxed at that rate. You will only keep 65 percent of the dividend after taxes (even less if you are subject to a state income tax).

Compared to direct ownership of property, REITs are a much less time-consuming way to invest in real estate. Because their portfolios of properties are diversified, their risks are spread. Their returns are, however, net of the fees and expenses taken out by the managers. These fees and expenses can have a significant impact on returns.

Certain operating companies own large portfolios of real estate, thereby making them real estate investment players.

A variety of different types of companies own so much valuable real estate that the liquidation value of their properties dwarfs the income-producing potential of their ostensible line of business. At one time, many movie companies owned Hollywood movie lots having very substantial development potentials. That real estate value often dominated the enterprise value that was derived from the profit potential of their moviemaking. Similarly, many railroads once owned vast tracts of land awarded to them by the federal government. These government land grants were designed to facilitate the westward expansion of their rail lines (western land grants). Today we find many agricultural enterprises in such places as Florida and California owning large tracts of land, some of which sits in the path of potential future development. Other types of companies may own valuable downtown properties. Indeed, the downtown switching yards of some railroads may offer substantial development potential. In most cases these real estate holdings are carried on the books at a small fraction of their current valuations. The total market value of their property may substantially exceed the value that the market has put on the enterprise.

Suppose the liquidation value of a company (after deducting any outstanding debt) is in the neighborhood of two or more times the value that the market places on the company's stock. You might expect that some profit-seeking investors would buy a controlling interest in the company and then liquidate it for a substantial profit. Many large investors have the resources for just such a move. The new owners would earn a nice return and those stockholders who hung on would share in the gains. At least one of two possible barriers frequently stand in the way of such an outcome. First, as an outside group seeks to take control of a company, the current management may put up roadblocks: A proxy fight with existing management may be the result, with the result uncertain. Second, an established family may already own a controlling interest in the firm. If, for example, the founder's family owns 50 percent or so of the firm's shares, no liquidation can take place without their blessing. The family's desire to maintain the current structure could explain why no liquidation has occurred to date. All is not lost, however. Often, once the founder (who may be rather elderly) turns control over to a new generation of owners, they may be much more likely to be interested in unlocking the underlying values by selling.

III
MARKET TIMING

Most financial economists believe that the market's fluctuations are essentially unpredictable. These experts think that timing your trades to take advantage of market cycles (concentrate your buying at the cycle's trough and selling at its peak) is virtually impossible. Or at the very minimum, such timing is thought to be nearly impossible to do with any degree of consistency. A substantial body of research underlies their beliefs. Thus buying at market bottoms and selling at market tops is a hopeless dream. You shouldn't even try. Market-timers inevitably undertake a lot of buying and selling in their efforts to catch the market's up and down cycles. They generally incur substantial trading costs, but usually fail to achieve above-average returns. Don't waste your time and money trying. And yet on occasion you may wish to see if you can enhance your portfolio's performance by timing your trades. Perhaps we can identify a few circumstances when market-timing efforts may be helpful. But you should not expect too much. Most investors are well advised to ignore the market's ups and downs. They should be content to try to assemble, and over time add to, a well-diversified portfolio of potentially undervalued assets. Nonetheless, most of us would still like to try to buy when things are cheap and sell when they are not. Read on.

12

Macroeconomic Trends

Clearly the performance of the stock and bond markets is related to the state of the economy. This chapter explores the various aspects of the relationships. First, we examine the role of recessions and large economic slowdowns, and their impacts on stock and bond prices are examined. Then the impact of the Fed and its influence on interest rates is explored, followed by a concept called "flight to quality." The chapter ends with a discussion of corners and cartels. All of these subjects constitute background material for an understanding of the economic impact of market cycles.

Perhaps an understanding of the level and direction of economic activity can help one with timing issues. The stock market (which is driven by fundamentals such as sales, profits, and growth) and the economy (which has a very large impact on a firm's fundamentals) do tend to move in sympathy with each other. The stock market is believed to lead the economy by about six months. That is, the market tries to anticipate where the economy will be about six months into the future and then attempts to price stocks accordingly. When the stock market falls significantly, that drop may well signal that the market expects (correctly or otherwise) that the economy is in for some tough times. The market's expectations may or may not be accurate. As Paul Samuelson (Nobel Prize–winning economist) once said: "The market has forecast nine out of the past five recessions." The stock market's economic crystal ball is often a bit cloudy. Nonetheless, the stock market does generally try to anticipate what is about to happen to the economy. While it is not always correct, often enough it is.

RECESSIONS AND ECONOMIC SLOWDOWNS
OF LESSER MAGNITUDE

One interesting phenomenon involves the stock market's behavior during recessions. A typical recession lasts a bit more than a year; thirteen months is about average. The stock market tries to look ahead by about six months. So when the market expects that a recession is coming, it will generally start to decline while the economy is still expanding. Then it will begin to rise early in the life of a recession while the economy is still declining. On the other hand, the stock market generally does not react positively when the economy turns up. This tendency for the stock market to rise when the economy is still declining and not rise when the economy does begin to expand seems paradoxical. But the investor should not be surprised. The stock market is focusing on the future rather than on the present. The above discussion suggests that *about six months into a recession could be an attractive time to invest in stocks.* Within a few months the market will begin to anticipate an economic upturn and start to rise. Similarly, about six months before a recession begins may be an attractive time to sell. Unfortunately, predicting a recession six months in advance of its start is very difficult, to say the least. Still, if you watch the Fed and the economic statistics that the Fed watches, you may be able to develop some expectations for the economy's future.

THE FED, INTEREST RATES, AND STOCK PRICES

Stock prices tend to move inversely with interest rates. That is, falling interest rates tend to cause stock prices to rise, and increasing interest rates usually depress stock prices. The Fed is likely to take steps designed to cause interest rates to rise (decline) when it sees a need to slow down (stimulate) the economy.

Falling interest rates tend to enhance stock values in several ways. Declining rates result in lower financing costs for companies that borrow. Low interest rates facilitate consumers' financing of large purchases such as houses and automobiles. Declining interest rates increase disposable income by reducing the portion of time payments that must be used to cover the interest charges. All of these influences tend to stimulate economic activity and thereby corporate profits and revenue growth. In addition, declining interest rates in the marketplace correspond to declining rates for discounting the projected income stream of stocks (dividends). Stimulating the economy by reducing interest rates tends to increase profitability. Similarly, lowering the rate at which the income stream is discounted tends to enhance investment values. Thus, most of the time stock prices will rise when interest rates fall. Rising interest rates tend to have the opposite effect on the economy and stock market. That is, rising interest rates tend to depress the economy and generally lead to falling stock prices.

The Fed's influence on interest rates provides it with a great deal of power to affect the level and direction of economic activity. Using its so-called open market operations tool, the Fed can inject funds (reserves) into or withdraw funds from the banking system, thereby increasing or reducing the supply of loanable funds. As the supply of loanable funds varies, so does its price (the interest rate). The Fed's strongest influence is at the short end of the market. That short end is where it implements its open market operations by buying and selling Treasury bills. The Fed generally does not buy, sell, or hold longer-term governments (or any other long-term security for that matter).

Note, however, that stock market participants closely monitor current and anticipated interest rate movements. The stock market also seeks to anticipate Fed actions. By the time the Fed has acted to reduce or increase interest rates, the stock market's reaction has generally already occurred. *Any attempt to take advantage of the relationship between the stock market and interest rates is likely to require anticipating what the Fed will do.* Even that strategy may not succeed, as the market is also trying to guess the Fed's next move.

FLIGHT TO QUALITY

Normally stock and bond prices move up and down together for the reasons discussed above. Declining (rising) interest rates have a positive (negative) impact on both stock and bond prices. Sometimes, however, interest rates will decline and stock prices will fail to rise (and may even decline). To understand how the two markets (stock and bond) can move in opposite directions, we need to explore what factors in addition to interest rates determine stock prices. Stock prices can be viewed as being determined by three factors (recall the dividend discount model that we discussed in chapter 5):

- The current level of dividends and earnings
- The expected rate of growth of dividends and earnings
- The rate at which expected future dividends and earning are discounted (market interest rates and risks)

If everything else (current levels and expected growth rates of dividends and earnings) stays the same, a decline in the rate at which dividends and earnings are discounted will cause a stock's market value to rise. That discount rate is strongly influenced by the level of market interest rates. Note, however, that the discount rate employed to determine the present value of the stock's expected income stream is composed of two factors: the market rate on risk-free assets and a risk premium applied to risky assets like stocks. The first of these two factors, the risk-free rate, is approximately equal to the rate on governments, a market interest rate. Governments are viewed as being essentially risk-free. The appropriate risk premium is another matter. In particular, this risk premium is not constant over time. Nervousness on the part of market participants may, on occasion, lead to an increase in the premium demanded by the market in exchange for accepting risk (*flight to quality*). This action could cause the discount rate on stocks to rise even as market interest rates on governments are falling. Thus in a flight to quality environment, stock prices tend to decline even when the interest rates on risk-free government bonds do not rise.

In addition, growth expectations may sometimes cause bond and stock prices to move in opposite directions. If the stock market's growth expectations become more pessimistic, a decline in interest rates may not result in higher stock prices. That is, the (negative) impact of declining growth expectations may dominate the (positive) impact of the interest rate fall. Indeed, a weakening economy may lead to both a decline in interest rates (bond prices rise) and a decline in growth expectations (stock prices fall).

CORNERS AND CARTELS

Very few, if any, individual investors will ever try to corner a market or be invited to join a cartel. Such activities are largely illegal in the United States (Sherman Antitrust Act of 1890). Moreover, few individual investors have sufficient resources even to think about trying to gain control of a market. Still, investors may on occasion find themselves involved in a market in which an attempted corner or cartel is under way. Accordingly, investors are likely to benefit from an understanding of what happens in a market that is subject to an effort to corner or cartelize.

A corner is an attempt to control (and generally to raise or at least stabilize) the market price of some type of asset by acquiring ownership of a very large part of the available supply. In the early 1980s, what was then the very wealthy Hunt family of Texas (the deceased father of the clan, H. L. Hunt, had made his fortune in oil) tried to corner the market first in soybeans (to a limited extent) and then in silver (to a much larger extent). They did so by acquiring large positions in the contracts traded on the Chicago futures market. At first, they were able to squeeze the market by the very act of accumulating their large positions. The world supply of silver was huge but the available supply of deliverable grade silver located in the designated Chicago warehouses was much smaller. Only silver refined to .999, and in the form of ingots stamped by a select list of refiners (e.g., Engelhard), is certified for delivery to satisfy a futures contract. By purchasing the contracts and then, upon their expiration, taking delivery of the silver ingots, the Hunt brothers—Bunker, Herbert, and Lamar (their sister was wise enough to stay out of the maneuver)—created an artificial shortage of the metal, or at least of that part of the market (certified ingots) that the futures market relied upon. As a result, the price of silver shot up from around $3 an ounce to over $50 an ounce. On paper, at least, the Hunts, who now owned a lot of silver, were fabulously wealthy. They could not, however, prevent additional silver from coming into the marketplace, particularly the futures market where they traded. And, of course, they were the principal large buyers. To whom were they going to sell?

Turning silver coinage, silverware, jewelry, and unrefined silver ore into the appropriately sized, refined, and stamped silver ingots needed to satisfy delivery on a futures contract required only enough time to refine and certify the medal. As time passed, more silver was turned into deliverable-grade ingots. Time, however, soon began to run out on the Hunts' effort to corner the silver market. They could maintain silver's high market price only by buying more and more of the metal. At first they used the collateral value of their silver holdings to finance additional borrowings. The resulting funds were used to buy more silver futures contracts. This pyramiding strategy worked well when the metal's price was rising, but not once it topped out. As the market price of silver declined, the collateral value supporting their loans began to erode. Soon thereafter, their collateral became insufficient to support their debts. Eventually the Hunts ran out of money and credit to buy any more silver or even to cover the loans on the silver that they had purchased. Their lenders reacted by calling in the loans. These calls forced silver sales, which in turn pushed the price down. A second problem faced by the Hunts was (ultimately successful) lawsuits by those who claimed to have been damaged by the Hunts' alleged market manipulation. When the dust settled, the Hunt brothers had gone from being billionaires to bankrupt, and the price of silver was back to about where it had started.

OPEC (Organization of Petroleum Exporting Countries) is an example of a cartel. It has at various times had some success in raising the price of crude oil. In the early 1970s, OPEC was able to take the price of crude oil first from under $3 to $12 and then to over $30 a barrel. It did so by persuading its members, especially Saudi Arabia, to restrict the supply. OPEC, however, could not forever maintain the high price level that it was able initially to achieve. Among its problems:

First, non-OPEC members increased their production, spurred on by the high market price OPEC had established. OPEC tried, with limited success, to persuade the non-OPEC oil exporters (e.g., Russia, Mexico, Norway) to cooperate by limiting their own production.

Second, users of crude oil both became more energy-efficient and shifted to other cheaper sources of energy (e.g., coal), thereby reducing their oil usage. That is a natural reaction to a price rise. The longer the time the market has to adjust to the higher prices, the greater the amount that buyers will conserve and shift to substitutes.

Third, OPEC members could not agree to limit production sufficiently and very generally failed to adhere to the limits that they did impose upon themselves. Cheating was rampant. Non-OPEC oil exporters were even less inclined to limit their production.

In other words, OPEC was, in the long run, unable to control either supply or demand for crude oil. Thus, the market price initially tended to fall back to the market clearing level. When the price of crude oil later rose, it did so because of a true scarcity, not because OPEC controlled either supply or demand. Other examples of cartels in coffee, sugar, bauxite, and so forth have had a similar experience.

The vast majority of corners and cartels eventually fail. Market forces almost always overwhelm the best efforts of those who would try to maintain an artificially high price. *The market clearing price is one that allows everyone who wants to buy at that level to purchase what they want from everyone who wants to sell at that market clearing level.* At the market clearing price, the quantity supplied equals the quantity demanded. As the price is pushed above the market clearing level, would-be buyers begin to disappear while the amount offered for sale increases. A gap emerges between the amount that market participants want to offer for sale (quantity supplied) and the amount willing purchasers are prepared to purchase (quantity demanded).

To raise the price above the market clearing level, supply must be restricted. The higher the price is pushed, the more supply must be restricted. One who manages a corner or cartel can do so by purchasing the excess or restricting the production that is under his or her control. Either approach is costly for the cartel members. Moreover, the higher the price, the more incentive outsiders (nonmembers of the cartel) have to sell into the artificially high-priced market. As time passes, the buyers find alternatives, and the noncartel group sellers offer greater and greater amounts for sale. Thus an ever-increasing excess supply needs to be removed from the market in order to maintain the artificially high price level.

You may on occasion suspect that a corner or cartel group is attempting to manipulate the market. If so, you can expect that the effort to produce an artificially high price will eventually collapse of its own weight. Does this mean you should bet against the market manipulator? Not on your life! What you don't know is how long the effort to manipulate the market will continue and how high the price will be raised before it collapses. Suppose that during the Hunt corner attempt you had concluded that at $20 an ounce, silver was very much overpriced. You could have sold silver futures contracts short at $20. The market would eventually have proven you correct. If you had had the resources and patience to hold on long enough, your position would have shown a profit. Silver's price did eventually fall back to below $5 an ounce. But along the way, you would have seen the market prices soar (to $50 an ounce) far above the level that obtained when you established your short position. Unless you had very substantial backup resources, your short position would have been liquidated when you could not meet the ever-rising margin calls. Even if you had been able to maintain your position, you would have had a lot to worry about as the price was rising against you and your short position.

For most investors, the best strategy for dealing with a corner or cartel is to stay out of the way. On occasion you may be on the favorable side of an effort by a corner or cartel to bid up the price. When that happens, you should take your profits (don't get greedy) and then move on. If you are on the wrong side and the market manipulation hurts you, you may want to hang on, but only if you have the staying power and the exposure is not too great. Otherwise, you should get out of the way and wait for the dust to settle.

———— 13 ————

Timing Strategies That Don't Work

A s Mark Twain once said, "It ain't what you don't know but *what you know that ain't so that gets you into so much trouble.*" Knowing what does not work may be as helpful as knowing what does. Avoiding mistakes can be every bit as important to successful portfolio management as taking advantage of profitable opportunities. This point is especially valid for efforts to time the market. A lot of self-appointed experts think they know how to time the market. You need to be able to see the shortcomings to their approaches. That way, you are much less likely to make the mistake of following their misguided advice.

Technical analyses as practiced by chart-readers is a waste of time.

Financial economists have differing views on many matters. Those same financial economists do, however, almost universally agree upon one concept: the validity of what is called the *weak form of the efficient market hypothesis,* or, as it was initially called, the *random walk hypothesis.* According to this hypothesis, security prices move randomly with respect to past price movements. Therefore, information on past prices and returns is said to be of no value in predicting future price changes. If this weak form hypothesis is correct, efforts to forecast where stock prices are going next by looking at charts of where they have been are bound to fail. That is not to say that the charts will never provide a correct signal. Rather, the signals derived from the charts are no better than those obtained from flipping a coin. They are, in a given instance, about as likely to be incorrect as correct. Even a broken clock shows the correct time twice a day.

Numerous studies utilizing a variety of statistical techniques have explored this matter. Virtually all of them have come to the same conclusion: *Stock prices move in a random fashion relative to a history of their past levels. You cannot tell anything about where a security price is going from where it has been.*

This conclusion not only means that you should not waste your time and money on books or articles dedicated to technical analysis, but also that you should not look for patterns in your everyday stock-trading. You might, for example, see a stock bounce back and forth between two apparent barriers. Suppose you see it reach a high of 22 and fall back to 20 and then climb back to 22 before falling back to 20. After several weeks of trading in the 20–22 range, you may conclude that you could make some money by buying at 20 and then selling at 22. You buy some of the stock the next time the price falls to 20 and then put in your sell order at 22. Well, you may be lucky and sell at 22. But according to the weak form of the efficient market hypothesis, that stock is as likely to fall to 18 as it is to go to 22. Seeing patterns where none exists is a well-known phenomena in psychology.

The "January indicator" is a sham!

According to the so called *January indicator,* if the stock market rises in January, the odds are about two-to-one that it will be up for the year. Historical research supports this proposition. The only problem with this so-called January indicator is that the stock market generally rises about two years out of three. January performance is no better at predicting the year's performance than is random chance.

Similarly, the idea that if the market falls two years in a row, it is very unlikely to fall in the third year has no incremental predictive value. Since the market rises in about two-thirds of the years, the odds are still about one-in-three that it will fall in a given year, regardless of its prior history. While the stock market rarely falls three years in succession, it did decline in 2002 after declines in 2000 and 2001.

Hot tips are radioactive.

Suppose your broker, bartender, brother, or bootblack tells you that he knows, on good authority, that important new information on a particular stock is about to be released. He goes on to say that once the market learns what he already knows, the stock is a sure bet for a big rise. He urges you to buy before the news comes out. Consider the following possibilities:

First, the person spreading the hot tip/rumor could be trying to stimulate interest in the stock in order to cause its price to rise. That person can then unload his or her own position into a rising market. This strategy is called *pump and dump*. Second, the person supplying the hot tip sincerely believes the rumor and that the stock's price will rise, but his or her information could be incorrect (the rumor is false). Third, the person actually knows something, but the recommendation is based on nonpublic information.

In all three of the above-mentioned circumstances, a trade based on the tip would be inadvisable. Clearly, if the tip is designed (illegally) to inflate the price, a buy is likely to turn out poorly for you or anyone else who trades on it. Once the market learns that the rumor is false, the stock price will almost certainly fall, perhaps dramatically. By then the source of the hot tip has probably dumped his or her own stock. He pumped; you bought; he dumped; you were left holding the bag.

Similarly, if the recommender is mistaken, investment results will be random at best. The third situation, however, is the most dangerous. *Trading on material nonpublic information is illegal.* The person providing you with access to such information for trading purposes is violating the law. You, too, become a lawbreaker if you knowingly trade on material nonpublic information. The penalties for trading on inside information can be severe. If you think that the odds of getting caught are small, think again. The regulators are likely to be very interested in any unusual trading activity that precedes a significant announcement. Once they become suspicious, the authorities will closely examine the relevant transactions in order to identify those investors who entered into profitable trades just prior to the public announcement. They will then explore who among the traders had a relationship with someone who had access to nonpublic information. Once they have the evidence, the regulators will vigorously pursue the case in the courts (ask Martha Stewart).

Don't expect a "greater fool" to bail you out.

Investors sometimes try to hop on to a stock whose price is rising, believing such theories as *the trend is your friend* or *don't fight the tape*. The stock is said to have a lot of momentum, which will continue to carry it higher, or so some may believe.

If, however, the price rise's underpinning is fluff, the market will soon enough realize its error and the price will stop rising. Then the price may start falling and eventually collapse. Make sure that you aren't buying into the idea that the price of this wildly overpriced stock will go even higher, allowing you to get out at a nice profit. You may find out that you were the *greatest fool*. You bailed the last guy out. But now no greater fool is available to pull your chestnuts out of the fire.

*Beware of backtest rules and strategies. Data-snooping
may explain the results.*

Much of what we have learned about stock market behavior has been
derived from studies of past tendencies and performance. The January effect,
performance of low PE stocks, stocks of bankrupt firms, companies that engage in reverse stock splits, and many other well-documented market tendencies have been explored by examining how the market reacted under
particular circumstances in the past *(backtesting)*. And yet, by no means do all
trading rules formulated from an analysis of the past continue to perform as
well as past history would suggest.

Data-snooping is one potential pitfall of rules derived from backtesting. The
history of a concept called *relative strength* illustrates the danger of relying
inappropriately on evidence from backtesting. In his dissertation (PhD in
finance, 1960s) Robert Levy introduced a concept that he called "relative
strength." Levy claimed that stocks that outperform the market over a prespecified time period exhibited a type of performance that tended to persist.
Such evidence of relative strength could, according to Levy, be taken as a
positive (buy) signal. These stocks would, again according to Levy, tend to
outperform the market at least for a time thereafter. Levy proceeded to for-
mulate and test a rule that purported to identify stocks possessing relative
strength. Levy's own backtesting seemed to show that stocks with relative
strength were likely to produce above-average returns. He even formed a
company to sell information on which stocks currently possessed relative
strength.

Michael Jensen, a highly respected financial economist, realized that the
patterns that Levy had claimed to find were inconsistent with weak form
market efficiency. Jensen, like most financial economists, was well aware the
vast array of empirical research in support of the weak form of market efficiency. He was therefore quite skeptical of Levy's findings and conclusions.
Accordingly, Jensen carefully retested Levy's concept. When Jensen applied
Levy's approach to a new set of data, relative strength's apparent success in
identifying profitable stock trade opportunities disappeared.

Jensen's reexamination of Levy's approach revealed the problem: Levy had
both designed and tested his trading rules on the same data set. Levy worked
the data very hard to find his rules. He tested many different forms of his rules
until he found a set of rules that "worked" on that particular set of data (time
period, set of stocks). If you try enough different formulations of a trading
rule, you will eventually find one that appears to work on the data set that you
tested. Indeed, according to one self-appointed expert: *Enough monkeys and
enough typewriters and one will write* King Lear. Levy had snooped through the
data until he found a rule that appeared to work on his test set. His trading
rule's apparent success, however, was not due to an underlying tendency of
the market. Rather, just by chance, it was successful on the particular data set

that he tested. That is why it did not hold up on a different data set. Levy was guilty of data-snooping.

Careful researchers seek to avoid being misled by this data-snooping problem. They begin their analysis by developing a specific theory without examining the relevant data too closely. Only when they have constructed a well-formulated concept that they believe may be worth exploring do they start testing it on an actual data set. Thus they try to avoid being led by the data. Second, they test only a few permutations and combinations of their concept. By avoiding tests of many different formulations, they reduce the possibility that what seems to work was just a statistical artifact of the particular data set studied. Third, and most important, they retest their relationships on a second, holdout sample of data. If, for example, a relationship is found for 1996–2005 data, it is retested on 1985–1995 data to see if the same relationship is replicated. If the relationship performs about as well on the holdout sample as on the original sample, the likelihood that it will continue to perform in the future is enhanced. Even this approach provides no guarantees. Financial markets may work one way at one time and a different way in a different time. Still, carefully retesting your finding on a second data set greatly reduces the likelihood that your results are a statistical artifact.

Whenever you learn about an investment strategy that has been tested on historical data and seemed to work well in the past, be wary of the possibility that the prior results may have been produced by data-snooping. Explore this matter before you act on such a backtested rule.

Be wary of the "100-year" storm. Such storms tend to occur much more frequently than once a century.

Many investment strategies are based on the belief that the future will be very much like the past. Indeed, those who advocate such strategies may believe that you can depend upon the apparent regularities that they have observed to continue to behave as if there is a law on the subject. Deviations from the expected relationships and tendencies are thought, by some self-appointed experts, to be as rare as one-hundred-year storms. All too often neglected is the possibility that the world will change. Hundred-year storms seem to occur much more frequently than advertised.

Some trading rules work very well right up to the time when they stop working. Consider an example. Many investment strategies have been based on the general tendency for long-term interest rates to be higher than short-term interest rates. And indeed, short rates are lower than long-raters, most of the time. But they are not always lower.

When short-term rates are below long-term rates, one who can borrow at the lower, short-term rates and lend at the higher, long-term rates will earn the spread in the rates. If the short rate is 4 percent and the long rate is

7 percent, a rate spread of 3 percent can be earned on a borrow-short-and-lend-long transaction. This borrow-short-and-lend-long strategy is, in fact, used extensively by commercial banks and other similar financial institutions (e.g., savings and loan associations). Banks generally try to hedge their positions in various ways (e.g., by making variable-rate loans). The strategy does, however, involve significant risks, even for banks.

Many investment strategies rely implicitly upon a particular type of relationship continuing into the future. For example, one who uses margin borrowing (interest charges based on a short-term rate) to invest in long-term junk bonds (a long-term, high-yield, high-risk bond) is relying upon the continuations of two relationships: (1) that the yield curve will continue to be upward-sloping; (2) that the default rate on junk bonds will remain relatively low. The strategy is effective just as long as these two relationships both continue to hold. When either of the relationships falls apart, so does the strategy. In the 1980s, a number of insurance companies and savings and loan associations employed a junk bond strategy, with disastrous results. They expected that their junk bond portfolios would continue to yield more than the cost of their short-term borrowings. The hundred-year storm that they encountered was a period of rising short rates, rising default rates, and collapsing junk bond prices. The bankruptcy of many S&Ls and insurance companies was the result. Various strategies involving derivatives may have at their core a dependence upon a similar kind of relationship. Orange County's (California) bankruptcy was one of a number of disasters that resulted from employing this type of strategy.

Short rates do not always stay below long rates. Sometimes the level of interest rates rises so high that almost everyone in the market is expecting them to fall from their current high levels. Investors rush into the long end of the market in order to lock in the high rates before they start to fall. When that happens, short-term rates often rise above long-term rates. Nor do interest rates always stay within a particular range. A rise in inflation fears generally causes the Fed to shift toward a tighter monetary policy. The result of this Fed tightening will be not only a rise in the general level of interest rates, but quite possibly a disproportionate rise in short-term rates. This phenomenon can result in short-term rates that are higher than long-term rates (a so called *inverted yield curve*). This inversion of the yield curve has happened on more than a few occasions.

Return to our example of the strategy of financing a long-term investment yielding 7 percent with short-term borrowing at 4 percent. A crisis in the Middle East could lead to a shortage in crude oil and a dramatic rise in inflationary expectations. The Fed could then tighten up on the money supply. Short-term rates could rise from 4 to 9 percent while long-term rates increase only from 7 to 8 percent. The investor could soon need to start financing the long-term asset not at a rather low 4 percent, but at a much higher 9 percent. Since the long-term asset was purchased to yield 7 percent, the positive interest spread has turned into a negative 2 percent ($7\% - 9\% = -2\%$). That negative yield spread, however, is not the worst of it. The bonds that were purchased when their yields were 7 percent are now trading in a market where they must be priced to yield 8 percent. Thus their market values would have fallen substantially. Accordingly, the investor not only faces a significantly negative yield spread, but his or her assets have also suffered a loss in market value. Even worse, the decline in portfolio value could lead to a margin call. The investor could be forced to sell his or her long-term assets at a substantial loss.

So we see how a strategy that seemed to work effectively most of the time might well encounter market conditions that would lead to large losses. The above scenario is not hypothetical. It has happened to a number of very sophisticated investors (including one with a Nobel Prize in economics). They were hit by what they thought was a hundred-year storm (a financial crisis in Russia) only a few years after they started their firm (Long-Term Capital Management). At first their firm's strategy was very successful. This initial success added to their confidence (hubris) and willingness to take additional risks by using ever-increasing amounts of leverage. When (after a default in Russian bonds) the market stopped performing the way they had expected it to, their exposure was great, as was that of their lenders. Only the Fed's intervention avoided a major financial panic.

A second strategy that can lead to trouble is to borrow at relatively low rates and invest the borrowed funds in higher-rate, higher-risk assets. So called subprime and asset-based lenders who extend credit at high interest rates to borrowers who have weak credit ratings represent one example of such an approach. Another example involved insurance companies and S&Ls that invested heavily in junk bonds.

True, higher risk is usually associated with higher returns. Moreover, a diversified portfolio of high-risk investments has generally offered a higher return than a diversified portfolio of investment-grade bonds (even after taking account of default losses). But, and it is a big but, *what usually happens does not always happen*. Indeed, at various times the market has turned very negative on low-quality bonds. Such bonds may on occasion (such as during a severe recession) experience unusually high default rates. Similarly, at times, the loss rate on loans to weak credit borrowers may turn out to be much higher than had been expected. In these cases the promised premium yield on high-risk instruments may be well below the level needed to offset the losses on those issues that do default. At such times a strategy that relied upon a tendency which generally worked in the past will fail because of that hundred-year storm. Some kind of hundred-year storm seems to occur every several years.

Potentially Useful Timing Rules

The preceding discussion may or may not be helpful to those seeking to apply market timing to the management of their portfolio. It should at a minimum help you understand why the market is doing what it is doing. Now let's turn to some potentially helpful timing rules. Don't get too excited. Most of these rules tend to work only in special circumstances and provide only a minor benefit. Still, some advantage is better than no advantage and a lot better than false promises that can lead you astray.

Take tax losses by November in order to avoid the depressing impact of tax-selling in December.

A substantial body of research has been devoted to what has come to be known as the *January effect*. According to these studies, stocks that had been depressed at year-end tend to rebound in January. Stocks whose prices are depressed in December may be beaten down by tax-selling. Investors often seek to reduce their tax liability by realizing losses before the calendar year ends. Indeed, they may be selling their losers to such an extent that the selling pressure pushes the relevant (already depressed) stock prices down even more. After the year ends, the selling pressure abates and the stocks that had been depressed by tax-selling may rebound somewhat.

Harvesting tax losses is often advantageous. An investment that is not working out as planned can at least be sold to realize a capital loss and thereby offset the tax liabilities on more successful transactions. If the stock is never destined to recover, the tax shelter provided by the tax loss is the only thing that is left to be salvaged. Taking losses sooner rather than later has the effect of accelerating the realizations of the tax benefit. One does not, however, want to exacerbate the pain by selling a losing position at the very bottom. Since most tax-selling tends to occur in the latter part of December, one who realizes losses earlier in the year is less likely to be selling during a period of heavy selling pressure (and therefore at especially depressed prices). Normally you can wait as late as November to realize your tax losses and still not get hit by the adverse effect of tax-selling. Alternatively, you can wait until January to do your selling, when the price may have rebounded somewhat. Waiting until January, however, pushes the tax benefit into the next year. You would generally prefer to realize the tax benefit before year end. That way you can use the realized loss to reduce your tax liability a year sooner.

When possible, avoid realizing gains late in the year. Postpone realizing those gains until the next calendar year in order to put off the tax liability.

For almost all taxpayers, December 31 is at the dividing line between events that lead to a tax liability in the current year and those that relate to taxes for the next tax year. Just as realizing losses in time to use them to reduce the current year's tax liability is generally advantageous, so is postponing gains realizations and the corresponding tax liability into the following year. One who might otherwise sell a gain-bearing position late in the current year could benefit tax-wise by deferring the transaction until the beginning of the following year. A gain realized in the last part of the current year will generally require a corresponding estimated tax payment on January 15 or, at a minimum, a tax payment on April 15 of the following year. That same gain realized in the first part of the following year will, at worst, result in an obligation to make four equal-sized tax payments starting with April and extending up to the following January. Thus by deferring the transaction into the following year, the tax liability is put off by an average of at least six months and typically more. Deferring a tax liability has the same financial impact as getting an interest-free loan from the government.

Options can be used both to protect a gain and to defer realizing it in order thereby to put off its associated tax liability.

Waiting until after January 1 to realize a gain exposes you to the risk that the market will move adversely before your position is liquidated. Your stock's price could decline while you wait for the year to turn. Several different techniques may be used to postpone a gain's realization while simultaneously protecting the gain itself. One such profit-protecting approach utilizes options.

Suppose you would like to realize the gain on a stock at the current price level. You bought the stock at 15 and it currently trades at 53. Your gain of 38 points per share will, if realized, give rise to a substantial tax liability. If you had owned 500 shares, your gain would be $19,000, and even at 15 percent the tax liability would amount to $2,850. If the gain is short-term and you are in the 35 percent tax bracket, the associated tax liability would amount to $6,650. You want to lock in your gain now but postpone incurring your tax liability until next year. This objective can be accomplished (with some risk of not succeeding) by writing an in-the-money call or (with no risk of failure) by buying a put. You could, for example, write a call with a strike of 50 that expires in January. If the stock's price remains above 50 when the option expires, the call would be exercised. You would sell your stock to the one who owns the call. The stock now priced at 53 has a reasonably good chance of staying above 50 until next year. The odds of an exercise would be even more in your favor if you wrote the call with a strike of 45 or 40. The lower the strike, however, the smaller the time value on the call that you write. This in-the-money call-writing strategy has the added bonus of obtaining a somewhat higher price for your position than an outright sale (the previously mentioned time value of the option). That is, you might be able to sell a three-month call with a strike of 50 on a 53 dollar stock for a price of 5. You would be paid immediately for the call and then receive the strike price for your stock when (if) the option was exercised. So, you would be paid 5 now and (hopefully) 50 later, for total sale proceeds of 55 for a stock now selling at 53 (assuming the stock's price stayed above 50 so that the option was exercised). You might even receive an additional dividend by holding the stock a bit longer.

You could also protect your gain by purchasing a put. A put with a strike of 50 would cost you something and protect you only against a stock price fall of greater than 3 points. Still, you would retain the benefit of any price rise in the stock as you waited for the year end to arrive.

Another way to defer a gain is to sell short against the box.

Rather than use options, you could defer but lock in your gain by *selling short against the box*. With this procedure, you would sell short an amount of the stock equivalent to the amount that you own. But you would not initially use your long position to cover your short position. As a result, your account would reflect both a long and a short position involving equal amounts of the same stock. Once the year ended, you would use your existing long position to cover your short position. Your taxable gain would thereby be assigned to the new year. One disadvantage of this strategy: You do not obtain access to the short sales' balance until the short position is closed. That is, even though you have essentially sold your stock, the sales proceeds will remain deposited in your short account until you actually cover your short position. And your broker will probably keep any interest earned on this short balance.

Use options to realize a loss and yet maintain your position.

Suppose you show a paper loss (unrealized) on an investment. You would like to realize this loss so that you can use it to lower your tax liability this year. You would also like to hold on to your position because you expect the price on the losing position to rebound. If you realize a loss but restore your position within thirty-one days (buying back either after or before the sale), the set of transactions would be viewed by the IRS as a *wash sale.* You are not allowed to recognize such a wash sale loss on your tax returns. Rather, the loss on your position becomes embedded in the basis of your restored position in the repurchased stock.

Options can, however, be used to avoid the adverse impact of the wash sale rule. One approach would be to sell the stock and simultaneously buy a call on the stock. As long as the call has an expiration date that is more than thirty days off, you can use it to buy the stock back without fear that the price will rise above the call's strike price. Moreover, if the stock's price declines below the strike price, you can buy the stock back on the market for less than your calls' strike price.

A second approach is to sell your stock at a loss and then write a deep in-the-money put on the same stock with an expiration date more than a month off. If the put is exercised, you will own the stock again. With this put strategy, you actually pick up some time value as opposed to paying for it with the purchase of a call. You will also have some temporary cash that you can use (invest it for a return or use it to pay down debt and thereby reduce the interest cost). The one risk with this strategy is the possibility that the stock price will rise above the put's strike price. But, if you write a put that is deeply in the money and has a short expiration, this risk is likely to be small.

Be mindful of the "cockroach rule."

Suppose you have the misfortune to walk into the kitchen, turn on the light, and see a cockroach scamper across the floor. You can be almost certain that you are sharing your living space with more than one cockroach. You saw the one that happened to be out and about. The others were not visible, but they certainly were hiding there someplace.

A similar kind of phenomenon often occurs when a stock that you have the misfortune to own releases very bad news, particularly when the news is truly awful. A company that begins to release news of a serious nature often tries to let its investors down slowly. Management is only now being forced to face up to reality. Only now is the company beginning to reveal just how bad things are. The first announcement of trouble may put an unrealistically favorable spin on the situation. But the bad news continues to come out. Things go from bad, to worse, to disastrous. We saw this phenomenon with both WorldCom and Enron. Accounting irregularities were discovered and disclosed. Then more and still more. The poor investor could not get a sense of where the bottom was because more bad news kept coming out. The result was horrendous. Not only was the released news very bad in and of itself, but also each new release contradicted things said in the last. The market soon lost all faith in each company's credibility.

The point for the investor is clear: *Bad news, truly bad news, is often followed by still worse news.* If you own stock in a company that is beginning to disclose very bad news, you may be inclined to hang in there and wait for things to turn around. That strategy will sometimes work. But the wait may be long and difficult. Think about the cockroach theory.

The market generally rises in a presidential election year.

Every four years (every leap year) we have a presidential election. Almost always the current president is either seeking reelection or supporting his or her party's nominee (often the current vice president). History has shown that if the economy is doing well, the party in power is usually reelected (Clinton, Reagan, Bush II), and it usually loses if the economy is thought to be doing poorly (Carter, Ford, Bush I). Accordingly, the administration currently in power would very much prefer for the economy to be strong and even improving going into the election. The government has a number of ways to influence the level of economic activity. Government spending and taxing (fiscal policy), Federal Reserve activity (monetary policy), activity in the international area (trade policy) and in the regulatory sphere (microeconomic policy) are all within the province of the federal government. The president has varying degrees of influence over the government's economic policy. The president can be expected to pursue policies designed to bulk up a weak economy or maintain the strength of a strong economy as the election approaches. On the other hand, the Fed may worry that too much fiscal stimulation may overheat the economy. Too much steam in the economy leads to shortages, bottlenecks, and eventually inflationary pressures. Sometimes the Fed's effort to fight inflation results in an economic slowdown just before an election (1960, 1992). Most of the time, however, the economy is strengthening as a presidential election approaches.

A strong economy does not necessarily translate into a strong stock market and vice versa. Still, in most presidential election years, we have seen the president's administration take action to stimulate the economy. This economic stimulation has also tended to help the stock market.

On more than a few occasions, economic stimulation prior to an election has ended up overheating the economy. When that happens, inflation rears its ugly head. Then the Fed feels the need to slow things down. Tight monetary policy leads to rising interest rates and falling stock and bond prices. The period after a presidential election is not always favorable for the financial markets, particularly if the economy has been overheated prior to the election.

The stock market prefers Republicans.

While the electorate is about evenly split between Republicans, Democrats, and independents, investors and business managers are disproportionately Republicans. Republicans tend to favor lower taxes and less government involvement in the economy. Most investors and managers have incomes and wealth levels that are well above those of average noninvestors. Such higher net worth individuals generally believe that they will be better off economically under the kind of policies that Republicans tend to support. As a result of the above considerations, the market generally reacts more favorably in the period immediately after an election (presidential or midterm) in which Republicans do well than in elections in which Democrats do better than expected. This impact is, however, very short run. Soon after the election, the market will turn its attention to other matters.

Republicans and Democrats prefer policies that tend
to favor different industries. Invest accordingly.

The policies pursued by Republicans tend to favor one group of industries while those pursued by the Democrats tend to favor others. For example, Republicans are generally more supportive of defense spending than are Democrats. On the other hand, Democrats tend to be more supportive of environmental issues. Thus, pollution control and alternative energy–related companies are likely to fare better under Democrats. Democrats would spend more public money on health care (universal health insurance), but would also be more inclined to put controls on its pricing (pharmaceutical prices). Industries such as timber, oil, and tobacco tend to perform better with Republicans. High-tech industries tend to be more favorably disposed toward the Democrats. Republicans tend to favor lowering trade restrictions (free trade) while Democrats are more inclined to resist the lowering of trade barriers. They would prefer to protect American (particularly union) jobs, even at the cost of higher prices on goods and services for consumers.

Investors should be mindful of the preferences of the two parties and the impact these preferences may have on particular companies and industries. Especially when a change of administration occurs, the impact (favorable or unfavorable) on various industries can be substantial.

15

Rules for Short Selling

S ome timing strategies seek to take advantage of anticipated declines in the price of various investment assets (stocks, bonds, etc.). One way to do so is to sell short. Short sellers reverse the normal investment process. Usually you buy an investment in hopes that its price will rise so that you can sell it later for a profit. The short seller, in contrast, sells first in the hopes that the price will fall so that the asset can be purchased later at a lower price. Most short sellers are short-term traders. Since the prices of most investment assets tend to rise over the long term, short sellers are in a sense swimming against the current. They would prefer not to need to swim upstream for too long. Ideally, short sellers would like to implement their short sales positions just before a big price decline, cover their short position immediately after the price drops, and move on to the next situation.

Short sellers seek first to identify and then to establish a short position in overpriced stocks (or other assets). Most other investors are seeking to identify and take a long position in underpriced assets. Stock prices do go down as well as up. Accordingly, short selling is quite capable of producing profits just as purchasing undervalued stocks may produce profit for investors who take a long position. On the other hand, selling short can be very risky. Read on.

Short selling is a risky practice that is generally best left to experienced investors.

Short selling involves not only all the risks inherent in more traditional investing. A stock that you thought was misvalued in one direction turns out to have been misvalued in the other direction. Short sellers are also exposed to an additional set of risks. Specifically, losses on short sales are technically unlimited. The absolute most you can make on a short sale is the amount of cash that was generated by the short sale transaction itself. If you sell a stock short at 20, your greatest possible profit on the transaction is the 20 points per share that you got for the stock when you sold the shares short. And to earn the entire 20 points would require the stock's price to drop all the way to zero. Since a stock's price has no upper limit, your exposure to losses when you sell short is unlimited. The stock that you sold short at 20 could rise to 40 or 50 or 100 or even higher. So, in theory at least, you could lose far more on your short sale than your maximum profit of 20 points per share. This matrix of potential payoffs for a short sale is the mirror image of that for an investor who takes a long position. With a long (short) position, the maximum loss (gain) is the initial cost and the maximum gain (loss) is unlimited.

Short sellers face another risk. They are subject to margin calls. When you sell short, you must not only leave the proceeds derived from the short sale with your broker, you must also provide additional margin collateral (cash or marketable securities) to act as a cushion in case the price of the stock that you sold short goes up. Indeed, if the price rises high enough, you will be required to put up additional collateral in order to maintain your position. Usually, you will not earn any interest on the funds on deposit in your short account. If you are a large investor who generates a substantial amount of business for your broker, you may be able to persuade the brokerage firm to pay you a modest rate of interest on the balance in your short account, but you will need to negotiate for it. You will not be offered interest on your short account balance. You will, however, be required to pay the dividends on any stock that you sold short.

Timing is crucial for short sellers. You may be correct in your analysis that a stock is overvalued. And yet the market may be slow to recognize the stock's underlying intrinsic value. To profit from a short sale, you must not only identify an overvalued security, you must also be able to establish and maintain your short position long enough for the market to recognize the correctness of your analysis. If the price of the stock that you sold short rises above the price that you realized in your short sale, your position will show a loss. You may choose to maintain your position (at a loss) in hopes that things will turn around eventually. If, however, the price of the stock that you sold short rises high enough, you will receive a margin call. If you cannot meet the margin call, you will be forced to cover your short position at a loss. Such a margin call could force you to liquidate your position even though your strategy might eventually have shown a profit, if only you had been able to continue holding the position.

Even if you don't encounter problems with your margin account, you still could be forced to cover your short position before you are ready. In order to sell a stock short, your broker must be able to borrow the shares needed to facilitate the short transaction. Your broker's ability to maintain your short position is dependent upon the brokerage firm's success in continuing to find enough shares of the stock that you want to short. On occasion you may be required to cover a short position because the broker was unable to continue to borrow the shares needed to maintain it.

In light of all of the above risks and disadvantages, inexperienced investors should generally steer clear of short selling. The risk of an adverse outcome is just too great.

If you own any shares in a company that complains that short sellers have targeted it, sell the stock.

Large, experienced short sellers do indeed target certain companies. First, some sophisticated short sellers identify a company whose stock they believe is overvalued. They then proceed to accumulate their own short positions. Once they have established a sufficiently large short position, they bad-mouth the targeted company to the press in hopes of helping its stock price fall. Ideally, they would like to cause the price to collapse. The sooner they can help the market see the stock's weakness, the quicker they can realize their profits and move on. Usually when short sellers target a company, they have what they think are good reasons for believing that its stock is overpriced. They have a story to tell or, should we say, a story to sell. Their analysis of the underlying values may not be correct, just as any other investors/analysts may or may not be correct in their own assessment.

If the short sellers' analyses are incorrect, the company whose stock they sold short will perform better (profits, sales, growth) than the short sellers expect. This favorable performance is likely to result in the stock price rising rather than falling. That often happens to short sellers, just like many times investors buy (take a long position in) a stock that goes down. On the other hand, the short sellers' analysis may have the ring of truth. The shorted stock price may decline.

Sooner or later, the managers of the targeted firm learn that a group of short sellers has taken aim at their company's stock and is trashing it to the press. Not surprisingly, the managers of the targeted firm take a dim view of such activity. They see the short selling as an attack on both their company and their own jobs as managers. The managers of the targeted company often decide to counterattack. The managers who decide to fight the shorts can take various steps, including threatening to sue the short sellers and/or urging shareholders to request physical delivery of their stock certificates. Shares held in the owner's physical possession cannot be borrowed to facilitate short sales. Only shares held in the brokers' street name are available for borrowing by the short sellers. A scarcity of shares available to be borrowed increases the difficulty of selling short.

Research on this issue has revealed that more often than not, when managers do try to fight the short sellers, the stock's price does nonetheless subsequently decline. Apparently, those managers who take short selling in stride and simply focus on proving the short sellers wrong by concentrating on improving company performance do okay by their companies. On the other hand, those managers who declare war on the short sellers are unintentionally signaling to the market that they fear that the short sellers may be correct. Often the short sellers are the ones who have the last laugh.

Those who wish to bet on a stock's (or other security's) price going down generally should utilize options rather than sell short.

Short sellers are exposed to the risk that the security sold short could rise dramatically, imposing huge losses and possibly margin calls. The potential loss on an unhedged short position is unlimited. Another way to bet on a particular stock's price falling is to purchase a put. Buying a put has an important advantage compared to selling short: Your loss exposure is limited to the amount that you pay for the put. The price of your put can fall to zero, but it can't go any lower. A put purchase offers additional advantages (compared to a short sale): You are not required to provide any margin collateral, are protected from a margin call, and do not have any dividend payments to make on shorted stock. Finally, with a put purchase, you can control more stock with much less money than with a short sale (margin deposits on the short sale versus cost of the put with a put purchase). If the price of the underlying stock moves as you hope, your profits as a percentage of the sum of money required to establish your position are likely to be much greater with a strategy of buying puts than with a short sale strategy.

While buying puts does have some advantages over short selling (as a means of trying to take advantage of an expected price decline), puts also have their own sets of drawbacks. A couple of disadvantages to using puts to bet against a stock are: (1) You must pay a price for the put that reflects a premium over the put's intrinsic value (i.e., you must also pay its time value) and (2) The put has a defined and limited life. This means that the price of the stock that you are betting against must fall further (by the amount of the put's time value) for you to begin to earn a profit with a put strategy. With a short sale, in contrast, your position begins to show a profit when the stock's price falls below the price at which you sold short by enough to offset transaction costs (not the time value). Second, if the price of the underlying stock does not decline sufficiently while you own the put, your position will show a loss even if the price does eventually drop as much as you expected. In such a circumstance, you were correct on direction but not on the timing. When that happens, you lose. To win with options, your strategy must be correct in both the direction and timing dimensions.

One alternative to purchasing a put is to sell short and simultaneously protect yourself against large losses by purchasing a call on the same stock. If the stock's price declines, your short position will show a profit. If it goes up, your call position will limit your losses. If you buy a call with a strike price equal to the price at which you sell the stock short, the combined position will have a very similar payoff matrix to that of a put. You may, however, choose to sell short at one price and protect yourself from a large potential loss by purchasing an out-of-the money call at a higher price. So, for example, you might sell a stock short at 50 and hedge your position by purchasing calls with a strike at 55 or 60. The higher strike call will be less expensive, but will also provide less protection. Still, some protection is better than none. If you do sell short, buying a bit of protection with an out-of-the-money call is usually a good idea.

One more way to try to take advantage of a stock whose price you expect to fall is to write (i.e., sell) a call on it. When you sell a call on a stock that you do not own, you are engaging in a stratagem called *naked writing*. If the stock price ends up below the call option's strike price when the option expires, the call will (almost certainly) not be exercised. The writer of such an option keeps the money that was paid for the option and has no further obligation to the option holder. In other words, the call writer earns the full amount of the premium in exchange for agreeing to stand ready to do something that he or she is, at the end of the day, never asked to do. So, if you think a stock's price is about to fall, you can write a call. You will be able to keep the sale proceeds if your expectation is validated by the market.

Naked call writing is, however, a very risky strategy. As with short selling, if the stock's price rises, the call writer is on the hook for the entire amount of the increase. Potential losses are unlimited. The naked writer will have to satisfy the call exercise by buying the needed stock at the market price, regardless of the price level that it reaches. Additionally, margin money must be provided and maintained when options are written by one who does not own the underlying asset (naked writing). Once again you would be exposed to the risk of receiving a margin call if the price moves against you.

You can limit your exposure to possible losses on a naked call sale by purchasing another call with the same expiration date and a higher strike price. So, for example, if you write a naked call with a strike of 30, you could buy a call with a strike of 35. Such a higher strike call would sell for a much lower price than the one that you sold with a strike of 30. If the stock's price should unexpectedly rise dramatically, your exposure would be limited to 5 points $(35 - 30 = 5)$ less the difference in the prices of the two options.

For example, if you wrote the 30 call for 4 and bought the 35 call for 1, the net difference in your two positions would be 3 points $(4 - 1 = 3)$. In other

TABLE 15.1. Ways to Profit from a Stock Price Decline

Sell short, no hedge	Unlimited risk
Sell short, hedge with a call	Risk limited, added cost
Purchase put	Risk limited, added cost
Write call, no hedge	Unlimited risk
Write call, hedge with higher strike call	Risk limited, added cost

words, you would net a positive 3 points per share from the two transactions. For a single set of 100-share contracts, 3 points would be the equivalent to $300. If both calls expired out-of-the-money, you would keep the net proceeds of 3. If, however, both of the calls were in-the-money at expiration, you would have to buy stock at 35 and sell it for 30, yielding a negative 5-point difference. This negative 5-point difference would be partially offset by the positive 3-point difference that you received in setting up the initial option transaction. Your maximum loss would be 2 ($5 - 3 = 2$). The final possibility is that the 30 calls are in-the-money at expiration, but the 35s are out-of-the-money. Suppose at expiration the underlying stock is trading at 32. At that price level the 30s would have an intrinsic value of 2. You would have to buy the stock at 33 and sell it at 30 (a negative of 2). But you would have taken 3 points out when you established the two call positions. So your net result would be a gain of 1 point per share ($3 - 2 = 1$). On the other hand, you would be out by 1 point per share if the stock traded at 34 at expiration.

To bet on a stock going up, you may want to write a deeply in-the-money leap put.

Leaps are long-term option contracts. A leap put is a long-term option to sell. Because it has a long life, a leap's price usually contains a substantial time value. If the put is deeply in-the-money, it will also have a substantial intrinsic value. Accordingly, such a put will sell for a relatively high price (a price well above its intrinsic value).

Suppose you are considering buying a stock that is now trading at 25. You could simply enter an order (market or limit) to purchase the stock outright at 25. That is what most investors who wanted to own the stock would do. But as an alternative you could write a one-year put with a strike of 30 on the stock. Such a put would probably be priced at around 7. At 7 the put would have an intrinsic value of 5 and time value of 2. You would be paid 7 for writing the put. If the stock's price stayed at 25, a year from now you would still have to buy it for 30. But since you were paid 7 for writing the put, your net cost for the stock would be 23 ($30 - 7 = 23$). Actually, you would do even better with the put-writing strategy because of the impact of the time value of money. You would receive the 7 immediately and thus be able to earn interest on that sum. You would pay the 30 a year later. Accordingly, you would save a year's financing cost on the purchase price and be able to earn interest for a year on the put sale proceeds. But what if the stock did so well that its price rose to 30 or above? At the end of the year, the put would expire and the $7-per-share put premium would be yours to keep. You would have no further obligation to the put-holder. That result would not be bad for you. You would be paid $7 a share for doing nothing. On the other hand, suppose the stock dropped to 20. You would still have to buy it at 30, but again your net cost would be 23. Had you bought the stock initially at 25, you would be underwater by 5 points. With the leap sale strategy you are down by only 3 points (and somewhat less because of the above-mentioned time value of money impact).

You give up one thing with this approach of writing deep in-the-money leap puts: the possibility of earning a really large gain on the stock that you might otherwise have bought outright. Your profits on a put sale max out once the underlying stock's price reaches the put's strike price. If, for example, the stock that you write a put on with a strike of 30 rises to 50 while the put is outstanding, you are no better off than if its price rise stopped at 30. You have given up the potential profit of 20 points per share that you would have earned if you had owned the stock rather than written a put on it. You could enhance your upside potential on this put-sale-strategy by writing a put with a higher strike. Usually, however, the highest strike is still relatively close to the stock's current stock price. Moreover, the greater the amount that your put is in the money, the lower is its time value.

_____ 16 _____

Rules for the Futures Market

W e have considered investing in a large array of different types of assets: stocks, bonds, options, mutual funds, real estate, and assets related to each of these asset types. We have even explored the pros and cons of some less traditional types of investments such as collectibles and tangibles. The one major class of investments that has not been discussed thus far is *futures contracts*. Futures are, nonetheless, a significant player on the investment scene. You may or may not wish to take a position (long or short) in the futures market. Nevertheless, to be a well-informed investor, you do need to understand the futures market and its impact on the securities market. Such an understanding is an important piece of the story that explains how securities markets behave.

Understand that unlike an option contract, a futures contract obligates both sides to follow through with the specified transactions.

A futures contract is a particular type of sales agreement between a buyer and a seller. Unlike the more typical spot market contract, both the buyer and seller of a futures contract agree to fulfill the terms of the contract at some specified time in the future. Neither side has an option. The buyer of the contract agrees to pay for and take delivery of the asset identified in the contract. The seller agrees to make delivery of that asset in exchange for the prespecified payment. The contract specifies the item to be delivered and its grade and quantity as well as the date and place where delivery is to take place. Futures contracts are standardized with respect to these features. The market price will fluctuate, but the terms will remain the same throughout the life of the contract. As a result, many individual contracts having identical terms are almost always being traded in the marketplace.

While a futures contract does obligate the buyer (seller) to take (make) delivery, either party can extricate him (her) self from the obligation prior to the delivery date by entering into an offsetting transaction. So, for example, if you have bought (sold) a futures contract, you could eliminate your obligation by selling (buying) an identical contract. The vast majority of futures contract obligations are *covered* in this way. Less than 1 percent of all futures contracts result in actual physical delivery.

While futures contracts began with agricultural products and moved into minerals, most of the futures market trading is now concentrated in the financial area.

Futures contracts started as one-of-a-kind agreements for deferred delivery of grain. A seller would commit to deliver and a buyer to pay for and take delivery of a specified amount of grain on a specified date at a specified location. At first these contracts were entered into and held by both original parties until the terms were fulfilled. Later the contracts began to be traded with third parties so that when delivery was due, one or both sides could be different from those who originated the contract. Still later, the contracts began to be standardized and eventually traded on an exchange. Most of this development took place in Chicago, but futures exchanges were also established in other cities. Major futures exchanges are now located in both Chicago and New York. As with stocks and bonds, futures trading also takes place around the world.

Futures contracts were developed in various agricultural commodities and then in metals and minerals. Finally, financial futures began to be developed and actively traded in the 1970s.

The three basic types of financial futures—stocks, bonds, and currencies—each have an impact on and are affected by their underlying cash markets.

Financial futures began with contracts calling for delivery of debt instruments such as Treasury bills. In effect, the players in this market are making a wager on where market interest rates will be when delivery is due. Such contracts now exist for various maturities and types of debt instruments.

Soon after the futures markets began trading debt instruments, equity or stock market futures were developed for various indexes. Much of the trading in the area of financial futures takes place in futures contracts on the S&P 500 index. Finally, currency futures were developed, calling for delivery of a quantity of one currency paid for in another currency. Such contracts represent a bet on futures exchange rates.

Agricultural and mineral contracts call for delivery of an actual physical commodity. Most financial futures, in contrast, are settled with a cash payment reflecting the economic value of the contract on the delivery date.

Because of the very large amount of leverage inherent in futures market trading, the risks to traders are enormous.

Both the buyer and seller of futures contracts are required to provide a deposit (margin or earnest money) equal to a percentage of the value of the contracts. The margin percentage is typically in the range of 5 to 15 percent of the total value of the contract. When you purchase a futures contract having a 10 percent margin requirement, you are committing yourself to pay the remaining 90 percent of the contract's value on the contract's delivery date. You are initially depositing only 10 percent of the total value of the contract. The other 90 percent will be due to the seller upon delivery. This amount of leverage (e.g., put up only10% margin) creates a great deal of risk for those who trade futures. If, for example, the contract terms call for a 10 percent margin deposit, a 10 percent move in the underlying asset's price would wipe out the original investment of one side while doubling the value in the account of the other. As with trading securities on margin, the margin account must be maintained at a sufficiently positive level, or the account's owner will receive a margin call. If that call is not cured, the positions in the account will be liquidated. Margin calls are frequent in futures trading, as are large losses.

Because of the high level of risk in futures markets, most individual investors should avoid this "investment" area.

Many of the players in the futures markets are sophisticated professionals, hedging large offsetting positions in the cash market. In a hedging transaction, risk is reduced by establishing positions on both sides of the market (e.g., long cash, short futures, or vice versa). Others have a very deep, specialized knowledge and understanding of the markets in which they operate. These professional players usually have massive resources and staying power. If anyone can make money buying and selling futures, these large, experienced traders would be expected to do so.

Futures market trading is a zero sum game. At the end of each day as well as at contract expiration and at every point in between, what one side wins the other side loses on every futures contract ever written. If the price rises (falls), the long position gains (loses) the same amount as the short position loses (gains). Indeed, the impact of commissions and other costs of trading reduce the performance for both sides of the trade. So futures trading is not even a zero sum game. Technically, it is a *negative sum game*. The large, experienced traders are quite likely on balance to be successful. Otherwise, they would not remain large traders and be able to continue gaining more experience. And if they are successful, they must be doing so by profiting at the expense of the rest of the market. You would be in that rest-of-the-market group.

As a result of the above considerations, small individual investors are advised to stay well clear of the futures market. The risks are just too great.

Program trading and particularly index arbitrage can have a significant impact on the behavior of the stock market, at least in the short run.

Much of the trading in financial futures involves systematic, complex, and to a degree automatically structured trades. Such mechanical trading systems are referred to as *program trading*.

The best-known and most widely practiced type of program trading is a set of related trades known as *index arbitrage*. Index arbitrage trades are designed to take advantage of differences in the pricing of futures contracts on an index and the prices of the stocks that make up that index.

We know that at the expiration of an index futures contract (such as the S&P 500), the price of the contract will be equal to the weighted sum of the prices of the stocks making up that index where the proportions correspond to their weights in the index. That is how such contracts are settled at expiration. Thus, at contract expiration, the market price of an S&P 500 futures contract and the corresponding market prices of the stocks making up that index will be precisely in line. Prior to the contract's expiration, however, the futures contract's price will be determined by supply and demand for the contract in the *futures* market. Supply and demand in the *stock* market will determine the prices of the individual stocks that are components of the index. No market forces guarantee that supply and demand in the two sets of markets and the resulting market prices will be in line with each other.

Not infrequently the price of the S&P 500 futures contract will be priced either appreciably above or appreciably below the combined prices of the stocks making up the index. Such price differences open up an opportunity for an index arbitrage trade. Suppose the S&P 500 contract is priced above the corresponding value of the stocks making up the index. The index arbitrage trader would buy a contract-sized unit of stocks in the proportions of the index and simultaneously sell a futures contract on the index. Because of the price differential, the cost of the stock purchase would be less than the proceeds derived from the sale of the futures contract. When the contract reaches its expiration date, the two positions would have identical market values. Accordingly, the trader would sell the stocks and buy a corresponding index futures contract (or just let the contract expire) and thereby extract the price differential that existed when the two positions were established.

In actual real-world practice, the index arbitrage transaction is more complex than outlined above. The establishing and the unwinding of the trades must take place close together in time and, to be profitable, must yield gross gains large enough to cover transactions costs, dividends, financing costs, and tax impacts. Still, a nimble trader can indeed extract an essentially riskless profit when the prices in the two markets are sufficiently out of line.

To be effective, index arbitrage trades need to be implemented in very large dollar amounts. According to one estimate, $5 million is the minimum for effectively undertaking such trades. On occasion, particularly when such contracts are about to expire, index arbitrage activity can move the market in a particular direction. If unwinding positions lead to a large quantity of stock sales, prices can be driven down. Alternately, a disproportionate amount of index arbitrage–motivated buying activity can drive prices up. Be mindful of this possibility and stay out of the way.

Options on futures contracts are costly, but they do limit one's risk.

If you absolutely must try your luck with futures, you should consider buying *options on futures*. An option on a futures contract provides the owner with the right but not the obligation to take a position in the futures market. So, for example, a call (put) option on an S&P futures contract would allow the owner to buy (sell) the futures contract at a set price over a set time period. If the S&P index rose (fell), the S&P futures contract price would also rise (fall). That rise (fall) is likely to increase the value of the call (put) option. The option could then be sold for a profit. The major advantage of buying the option versus just buying the futures contract is the limitation on risk provided by the option on the futures contract. If you own or are short a futures contract and the market moves against you, the more it moves against you, the more you stand to lose. With an option on a futures contract, the most you can lose is the cost of the option contract.

Conclusion

This book lists and explains a series of easy-to-understand rules. Each rule is designed to help investors make informed investment decisions. Many of the rules are designed for those with no more than a modest amount of experience. Care is taken to explain that the rules will only *tend* to help the investor *at the margin*. Readers of this book should realize both that successful investing is not easy and that extremely high returns (20% or more) are not to be expected. Those who suggest the contrary are promising too much. The long-term average stock market return of 9 to 11 percent is an attractive and realistic objective for most investors. You may be able to do a bit better, but you will do just fine if you avoid doing worse.

A substantial part of this book is devoted to debunking false claims. Knowing what does not work is, in many cases, every bit as important as knowing what does. Another set of rules is designed to help you avoid making *unnecessary* mistakes. Making mistakes as an investor is easy. Avoiding them is more problematic. Still other rules should give you a slight edge in an inherently difficult market. This book's goal is to help you get rich slowly by working with modest advantages here and there and using patience and the power of compound interest. Others may promise quick riches. I seriously doubt if they can deliver. I believe that I can deliver on my more realistic goals.

The book itself begins with a discussion of the power of compound interest. We then move on to three important investment topics: investment mechanics, investment selection, and market timing. Separate sections are devoted to each of these topic areas. In each section rules are explored that may, in particular circumstances, help the investor add to his or her return. None of these rules works every time. None should be expected to produce miracles. On the other hand, each is designed to help in particular situations, hopefully adding a few basis points to your average returns. Every little bit of higher return can make a significant difference via the impact of compounding. Remember, *investing is a game of inches.*

While each of the rules discussed here is designed to be helpful, they are by no means of equal value. Without going into detail, I shall now remind the reader of what we covered by listing some of what I consider to be the more important rules.

IMPORTANT RULES

Do not invest in:

1. *Something you do not understand*
2. *Anything that offers returns that seem too good to be true*
3. *A stock or other security based on a hot tip or nonpublic information*
4. *Collectibles or intangibles, unless you really understand what you are doing*
5. *Futures contracts, unless you are an expert in the area*
6. *Potential takeover candidates, unless you like the asset on its own merits*
7. *The stocks of IPOs in the immediate aftermarket (just after they have gone public)*
8. *The stocks of bankrupt firms (prefer their bonds)*
9. *The stocks of firms that engage in reverse splits*
10. *The stocks of firms whose managers are fighting with short sellers*

Do not invest in the following types of (mutual, closed-end, hedge) funds:

1. *Closed-end funds at their new issue price*
2. *Funds of funds*
3. *Load funds*
4. *Actively managed funds, unless you have a good reason to believe that the manager has superior ability*
5. *Limited partnership tax shelters*

Do not rely upon:

1. *Any investment recommendation based on technical analysis*
2. *Any investment recommendation based on the write-up of an investment analyst*
3. *The January indicator's signals*
4. *Backtested rules that were tested on only one data set*

Do not:

1. Let any single asset, especially the stock of your employer, account for more than 10 percent of your portfolio
2. Sell short, without hedging your positions
3. Write naked options, without the protection of a hedge
4. Let tax considerations override sound investment decisions
5. Hire a personal investment manager, unless you have a very large portfolio

Do invest in:

1. Index funds, especially those with low expense ratios
2. Interval funds, but only if you like the fund on its own merits
3. Takeover candidates, but only if you like the company on its own merits
4. Stocks with high dividend rates that qualify for the 15 percent tax rate, if they are otherwise attractive
5. Agencies rather than treasuries
6. Real estate by buying your own home, but only if you can afford it and plan to live there for at least several years
7. No-load and closed-end funds that you like on their merits
8. The bonds of bankrupt companies, if your analysis indicates they are undervalued

Do:

1. Have patience and allow the power of compound interest to work for you
2. Take an eclectic approach to investing
3. Construct your own homemade diversified fund of funds
4. Diversify internationally
5. Tender closed-end funds or other assets when you can do so above the market price (replace)
6. Take maximum advantage of tax shelters such as IRAs
7. Use options as a vehicle both to buy and sell securities and to manage tax losses
8. Use margin borrowing as a source of low-cost credit, but do so with care
9. Use limit orders to buy and sell securities
10. Take account of the impact of taxes on the returns that you earn; invest accordingly
11. Put off or reduce tax liabilities when you can do so advantageously by, for example, the use of versus purchase orders and options
12. Concentrate high-tax-liability investment income in retirement accounts and lower-tax-liability assets in your nonretirement account
13. Use an internet or discount broker to minimize trading costs
14. Obtain a full quote, including "size," before you enter an order to buy or sell
15. Take tax losses before December selling pressure begins
16. Participate in dividend investment plans, but only if you want to own more of the stock

Glossary

abnormal rate of return: The amount by which an asset's return departs from its expected rate of return where that expected return is based on the market's rate of return and the security's relationship to the market.

absolute priority of claims principle: The general rule in bankruptcy law that requires each class of liability claims to be repaid in full before the next highest priority category can receive even a partial payment.

accelerated depreciation: The writing off the recorded balance sheet values of assets at a more rapid rate than proportional to their pro rata life expectancy. See straight line depreciation.

acceptance: See banker's acceptance.

accrued interest: The amount of the pro rata interest obligation on a bond or other debt instrument that has accumulated since the last (typically semiannual) payment date. Most bonds trade at a price that reflects their net market price plus accrued interest. Defaulted and certain other bonds, however, trade "flat" (which see).

acid test ratio: Cash and accounts receivable divided by current liabilities; used as an index of short-term liquidity. Also called the quick ratio.

actuarial tables: Data tables containing statistics on the probabilities of death for members of a particular age group; based on past experience, with separate tables for men and women and certain hazardous occupations. An actuarial table might indicate that at age 25 a male would have 1 chance in 750 of dying within the next year and is expected to live 50 more years (to age 75). A 65-year-old male's chance of dying in the next year might be reported as 1 in 50 and his future life expectancy as 16 years (to age 81).

adequate protection: Not specifically defined in the Bankruptcy Code. Generally refers to the concept of protecting a creditor's interest in property owned by the debtor. Several nonexclusive methods for providing adequate protection for creditors are specified, including periodic cash payments to a lien creditor equal to a decrease in the value of the creditor's interest in the collateral. Another example would be an additional lien or substitute lien on other property to protect against a decline in value. An additional concept would be to provide a secured creditor with the "indubitable equivalent" of its bargain with the debtor.

adjusted gross income (AGI): An interim figure that is reached on the way to computing a taxpayer's tax liability; consists of total income less allowed adjustments, which include such items as moving expenses, IRA and Keogh contributions, alimony payments, and employee business expenses (above a defined threshold). Taxable income is obtained by subtracting deductions and the allowance for exemptions from adjusted gross income. See taxable income.

administrative priority: A claim incurred after a company has filed for bankruptcy. The claim must be paid before prepetition unsecured claims holders receive a distribution.

ADR (American depository receipt): A U.S.-traded security representing ownership of stock in a foreign corporation.

adviser's sentiment index: A technical market indicator based on a composite of investment advisers' forecasts; index users believe that bullish (bearish) advisers' sentiment forecasts a market decline (rise).

affiliate: An entity that directly or indirectly owns control or holds power to vote 20 percent or more of the debtor or an entity that operates the business or substantially all of the property of the debtor under a lease agreement.

after-tax cash flow: The difference in the actual cash income and outgo for an investment project after taking account of (subtracting) the tax impact.

after-tax return: The rate of return an investor receives on an investment after adjusting for its associated tax liability. Thus, for example, a fully taxable 10 percent return corresponds to a 7.5 percent after-tax return for one in the 25 percent marginal tax bracket.

agency security: A debt security issued by a U.S. federal government agency such as GNMA. Such securities may or may not be backed by the full faith and credit of the U.S. Treasury.

agent: A person who acts on behalf of one or more of the principals involved. The agent may, for example, be an investment banker or an attorney representing the debtor or one of its creditors.

air rights: The right to build and occupy a structure over someone else's property as, for example, the right to build an office complex above a downtown railroad switching yard.

all-or-nothing order: An order to purchase or sell securities that must either be immediately executed in its entirety or, if that is not possible, not at all.

allowed claim: A claim that has been both (1) timely filed (see "Bar Date") and (2) agreed to in amount by the debtor and the creditor. If such a claim has not been agreed to, it is referred to as "disputed." See "disputed claim."

alpha: The intercept term in the market model; provides an estimate of a security's return for market return of zero.

alternative minimum tax (AMT): A special tax liability computation that may be applicable to those with large amounts of otherwise sheltered income (preferences) such as accelerated depreciation deductions; applies when the AMT tax liability computed (after disallowing these preferences) exceeds the liability when the tax is computed the normal way.

amalgamation: A merger-like transaction combining more than two firms into a single company.

American Association of Individual Investors (AAII): Organization designed to help and promote the interests of small investors.

American option: An option contract (put or call) that can be exercised at any time over its life up until it expires. See European option

American Stock Exchange index: A value-weighted index of AMEX stocks.

Americus Trust certificate: A type of security that divides the ownership of certain stocks into two categories of instruments: the primes receive dividends and are entitled to a liquidation value equal to the price of the stock at termination or a predetermined value, whichever is lower; the scores are entitled to the remaining termination values (if any).

AMEX (American Stock Exchange): The second-largest (in terms of primary security listings) U.S. stock exchange (after NYSE); occasionally abbreviated as ASE; listed firms tend to be of medium size compared with the larger NYSE issues and the typically smaller OTC issues. AMEX lists a disproportionate number of energy stocks.

amortization: The process of periodically writing down (for accounting purposes) an asset's or liability's stated book value, particularly a paper asset or liability.

annual percentage rate (APR): The yield to maturity on a fixed-income investment or the interest rate charged on a loan; computed using a compounding factor reflecting the balance still due.

annual report: A yearly report to shareholders containing financial statements (balance sheet, income statement, changes in financial position statement, and funds statement), auditor's statement, president's letter, and various other information about the firm.

annuitant: One who holds an annuity. See annuity.

annuity: An investment-like asset that provides a payment stream to its owner. The annuity usually promises to pay a fixed amount periodically for a predetermined period, although some pay a sum for an individual's lifetime (life annuity); certain annuities' values are variable: thereby depending upon the issuer's investment experience. Most annuities are sold by insurance companies.

anomalies: Security price relationships that appear to be inconsistent with the efficient market hypothesis. Examples include the January effect, size effect, Value Line enigma, and so on.

antidilution clause: A provision in a convertible bond or other security's indenture restricting the issuance of new shares.

anxious trader effects: Short-run price distortions caused by sales or purchases of impatient large traders.

appreciation: Increases in the value of an asset over time.

appreciation mortgage: A mortgage in which the lender is assigned the rights to a percentage of any price appreciation that is realized when the property is sold. In exchange for giving up part of this profit potential, the borrower usually is charged a more attractive interest rate (lower) than that charged on a standard loan.

arbitrage (pure): Simultaneously buying in one market and selling equivalent assets in another for a certain but usually modest profit. See also risk arbitrage.

arbitrage pricing theory (APT): A competitor to the capital asset pricing model that introduces more than one index in place of (or in addition to) CAPM's market index. See CAPM.

arithmetic mean return: The simple average return found by dividing the sum of the separate per-period returns by the number of periods over which they were earned. See geometric mean return.

ARM (adjustable rate mortgage): A type of mortgage in which the interest rate charged by the mortgage holder is periodically adjusted as market interest rates change.

arrearage: An overdue payment, as in passed preferred dividends; if the dividends on the senior security are cumulative, arrearage must be made up before common dividends are allowed to be resumed.

ask: The lowest price at which a security is currently offered for sale; may emanate from a specialist (exchange), market maker (OTC), or unexercised limit order.

asset: Any item of value; often income-producing; appears on the left side of the balance sheet.

asset allocation: A compromise or more balanced approach to market timing (as compared to pure market timing). The asset allocator divides his or her portfolio among a number of categories such as stocks, bonds, and cash. The percentage of the portfolio invested in each of these categories is varied depending upon whether the asset allocator's outlook is positive or negative.

asset class: Securities that have similar characteristics. Examples include stocks, bonds, options, futures, and the like.

asset divestiture: Disposition of an asset by a company. Frequently companies will divest an asset that is not performing well, not vital to the company's core business, worth more either to a potential buyer or as a separate entity than as part of the company, or in order to raise cash to fund continuing operations.

asset play: A firm whose underlying net assets are worth substantially more (after deducting the firm's liabilities) than the market value of its stock.

assets under management (AUM): The total market value of the assets managed by an investment manager.

at-the-close order: An order that must be executed at or near the time of that day's close.

at-the-money: An option for which the exercise price and the market price of the underlying asset are identical.

at-the-opening order: An order that must be executed at that day's market opening.

auditor's statement: A letter from the auditor to the company and its shareholders in which the accounting firm certifies the propriety of the methods (GAAP) used to produce the firm's financial statements. See GAAP.

automatic stay: When a company files for bankruptcy protection, the code automatically provides a stay against secured creditors seeking to foreclose on assets or otherwise enforce their liens. Such a stay is integral to the debtor's rehabilitation process. It may be lifted only through a judicial process, after the creditor has shown it would otherwise suffer damage.

average tax rate: A taxpayer's total tax liability divided by his or her total income.

avoidance: The debtor in a bankruptcy proceeding has the ability to set aside, or "avoid," certain transactions. If, for example, a transaction of questionable merit involving insiders had occurred just prior to the company's filing for bankruptcy, the court might avoid (reverse) the transaction and force rescission.

backwardated: A set of futures market prices in which the current contract price is less than the current spot price for the underlying asset. Thus the cost of carry is negative. See cost of carry.

backtesting: Simulating a proposed investment strategy on historical data in order to determine if it would have been profitable to employ in the past. Successful backtesting does not necessarily prove that the tested rule will work (be profitable) in the future; past experience may not reflect the future market environment.

balance of payments: The difference between a country's international payments and its international receipts.

balance of trade: The difference between a country's expenditures on imports and its revenues from exports.

balance sheet: A financial statement providing an instant-in-time picture of a firm's or individual's financial position; lists assets, liabilities, and net worth as of the date of the statement.

balanced fund: A mutual fund that holds both stocks and bonds in its portfolio; may own both common and preferred shares as well as bonds.

balloon payment: A final large principal payment on a debt instrument whose interim payments either incompletely amortized or did not amortize the initial principal at all.

banker's acceptance: A money market instrument that usually arises from international trade; made highly secure by a bank's guarantee or acceptance. Also called acceptance.

Bankruptcy Code: The body of laws (as modified by court interpretations) that governs bankruptcy proceedings for businesses, individuals, and government entities. The relevant sections for most corporations are Chapter 11 (governing reorganizations) and Chapter 7 (governing liquidations).

bankruptcy proceeding: A legal process under Title 11 of the United States Code for dealing formally with an entity seeking protection from creditors; may result in a liquidation (Chapter 7) or reorganization (Chapter 11).

bankruptcy remote vehicle: Secure creditors are frequently unable to collect on amounts due from a bankrupt debtor. See "automatic stay." In response, attorneys and investment bankers have devised structures that seek to get around the bankruptcy laws. For example, a company could sell receivables to a newly formed subsidiary. This subsidiary could then borrow money secured by the receivables. The proceeds could be upstreamed to the parent. If the parent seeks bankruptcy protection at a later date, the secured creditors lending to the newly formed subsidiary would expect that their legal rights to the receivables would be unaffected by the parent's bankruptcy—hence "bankruptcy remote."

bankruptcy trustee: Generally, a representative of the estate. The filing of a bankruptcy petition leads to the creation of an estate consisting of all of the property of the debtor at the time of the bankruptcy filing that is not exempt. This estate is a separate legal entity, and the trustee is the representative of this entity.

bar chart: In technical analysis, a type of graph that contains plots of the price over time; typically contains data on the high, low, and closing prices as well as the volume of trading.

bar date: To assert a claim in a bankruptcy, creditors must file a proof of claim before a deadline set by the court—the "bar date." Claims asserted after the bar date are automatically disqualified (unless allowed by the court as late claims).

Barron's: A major weekly investment periodical published by Dow Jones Inc.

Barron's **Confidence Index:** A technical market indicator series based on the yield differential between high-grade and average-grade corporate bonds, with a small differential signifying confidence in the future and a large differential signaling a lack of confidence.

basis (commodity): The difference between the spot price and the futures price of the asset underlying a futures contract.

basis (taxable): The acquisition cost of an asset as adjusted for any capital distributions, depreciation, or amortization, for example. The taxable gain equals the difference between the basis and the sale proceeds.

basis point: A unit of measurement equal to one-hundredth of one percentage point; primarily used with interest rates.

basis risk: The risk that the basis of a commodity contract will move adversely.

bear: One who expects a declining market.

bear market: A declining market.

bear raid: An attempt (often by a group of short sellers) to drive prices down by selling short.

bearer bond: An unregistered bond whose ownership is determined by possession of the bond certificate

before-tax return: The gross return on an investment prior to any adjustment being made for the impact of income taxes.

behavioral finance: The analysis of various psychological traits of investors or managers of businesses and how these traits affect how they act.

benchmark error: An error that results from using an inappropriate or incorrect benchmark to compare and assess portfolio returns.

benchmark portfolio: A comparison standard of risk and assets referenced in the policy statement and similar to the investor's risk preference and investment needs; can be used to evaluate the investment performance of the portfolio manager.

benefactor: A person named to receive property or other resources, as in a will or insurance policy.

Bernhard, (Arnold) and Company: The firm that owns over 80 percent of the stock of the investment periodical *Value Line*. See *Value Line*.

best interest of creditors test: Bankruptcy Code rule which requires that any departure from absolute priority be such that all creditors still receive a distribution that is worth at least as much as they would have received in a liquidation.

beta: A parameter that relates stock performance to market performance; for a z percent change in the market, a stock's price will tend to change by (beta) z percent.

bid: The highest currently unexercised offer to buy a security; may emanate from a specialist (exchange), market-maker (OTC), or limit order. See ask.

Big Board: A popular term for the New York Stock Exchange, the largest U.S. stock exchange.

bills: Government debt securities issued on a discount basis by the U.S. Treasury for periods of less than one year.

Billy Martin indicator: A whimsical technical market indicator that hypothesized that anytime the New York Yankees name Billy Martin to be their manager, the stock market would decline. Inoperative since the death of Mr. Martin.

binomial option pricing model: An option valuation equation based on the assumption that the price of the underlying asset changes through a series of discrete upward or downward movements.

black knight: A potential acquirer who is opposed by existing management and to which management would prefer to find an alternative (i.e., a white knight).

Black/Scholes formula: An option pricing formula based on the assumption that a riskless hedge between an option and its underlying stock should yield a riskless return; thus an option's value is a function of the stock price, striking price, stock return volatility, riskless interest rate, and length to expiration.

blind pool offerings: Bonds issued, the proceeds of which are to be used for some as-yet-to-be-stated purpose.

block trade: A stock trade involving 10,000 or more shares; the transaction is usually handled by a block trader.

block trader: One who, for a fee, assembles the passive side of a block trade in order to facilitate the transaction for the active side.

Bloody Monday: October 19, 1987, when the stock market experienced its worst one-day decline in its history; the Dow Jones Industrial Average dropped by 508 points, which corresponded to a 23 percent decline.

blue chip stock: Shares of a large, mature company with a steady record of profits and dividends and a high probability of continued healthy earnings.

blue sky laws: State laws designed to protect investors from securities frauds.

Blume adjustment: A method for adjusting estimated betas toward unity in an effort to improve their general accuracy and reliability.

boiler room operations: High-pressure selling programs often associated with investment scams such as Ponzi schemes; characterized by aggressive sales forces utilizing banks of telephones and cold-callers in order to extract "investments" from unsophisticated individuals for risky and often worthless ventures. See Ponzi schemes.

bond: A debt obligation (usually long-term) in which the borrower promises to pay an almost always fixed (not variable) coupon rate until the issue matures, at which time the principal is to be repaid; sometimes secured by a mortgage on a specific property, plant, or piece of equipment. See also debenture, collateral trust bond, equipment trust certificate, zero coupon bond, variable rate note.

bond rating: An estimated index of the bond's investment quality and default risk. See Moody's, Standard & Poor, Fitch.

bond swap: A procedure in the managing of a bond portfolio that involves selling some bonds and using the proceeds to buy others; may be designed to achieve benefits in the form of taxes, yields, maturity structure, or trading profits.

book value (of common shares): The total accounting value of the assets of an enterprise minus its liabilities, minority interests, and the par value of any preferred stock, divided by the number of outstanding common shares.

borrower life insurance: An insurance policy on the borrower's life having coverage equal to the outstanding loan principal and naming the lender as the beneficiary.

Boston Consulting Group (BCG): A strategic planning consulting firm famous for its growth-share matrix (BCG matrix) and learning curve concepts.

bottom up approach: An approach to fundamental analysis that begins with the individual investments (e.g., the firm and its stock) and then examines the relevant environment (economy).

box spread: A type of option position in which the investor assembles a vertical spread with calls and a similar but offsetting vertical spread with puts.

Brady Commission: One of a number of commissions that studied the causes for the stock market crash of October 19, 1987; set up by the U.S. Congress and named after Nicholas Brady, former New Jersey senator.

breakeven: The period of time required for an investor to recoup the amount of the conversion premium from the coupon income on a convertible instrument.

breakup fee: A penalty payment that one side to a negotiated merger agreement must pay to the other side in order to voluntarily exit from the deal.

breakup value: The sum of the values of a company's individual assets, if sold separately.

broker: An employee of a financial intermediary who acts as an agent in the buying and selling of securities (or other types of assets). A broker, unlike a dealer, never owns the securities that he or she trades for his or her customers.

broker call-loan rate: The interest rate charged by banks to brokers for the loans that brokerage firms utilize in order to fund their margin loans to their own customers.

brokerage firm: A firm that offers various services such as access to the securities markets, account management, margin loans, investment advice, and underwriting.

bull: One who expects a rising (usually stock) market.

bull market: A rising market.

bullion: Gold, silver, or other precious metals in the form of bars, plates, or certain coins minted to contain a specific unit of weight (bullion coins).

burn rate: The rate at which a firm with negative cash flow is using up its available cash.

business cycle: The pattern of fluctuations in the level of economic activity.

Business Week: A popular business periodical published weekly by McGraw-Hill Inc.

business risk: The variability of operating income arising from the characteristics of the firm's industry. Sources include sales variability and operating leverage.

butterfly spread: A type of option spread in which two call contracts are sold at one striking price and one call contract each is purchased at striking prices above and below the striking price for the contracts that were sold; or a similar configurations with puts.

buying power: The dollar value of additional marginable securities that can be purchased with the current equity in the customer's account.

buy-and-hold strategy: A portfolio management strategy in which securities are bought and held until maturity if bonds, or held for a lengthy period of time if stocks or other assets.

call: An option contract to buy stock or some other asset at a prespecified price over a prespecified time period. The standard contract size for a call is 100 shares.

call-loan rate: See broker call-loan rate.

call market: A market for individual stocks in which trading takes place only at specific times. All of the available offers to buy and sell are assembled. The market administrators can then specify a single price designed to clear the market at that time.

call premium: The amount in addition to a bond's face value that the issuer must pay to bondholders in order to retire a callable bond prior to its stated maturity.

call price: The price at which a bond, preferred stock, warrant, or other security may be redeemed by the issuer prior to its maturity; the call price usually begins at a significant premium over the face value; the premium then declines as the instrument approaches its stated maturity. Also called the redemption price.

call protection: An indenture provision preventing a security (usually a bond or preferred stock) from being redeemed earlier than a certain time period after its issue; for example, a twenty-year bond might not be callable for the first five years.

call right: A feature in the indenture of a bond or preferred stock. An option that allows the issuing company to repurchase the securities at a set price over a prespecified period (prior to maturity).

call risk: The danger to the holder of a callable bond or preferred stock that the security will be redeemed early (called) by the issuer.

callable: The characteristic of certain securities that allows the issuer to redeem them prior to maturity. See call right.

cap agreement: A contract that, on each prespecified settlement date, pays the holder the greater of zero or the difference between the reference (interest) rate and the cap rate.

capacity effect: The tendency of inflationary pressures to accelerate when the economy approaches the full employment level.

capital asset: Virtually any asset held as an investment. To qualify as a capital asset (and thus be subject to the advantages, if any, of long-term capital gains treatment), an asset must be held as an investment rather than in inventory as an item of trade.

Capital Asset Pricing Model (CAPM): A theoretical relationship that is designed to explain returns as a function of the risk-free rate, market risk, and the return on the market portfolio.

capital distribution: A dividend paid out of the firm's capital rather than from its earnings. Such distributions are not taxable when received, but do have the effect of reducing the investment's basis.

capital gains (losses): The difference between the basis of an investment asset and its sales price.

capital market line: The theoretical relation between an efficiently diversified portfolio's expected return and risk derived from the capital asset pricing model.

capital preservation: An investment objective in which the investor seeks to limit the risk of loss even at the sacrifice of some upside potential.

capital structure: The composition of the ways in which a firm has obtained the capital needed for its business activities (short-term debt, long-term debt, common equity, and preferred equity).

capitalizing of expenses: Placing on the business's balance sheet as assets sums expended for current business expenses. Such "asset" values can then be written off over time rather than expensed all at once, thereby spreading out their cost impact for accounting purposes.

carry: The cost of holding and maintaining a physical commodity until it becomes deliverable under the terms of a futures contract; the primary components of the carry are storage and financing costs. Also called cost of carry.

cash cow: A company subsidiary or division of a company that, in the normal course of its operations, throws off a substantial cash surplus.

cash flow: Reported profits plus the sum of the noncash expenses of depreciation, depletion, and amortization.

cash flow bond: A debt instrument that pays greater coupon amounts if the reorganized company produces better earnings.

cash management account: An individual financial account that combines checking, credit card, money fund, and margin accounts. Funds and liabilities are swept from account to account in order to maximize returns and minimize interest charges on transaction balances.

cash market: A market in which physical commodities (spot) are bought and sold for immediate (as opposed to future) delivery.

cash surrender value: The accumulated savings element of a life insurance policy. Under the terms of the policy, this cash value can be recovered by canceling the policy. The policy's cash value can also be borrowed against at an interest rate specified in the policy's contract.

cause of action: A fact pattern that gives rise to the owner of the cause of action the right to file a lawsuit.

CBOE (Chicago Board Options Exchange): The largest of the option exchanges; originator and promoter of organized options trading.

CBT (Chicago Board of Trade): The largest of the commodity exchanges; lists futures contracts on a variety of physicals including wheat, corn, oats, soybeans, plywood, silver, stock indexes, GNMA, and long-term bonds.

CD (certificate of deposit): Special redeemable debt obligation issued by a bank or other depository institution.

CEA (Commodity Exchange Authority): A former government agency that once had regulatory authority over agricultural futures markets; now regulated by the CFTC.

Central Certificate Service: An organization that allows clearing firms to effect security deliveries with computerized bookkeeping entries.

central market: A congressionally mandated concept for a complete linkup of the various markets in which securities are traded; the development was under way but incomplete as of 2006.

central unemployment rate: The unemployment rate for males in the 25 to 45 age group or the unemployment rate for some similar high-employment component of the labor force.

CFTC (Commodity Futures Trading Commission): The federal agency that regulates the futures markets.

changes in financial position statement: An accounting statement that contains reports on a firm's cash inflows and outflows. Formerly called source and application of funds statement.

Chapter 7 bankruptcy: Provides for a liquidation of a debtor under the Bankruptcy Code.

Chapter 11 reorganization: Contemplates a rehabilitation and restructuring of a debtor under the Bankruptcy Code.

Chapter 22: A term for companies that return to the bankruptcy court once they fail after being reorganized the first time.

characteristic line: The relationship between a security's expected return and the market return; defined by the security's α (intercept) and β (slope parameter).

chart-reading: A method for attempting to forecast stock price changes using charts of past price and volume data.

Chicago Mercantile Exchange (the Merc): Second-largest of the U.S. commodity exchanges; lists futures contracts on a variety of physicals including cattle, hogs, pork bellies, fresh broilers, lumber, stock indexes, currencies, and debt securities.

chicken (strategy): A negotiation tactic where one negotiator takes and aggressive and potentially self-destructive position and waits for the other side to blink first.

churning: Overactive trading of customer accounts designed to generate commissions for the manager/broker without necessarily benefiting the customer.

circuit breakers: A procedure calling for the suspending of trading when a market move reaches a prescribed threshold; for example, stock trading might be halted for thirty minutes whenever the DJIA moved 150 points during a single day.

claim: A right to seek payment.

classified common stock: Different categories of common stock, some of which may be nonvoting and others non–dividend receiving.

clearinghouse: An organization that keeps track of and guarantees fulfillment of futures contracts or options contracts.

Clifford Trust: A device for shifting tax liability on income, usually from parent to dependent child; trusts set up since the Tax Reform Act of 1986 do not achieve the desired tax-shifting goal.

CLOB (consolidated limit order book): A composite book of limit orders that could be executed in any market where a security is traded; a feature of the proposed central market. See central market.

closed-end fund: A type of investment company that is organized as a public corporation with its stock traded in the same markets as other stocks; its market price may vary appreciably from the fund's net asset value.

closing costs: Costs associated with obtaining a real estate loan and completing the purchase; may include the costs of a title search, points, transfer taxes, and various other fees.

Coffee, Sugar and Cocoa Exchange: A commodity exchange located in New York City that lists futures contracts for coffee, sugar, and cocoa.

coincident indicators: A set of economic variables whose values tend to reach peaks and troughs at about the same time as the aggregate economy.

cold call: An unsolicited call (by phone or in person) by someone who is trying to sell something to a targeted individual who may very well have no interest in even hearing the seller's pitch.

collar merger offer: A takeover offer in which the consideration is in the form of stock in a ratio to be determined by the average price of the acquiescent shares shortly before the transaction closes.

collateral: Asset pledged by the borrower to assure repayment of debt to the lender; the lender may take ownership of the collateral (foreclose) if the loan is not repaid as promised.

collateral trust bond: A secured bond; for example, an equipment trust certificate secured by such collateral as railroad rolling stock or airplanes.

Collateralized Mortgage Obligation (CMO): A debt security based on a pool of mortgages that provides a relatively stable stream of payments for a relatively predictable term.

combination security: An asset combining characteristics of more than one type of security; includes convertible bonds, convertible preferred stocks, hybrid convertibles, equity notes, commodity-backed bonds, and stock-indexed bonds.

commercial paper: Short-term, usually low-risk debt instruments issued by large corporations with very strong credit ratings.

commingled real estate fund (CREF): In effect a self-liquidating unit investment trust with a managed portfolio of real estate.

commissions: Fees charged by brokers for handling investment transactions such as those involving the buying and selling of securities or real estate.

commodity: In general, any article of commerce; in investments, any of a select group of items traded on one of the commodity futures exchanges either spot (for immediate delivery) or in the futures market (for delivery at a prespecified future date).

commodity board: An electronic sign in the trading room of a commodity exchange that displays current market statistics.

commodity option: A put or call option to purchase or sell a futures contract.

common stock: Security that represents proportional ownership of an incorporated enterprise; common stockholders are the residual claimants for earnings and assets once all creditors and holders of preferred stock have received their contractual payments.

company analysis: Evaluating the strengths and weaknesses of a firm and its investment appeal vis-à-vis its markets and competitors. Also called firm analysis. Step three of the three-step-top-down-approach of fundamental analysis. See three-step top-down approach.

competitive bid: An underwriting alternative wherein an issuing entity specifies the type of security to be offered and characteristics of the issue. The issuer solicits bids from competing investment banking firms. The issuer agrees to accept the highest bid from the bankers.

completeness fund: A specialized index used to form the basis of a passive portfolio. Its purpose is to provide diversification to a client's total portfolio by excluding (including) those segments in which the client's active managers (do not) invest.

composition of creditors: Contract between a debtor and two or more creditors in which the creditors consent to take a specified partial payment in full satisfaction of their claims. This arrangement is generally arrived at outside of bankruptcy law and is frequently referred to as a "formal workout."

compound interest: Interest earned on prior interest payments as in a result of reinvesting one period's income to earn additional income in the following period. For example, $100 earning 9 percent compounded annually will yield a payment of $9 the first year. The investor will therefore start the second year with $109. The 9 percent yield will be applied to $109 for a return of $9.81 in year two. In the third year the principal will have grown to $118.81 ($100 + 9 + 9.81$), and another 9 percent yield applied for that sum will earn about $10.62. This process continues, with the interest rate being applied to a larger and larger principal.

compound value: The end-period value of a sum earning a compounded return.

COMPUSTAT Data Tape: A data source containing balance sheet, income statement, and other financial information on a substantial number of companies for the most recent twenty years.

concentrated position: A margined portfolio having a disproportionate amount of its value represented by one or a few securities; such a concentrated position account may be assigned a higher margin maintenance percentage than that set by brokerage firms for more diversified accounts.

conditional forecast: A prediction based upon some exogenous factor such as a stock performance forecast relative to market performance.

Conference Board: An organization that compiles quarterly capital appropriations statistics and reports them in *Manufacturing Industrial Statistics.*

confirmation: To be consummated, a plan of reorganization must be "confirmed" by the bankruptcy court. The confirmation hearing occurs after the voting process has been completed. The court must determine that the claims and interests have been appropriately classified, that the voting process met certain technical requirements, and that the requisite number of claims (by both dollar amount and number of creditors voting) and interests (by number of shares voting) approved the plan. The courts must also find that the plan is "feasible" that creditors receive more than they would under a hypothetical Chapter 7 liquidation, and that no creditor receives value for more than 100 percent of its claims.

conflicts of interest: The company's former advisers and principals may have their own selfish agendas, such as limiting any liability they may have for the organization's demise. Moreover, certain professionals and other participants in the case may have relationships with other entities also in the case. These agendas and relationships can cause an individual or firm to have conflicted loyalties to the debtor and its best interests. To deal with these "conflicts of interest," the participants in the case must disclose their conflicts. The court then determines whether a firm or individual may continue to be engaged in the case.

conglomerate: A company with a diversified portfolio of business units; particularly one formed through a merger of a diverse array of formerly independent companies.

consideration: The payment made in exchange for an asset, claim, or interest. Such a payment may be in the form of cash, debt, stock, or other form of currency.

consol: A perpetual debt instrument that pays a set coupon each period but never matures and thus never returns the original borrowed principal.

consumer credit: Personal debt as represented by credit card loans, finance company loans, or similar debts.

consumer durables: Long-life consumer assets such as furniture or appliances.

Consumer Price Index (CPI): A monthly cost-of-living index prepared by the Bureau of Labor Statistics, U.S. Department of Labor. One of the primary indexes used to measure the rate of inflation.

Consumer Reports: A periodical that (among other things) frequently contains personal finance oriented articles.

consumption expenditures: Spending by individual consumers on final goods and services.

contango: A price structure in the futures market in which the later delivery futures contract price is greater than the underlying asset's current spot price.

contingent deferred sales load: A mutual fund that imposes a sales charge when the investor sells or redeems shares. Also referred to as *redemption charges.*

contingent liability: A potential claim against a company or other entity; for example, an unresolved lawsuit seeking to recover damages would represent a contingent claim against the defendant.

contrarian: An investor who attempts to buy (sell) securities on which the majority of other investors are bearish (bullish).

contrary opinion: An investment approach that concentrates on out-of-favor securities; contrarians assert that what is not wanted today may be quite desirable in the future. The approach is similar to buying Christmas ornaments in January.

convenience yield: An adjustment to the theoretical forward or futures contract delivery price that reflects the preferences that consumers have for holding spot positions in the underlying asset.

conversion: A complicated set of security market transactions in related assets. Specifically, a conversion involves purchasing options, shorting the underlying stock, and reinvesting the sale proceeds; a technique used by brokerage firms that is designed to earn substantial returns when option and stock prices are not in line with their theoretical relationship.

conversion premium: The amount by which the price of a convertible (bond or preferred) exceeds the corresponding market price of the package of underlying instruments into which it is convertible.

conversion price: The face value of a convertible bond divided by the number of shares into which it is convertible.

conversion ratio: The number of common shares into which a convertible bond or preferred stock may be converted.

conversion value: The market price of the underlying stock referenced in a convertible bond or convertible preferred stock times the number of shares for which the convertible may be exchanged. In other words, the value of the stock embedded in the convertible security.

convertible: A bond or preferred stock that may be exchanged for a specific number of common shares.

convertible debenture: A debenture bond that may, for the bond's life, be exchanged for a specific number of shares of the issuing firm's common stock.

convertible preferred: A preferred stock that may be exchanged for a specific number of shares of the issuing company's common stock.

convexity: The degree to which a bond's price-yield relationship departs from a straight line. The characteristic reflects a bond's price variability for a given change in yields.

corner: The act of acquiring a large, often controlling, interest in a security issue or other specific type of asset that restricts supply and thereby pushes the market price to a very high level; corners can be especially damaging to short sellers who may need to cover their short positions at very disadvantageous prices. Corners are generally illegal.

corporate bond fund: A mutual fund holding a diversified portfolio of corporate bonds.

corporates: Corporate bonds; bonds issued by incorporated enterprises.

correlation coefficient: A measure of the comovement tendency of two variables, such as the returns of two securities. See covariance.

cost of carry: The cost of holding an asset in inventory; including financing, storage, and insurance costs.

counterparty: A participant (buyer or seller) in a derivative transaction.

country fund: A type of mutual fund that assembles and manages a portfolio of securities that were issued by enterprises located in a single country, such as the Japan Fund or the Mexico Fund.

country risk: Uncertainty of future investment values due to the possibility of major political or economic change in the country or region where an investment is located. Also called *political risk*.

coupon: The sum of money paid on a fixed-income instrument as interest or preferred dividends. The coupon is generally stated as an annual rate (i.e., 10%). It may be payable annually, semiannually, quarterly, or otherwise.

coupon bond: A bond with attached coupons that the owner must periodically clip and send to the issuer in order to receive the scheduled interest payments.

coupon clipping: Claiming income on coupon bonds by detaching each physical coupon and presenting it to the issuer for payment when due.

coupon effect: The price impact of differential yield components derived from coupon versus price appreciation as a bond moves toward maturity. Thus a deep-discount, low-coupon bond will offer a yield to maturity that includes a substantial component of tax-deferred capital gains; such a bond's price will usually be affected favorably by the coupon effect.

coupon-equivalent yield: Yield calculation for an investment that provides a discount yield (e.g., a T-bill) computed to correspond with (make it comparable to) a bond that pays a semiannual coupon.

coupon rate: The stated dollar return of a fixed-income investment. For example, a coupon rate of 6 percent on a $1,000 bond implies an annual coupon rate of $60.

coupon reinvestment risk: The component of interest rate risk due to the uncertainty regarding the future level of market interest rates at which coupon payments can be reinvested.

covariance: A statistic that reflects the degree of covariablilty of two variables. The covariance of variables x and y is: $Cov = E\{[-E(x)] [y - E(y)]\}$ here $E(z)$ is the expected value of z. If x and y tend to be above their means simultaneously and below their means simultaneously, the covariance is positive. If one is above when the other tends to be below, the covariance is negative. If they are independent, the covariance is zero.

covenants: Legally binding pledges between bond issuers and bondholders contained in indentures.

covered interest arbitrage: Trading strategy involving borrowing money in one country and lending it in another in an effort to exploit deviations from the parity interest rate.

covered writing: Writing options against existing stockholdings. Or writing options against an existing position in other similar but more senior options.

covering: Repurchasing securities or other assets such as options or futures contracts that have been sold short.

crack: Combination future market trade in which the trader buys crude oil futures and sells corresponding amounts of heating oil and gasoline futures. See reverse crack.

cramdown: Acceptance by the bankruptcy court of a reorganization plan when less than every class of creditors votes in favor of the plan. Certain additional requirements exist that must be satisfied, including (a) at least one impaired class of claimants has accepted the plan; (b) the plan does not discriminate unfairly; and (c) the plan is fair and equitable.

Crash of 1987: The largest one-day decline in stock market history; on October 19, 1987, the Dow Jones Industrial Average dropped 508 points, which corresponded to 23 percent of its value as of the previous close.

crawling peg approach: A technique whereby a protective stop loss order is entered on a stock position, and as the stock's price rises, the threshold on the stop loss order is also raised.

credit: In this context "credit" is used as a synonym for "company" or "high-yield issuer."

credit analysis: A type of bond analysis used to facilitate a type of active bond portfolio management strategy that is designed to identify bonds that are expected to experience rating changes (upgrades or downgrades).

credit balance: A positive balance, as in a brokerage account.

credit derivative: A type of option that provides a guarantee against default loss for specified debt investment.

credit union: A cooperative association offering many banking-like services in which the members' pooled savings are made available for loans to the membership.

creditors: Entities that have a debt claim against a debtor.

creditors' committee: An organized group of people that the United States Trustee is instructed to appoint; composed of the largest unsecured creditors willing to serve. This committee consults with the trustee or debtor in possession and investigates the debtor's acts and financial condition as well as participates in the formulation of the plan of reorganization.

Creditwatch: One of several short-term credit analysis services. A bond in danger of being downgraded would be likely to be placed on S&P's Creditwatch list once some degree of trouble is spotted.

CREF: See commingled real estate fund.

CRISPE data tape: A data source containing daily stock price information.

cross-border: A transaction involving entities from various countries.

cross hedge: A set of trading positions in which the price volatility of a commodity or security position is hedged with a forward or futures contract based on a different underlying contract.

crown jewel option: Antitakeover defense in which the most sought-after subsidiary of a target firm is spun off, thereby making its takeover unattractive.

crown loan: An interest-free loan, usually from a parent to dependent child, designed to shift taxable income from a high- to low-bracket individual. The Tax Reform Act of 1986 ended the tax advantage of this type of transaction.

crush: A combination trade involving futures contracts, especially a commodity trade in which soybean futures are bought and corresponding amounts of soybean oil and meal futures are shorted.

cum-rights period: The time prior to the day of record that determines when shareholders receive a rights distribution; securities that sell cum-rights will reflect the imputed value of the rights to be distributed. See ex-rights period.

cumulative preferred: A preferred stock for which any unpaid dividends in arrears are accumulated and must be paid before common dividends can be resumed.

cumulative voting: A method of voting for corporate directors that assigns each shareholder votes equal to the product of the number of shares held times the number of director slots; allows a group of shareholders with a substantial but minority position to concentrate their votes on one or a few candidates and thereby elect their proportional share of directors.

Curb Exchange: The American Stock Exchange, which until 1953 was called the New York Curb Exchange. Relates back to the time when the predecessor to the AMEX was an outdoor trading vehicle.

currency: Any form of money accepted by a country and in actual use within that country as a medium of exchange.

currency swap: An asset or liability swap transaction in which the cash flows, which can be either fixed or variable, are denominated in different currencies.

current assets: Assets that are expected to be converted into cash within the next year or next operating period, whichever is longer; primarily cash, accounts receivable, and inventory.

current income: A return objective in which the investor prefers to generate spendable cash income rather than earn capital gains.

current liabilities: Liabilities that are scheduled to become due and payable in the next year or the next operating cycle, whichever is longer; includes accounts payable, short-term bank loans, the current portion of long-term debt, and taxes payable.

current ratio: The ratio of a company's current assets to its current liabilities; a measure of short-term liquidity.

current yield: A bond's coupon rate divided by its current market price or, in the case of a stock, its indicated dividend rate divided by its current per-share price.

cyclical change: An economic trend arising from the business cycle.

cyclical company: A firm whose earnings tend to rise and fall largely with the general level of economic activity.

day of record: The date on which ownership is determined for deciding to whom to pay that quarter's dividends or for the issuance of some other distributions such as rights.

day order: An order that is canceled at the day's end if it is not executed sometime during the day that it was entered.

day trader: A commodity trader who closes all of his or her positions by the end of each day, thus all day trader transactions are opened and closed on the same day.

dead cat bounce: A small rise in the market following a major decline and followed by a further decline.

dealer: A security trader who acts as a principal rather than as an agent; thus a specialist or a market maker would be a dealer, but a broker would not (brokers are agents).

death benefit: Payment to a beneficiary upon the death of the annuity owner, usually the greater of the annuity value or the payments for the annuity. Also, payment to the beneficiary of a life insurance policy.

death spiral preferred: An instrument issued by a company in financial distress. Such a security may be convertible into the underlying common stock of the issuer at a price fixed at issuance. If however, the price of the company's stock subsequently drops, the conversion price would be reduced in accordance with a formula based on the lower stock price. This security could ultimately be convertible into virtually all of the company's pro formula equity if the stock price fell sufficiently.

debenture: A long-term debt obligation that, unlike a collateralized bond, provides the lender with only a general claim against the borrower's assets. In a default, the debenture holder has no claim against any specific assets.

debit balance: A negative balance (debt) in a margin account.

debt: A liability or a claim.

debt capacity: The maximum debt that can be issued by a firm or secured by a specific asset.

debt-equity ratio: The ratio of total debt to total equity.

debt securities: Bonds and similar securities that call for the payment of interest until maturity and principal at maturity. A firm that defaults on its interest or principal obligations is likely eventually to be forced into bankruptcy, unless it quickly cures the default.

debtor: A person for whom a case under the Bankruptcy Code has been commenced.

debtor in possession (DIP): The party in bankruptcy that is operating the bankrupt estate under the supervision of the court.

decreasing term: A type of term insurance in which the dollar value of protection decreases with the insured's age. Typically, the annual premium payment remains constant.

dedication: An investment management technique in which the dollar value of the portfolio's cash flows are structured so that they can be directly used to retire a set of liabilities over time.

deduction: In a tax computation, an amount that is to be subtracted from the taxpayer's adjusted gross income in order to determine his or her taxable income, if the taxpayer itemizes. Deductions include: state income taxes, charitable contributions, mortgage interest expenses, and certain other expenses.

deep-discount bond: A bond selling for substantially less than its par value.

default: Failure to live up to any of the terms in an agreement, especially a debt contract (indenture).

default risk: The risk that a debt security's contractual interest or principal will not be paid when due.

defeasance: The process whereby a debtor offsets the cash flow impact of a portion of its debt by purchasing high-quality debt instruments (usually governments) whose payments are structured to cover the payment obligations of the debt issue.

defensive recapitalizations: A form of leveraging a company where the majority of historical equity ownership is maintained. Assets are not generally written up to fair market value for balance sheet purposes.

deferred annuity: A contract which provides that the annuitant will not begin receiving income payments until some specified time in the future.

deferred compensation plan: A procedure whereby employees are permitted to set aside and thereby defer the income tax liability on a portion of their wages and salaries. The funds set aside are then paid into qualified investment plans.

defined benefit pension plan: An employee benefit plan in which the company contributes a certain sum each year for the benefit of each employee. That account (pension fund) provides employees with an income after they retire based on factors such as workers' age, salary, and time of employment.

defined contribution pension plan: An employee benefit plan in which worker benefits are determined by the size of employees' contributions to the plan and the returns earned on the fund's investments.

deflation: An increase in the purchasing power of the dollar or some other currency unit; the opposite of inflation.

delisting: The act of removing a security from the list of securities authorized to trade on an exchange.

delta: The change in the price of the option with respect to a one-dollar change in the price of the underlying asset; the hedge ratio; the number of units of the underlying assets that can be hedged by a single option contract.

depletion: The writing off (for accounting statement purposes) of the book valuations of assets as they are exploited, particularly mineral assets such as oil or natural gas.

Depository Trust Company: A financial services firm that facilitates securities trading between exchange members by using bookkeeping entries rather than physically delivering the stock certificates.

depreciation: A sum deducted from a firm's revenues in the process of producing its reported income. Depreciation allocates the acquisition costs of fixed assets over the course of their useful lives for the purpose of computing per-period income.

depression: An economic collapse during which unemployment rises to a high level and economic growth turns very negative.

derivative security: An instrument whose market value depends upon (or is derived from) the value of a more fundamental investment vehicle (the underlying asset). Examples include options and futures contracts.

dilution: Issuing additional shares of a corporation and thereby reducing proportional ownership of existing shareholders.

DIP financing: Funds obtained by a bankrupt debtor. The Bankruptcy Code provides incentives for lenders to provide new capital. These incentives include "super-priority" status. The new DIP loan can be repaid before any other unsecured claim. The DIP financer may even obtain a senior interest in the collateral of the estate.

disability insurance: Insurance protection designed to provide an offset to a potential income loss from a health condition that reduces or ends the insured's ability to earn an income.

discharge: A release from and forgiveness of certain debts of a debtor taking place in a bankruptcy proceeding. Certain debts (e.g., tax liens, environmental liabilities, etc.) are not dischargeable as part of a bankruptcy proceeding. In general, a discharge protects a debtor from any further personal liability on account of the debts that are discharged.

disclosure statement: As part of the reorganization process, the debtor issues a prospectus-like document called the "disclosure statement." It is supposed to contain all material information needed for a claimant or interest-holder to make an intelligent decision whether to support or oppose the plan. The statement must include historical and forecasted financial information, a description of the business, its history and prospects, and a summary of the plan. Prior to its dissemination, the court must find the disclosure in the document to be "adequate."

discount bond: A bond selling at a price below its face value.

discount brokers: Brokers who charge below-retail commission rates and usually offer a more limited set of investment services than do full-service brokerage firms. See Internet brokers.

discount loan: A short-term loan from the Federal Reserve System to a member bank. The loan is extended in order to cure or avoid a temporary reserve deficiency. The Fed emphasizes for the borrowing bank that its access to discount loans is a privilege, not a right to the borrower.

discount rate (for Fed members): The interest rate charged by the Federal Reserve System on discount loans to member banks.

discount rate (for income stream): The interest rate applied to an actual or expected income stream that is used in estimating or calculating its present value. The appropriate discount rate will vary with the level of the expected income stream's risk.

discount yield: A yield computation in which the return is based on the final value of the asset; thus a Treasury bill that sells for 100 minus x and matures in one year for 100 has a discount yield of x percent.

discounted cash flow analysis (DCF): The method of discounting a projected stream of cash flows in order to compute its present worth. Similar to interest operationing in reverse. A method for determining the worth of dollars to be received in the future in terms of their present worth.

disinflation: A slowing in the rate at which prices increase. A slowing down of the inflation rate.

disinterested: The opposite of "conflicted."

disintermediation: The movement of funds out of intermediaries and into direct investments. An example is the tendency of high market interest rates to draw funds out of thrift institutions and therefore away from the mortgage market.

diversifiable risk: Firm-specific or industry-specific risk as opposed to overall market risk; diversifiable risks tend to offset one another and thus average out in an efficiently diversified portfolio.

diversification: A technique used to reduce portfolio risks by assembling an investment portfolio with components spread out over different industries, companies, investment types, and risk levels; used to reduce risk by not having "all of your eggs in one basket."

dividend capture: A strategy in which an investor purchases dividend-paying stocks timed so as to own them on the day of record and then quickly sells them; designed to capture the dividend payment but avoid the risk of a lengthy holding period.

dividend discount model: An approach to stock valuation that is used to evaluate stocks on the basis of the present value of their expected stream of dividends; the basic formula is $P = d/(r - g)$ where: $P =$ stock price, $d =$ next year dividend, $r =$ appropriate discount rate, and $g =$ expected growth rate in the dividend.

dividend exclusion: An amount of qualifying dividends that an individual could at one time have excluded from taxable income. The Tax Reform Act of 1986 ended this exclusion.

dividend reinvestment plan (DRIP): A company program that facilitates the dividend payments to its shareholders being reinvested in additional shares of the dividend-paying company. The shares distributed to the participants are often newly issued by the company and may be sold to the shareholders at a discount from the current market price. Some plans also provide an option for additional share purchases with cash.

dividend restriction: The limitation placed on dividend payments in a bond indenture.

dividends: Payments made by companies to their stockholders out of the company's assets; usually financed from after-tax profits.

divisor: The number that is divided into the sum of the prices of the Dow Jones 30 stocks in order to calculate the value of the Dow Jones Industrial Average. Whenever a DOW component stock is split, the divisor is adjusted to preserve time series consistency.

dollar averaging: A formula-investment-plan requiring periodic (such as monthly) fixed-dollar-amount investments. This practice tends to "average" the unit purchase costs of an investment program made over time. A greater number of units are purchased when asset prices are lower, thereby reducing the average cost per unit.

DOT (designated order transmission): A system on the New York Stock Exchange in which orders are routed electronically to the trading posts where the securities are traded; often used by program traders to effectuate their index arbitrage trades.

Dow: See Dow Jones Industrial Average.

Dow Jones Inc.: The firm that publishes the *Wall Street Journal* and *Barron's* and also compiles Dow Jones stock indexes.

Dow Jones Industrial Average: The most commonly referred to index of stock prices; computed as the sum of the stock prices of thirty leading industrial firms divided by a divisor that is adjusted to reflect splits of its components. Dow Jones indexes are also computed for utilities and transportation companies. Also called simply the Dow. See divisor.

Dow Theory: A charting theory originated by Charles Dow (Dow Jones Inc.). According to the Dow Theory, a market uptrend is confirmed if the primary market index (such as the Dow Jones Industrial Average) reaches a new high that is soon followed by a high in the secondary index (such as the Dow Jones Transportation Index). A downtrend is signaled in a similar fashion for down moves in the indexes.

downtick: A price decline in a transaction price from the previous transaction price.

draft: A checklike instrument that calls for payment upon receipt.

dual fund: A type of closed-end investment company that divides its returns between two classes of fundholders: (1) dividend-receiving fundholders, and (2) capital gains–receiving fundholders.

dual listing: A security listed for trading on more than one exchange.

due diligence: The process of investigating the risks, merits, prices, and overall potential of an investment opportunity.

Dun & Bradstreet: A firm that evaluates and then rates the creditworthiness of many borrowers and generates benchmark financial ratios for many industry groups.

Dupont Equation: A profitability relationship that relates return on equity to several components; $ROE = ROS \times Sales/Assets \times Assets/Equity$. In words, return on equity equals the product of margin, turnover, and leverage.

duration: The weighted average rate of return of a bond's principal and coupon payment; a superior index of the payback rate. The length to maturity, in contrast, ignores the impact of payments received prior to principal repayment.

Dutch auction: A type of exchange or tender offer in which the company does not set a specific tender price. Rather, the holders are encouraged to submit offers to the company indicating the amount of securities and price that they would be willing to accept. The company then notifies the holders as to which securities will be purchased and at what price.

earnings momentum: A portfolio management strategy that identifies and selects stocks of firms with rising (accelerating) earnings.

earnings per common share (EPS): The net income of a company, minus any preferred dividend requirements, divided by the number of outstanding common shares; provides the investor or potential investor with information relevant to the sustainability of the dividend rate and capital gains potential; is considered one of the most important determinants of the value of common stock.

earnings surprise: An earnings announcement that differs from analysts' expectations.

EBIT: "Earnings Before Interest and Taxes," a measure of profit. It is used as a base to derive values for the "enterprise value" of the company.

EBITDA: "Earnings Before Interest, Taxes, Depreciation, and Amortization," a measure of profits, sometimes called "pretax cash flow." EBITDA is often viewed as an estimate for how much money (in the very short term) a company can afford to pay for debt service. Both EBIT and EBITDA are used to derive estimates for the "enterprise value" of the company.

econometric model: A model based on an analysis of economic data; particularly models of the economy.

econometrics: The statistical analysis of economic data.

economic analysis: An evaluation of a firm's investment potential within its economic setting.

economic value added (EVA): A management performance measure that compares net operating profit to the total cost of capital. Reflects how profitable company projects are as a sign of management performance.

efficient frontier: A set of investment portfolios with risk-return trade-offs, each of which offers the highest expected return for a given level of risk.

efficient market hypothesis: The theory that the market correctly prices securities in light of the known relevant information. In its weak form the hypothesis implies that past price and volume data (technical analysis) cannot be profitably used in stock selection. The semistrong form implies that superior valuation analysis which utilizes only public data is impossible; thus such data cannot be used to improve stock selection over what is possible through random selection. In the strong form of the hypothesis, even inside (nonpublic) information is thought to be reflected accurately in prices.

efficient portfolio: A portfolio on the efficient frontier of the capital asset pricing model. Such a portfolio offers the highest expected return for that risk level.

election-year cycle: The alleged tendency for the stock market to reach a peak about seven months after a presidential election and then fall to a low about eleven months later.

enhanced death benefit: An increased death benefit for which an annuity owner pays an extra fee.

enterprise value: The aggregate value of the financial debt and equity, net of cash on the balance sheet. It represents the value of owning all of the financial interests of the company.

equipment trust certificate: A type of bond collateralized by equipment, particularly railroad rolling stock or airplanes.

equity: See net worth.

equity accounting: Partially consolidating (on a pro rata basis) income and equity of affiliates that are 20 percent or more owned by the parent firm.

equity buyback: When a company repurchases its own stock.

equity capital: That part of a business's assets, financed by the owners as opposed to the part financed by the creditors.

equity kicker: A sweetener (such as a warrant) designed to make a debt issue more attractive by giving its owner an opportunity to benefit from the borrower's success (if any).

equity notes: Debt securities that are automatically converted into stock on a pre-specified date at a specific price or at a price level based on a formula that is prespecified. Also called mandatory convertible notes.

equity security: A share of ownership in a corporation, whether or not transferable; common or preferred stock, or a similar security.

ERISA (Employee Retirement Income Security Act): A 1974 federal law that protects pension benefits that have been promised by employers to their workers.

escrow account: In general, an account designed to hold a sum of money for a specific purpose; in a real estate transaction, the fund is normally set up for monthly deposits of the expected pro rata amount of real estate taxes.

ESOP (Employee Stock Ownership Plan): A federally sanctioned program in which a corporation contributes newly issued company stock worth up to 15 percent of employee payrolls into what amounts to a tax-sheltered profit-sharing plan.

estate: A person's total worth as determined by his or her vested interests in property and other assets, exclusive of any liabilities. Also the business of a debtor in a bankruptcy proceeding.

estate tax: A progressive tax on the assets left by deceased parties. Also called the "death tax."

Eurobonds: Bonds that may be denominated in dollars or some other currency but must be traded internationally.

Eurodollars: Dollar-denominated deposits held in banks based outside of the United States, mostly in Europe, but some are deposited in Asian and other area banks.

Euromarkets: Financial markets that operate outside of any national jurisdiction and deal in securities that may pay relatively high interest rates. The securities are usually based on deposits of large, international corporations or governments of nations involved in extensive foreign trade.

European option: An option contract that can be exercised only on its expiration date (not before). See American option.

ex ante: Before the fact; thus a procedure that consistently identifies attractive investments ex ante would generally facilitate a profitable trading strategy. See ex post.

ex post: After the fact; thus a procedure that identifies attractive investments but relies on ex post data to do so would not, by itself, facilitate a profitable trading strategy. See ex ante.

examiner: A court-appointed individual that the United States Trustee selects who (does not run the debtor's business) examines certain facts concerning the debtor and files a report on the investigations.

exchange offer: An out-of-court restructuring attempt. The debtor may offer to swap cash or newly issued common stock or bonds in exchange for outstanding indebtedness.

exchange rate risk: Uncertainty due to the pricing of an investment in a foreign currency.

exclusivity: The Chapter 11 debtor has the exclusive right to file a plan of reorganization for a period of months after bankruptcy filing.

ex-dividend date: The day after the day of record. Buyers who completed their purchase on or after the ex-dividend date do not receive that period's dividend even if the stock is held on the payment date.

executor: The person appointed to carry out the provisions of a will.

exempt property: See reaffirmation agreement.

exemptions: In tax laws, a dollar sum per dependent that may be subtracted from the taxpayer's adjusted gross income in order to compute the individual's taxable income. Note that the tax benefit of exemptions is subject to phaseout as the taxpayer's income level rises.

exercise value (put): The striking price of a put less the market price of the associated stock, if positive. Defined as zero if the difference is negative. Also called intrinsic value.

exercise value (warrant, call, or right): The market price of the associated stock less the striking price of the option, if positive. Defined as zero if the difference is negative. Also called intrinsic value.

exordium clause: The introductory portion of a will or other legal document.

expected rate of return: The expected return that analysts' calculations suggest a security should provide based on the combined impact of the market's rate of return during the period and the security's market risk.

expected value: The sum of the probabilities multiplied by their associated outcomes; the mean or average value.

expense deferral: An accounting technique whereby, for the purpose of computing reported income, expense recognitions are spread over time.

explanatory notes: Additional information in the form of footnotes; keyed to stock and bond quotations by letter symbols.

ex-rights period: The time period subsequent to the day-of-record for a rights distribution.

extraordinary gain (loss): An unusual nonrecurring gain (loss).

face value: The maturity value of a bond or other debt instrument; sometimes referred to as the bond's par value.

fairness opinion: "Fairness" is a financial concept that applies to a variety of negotiated transactions, including both mergers and reorganizations. Fairness addresses the question of whether the consideration received by a given constituency is sufficient.

FASB (Financial Accounting Standards Board): An accounting organization that establishes rules for preparing financial statements.

FDIC (Federal Deposit Insurance Corporation): A federal agency that insures deposits at commercial banks and thrifts. The insurance provides protection of up to $100,000 per depositor per institution.

Fed: See Federal Reserve System.

Fed call: A type of margin call that the Federal Reserve requires be issued when a margin borrower's equity falls below 25 percent of the borrower's account value. See house call, margin call.

Federal Funds Market: The market in which banks and other financial institutions borrow and lend immediately-deliverable reserve-free funds, usually on a one-day basis.

Federal Reserve Board of Governors: The governing body of the Federal Reserve System, comprised of seven members appointed by the president for long and staggered terms.

Federal Reserve System: The federal government agency that exercises monetary policy through its control over banking system reserves. Also called the Fed.

fee-only financial planner: An investment adviser who, for a fee, assists individuals with their financial planning but does not generate his or her compensation by recommending investments that would produce a commission for the planner.

FHA (Federal Housing Administration): A federal government agency that insures home mortgages for qualified borrowers.

fiduciary: A person who supervises the investment portfolio or manages the property of a third party and makes decisions in accordance with the owner's wishes and objectives.

FIFO (first in, first out): An inventory valuation method. With FIFO, items taken out of inventory are, for accounting purposes, assumed to have cost the amount paid for the earliest unused purchase. See LIFO.

fill-or-kill order: A type of security market order that must be either filled immediately or canceled.

filter rules: Any mechanical trading system, such as a rule to buy stocks when their PE ratios fall below some predetermined level or to trade whenever a particular price pattern is observed.

financial ratio: A ratio such as the debt/equity or times-interest-earned ratio; designed to reflect a firm's long-term financial strength.

financial risk: The variability of future income arising from the firm's financing costs. Fixed financial charges that magnify the effect of changes in operating profit on net income and earnings per share.

firm analysis: See company analysis.

fiscal policy: Government tax and spending policy that affects the level of economic activity.

fiscalists: A group of economists who believe that fiscal (rather than monetary) policy is the economic tool having by far the greatest impact. See monetarists.

Fitch Investors Service: A bond rating service; respected but somewhat less well known than Moody's or Standard & Poor's.

fixed asset value: The present value of the free cash flows expected to be generated by a business, plus the residual asset value.

fixed assets: Tangible assets with relatively long expected lives (greater than a year) that are not intended for resale and are used in the operation of the business; includes plant and equipment but not inventories or accounts receivable.

fixed costs: Costs of operating a business that do not vary with the firm's level of output, in the short run.

fixed-income security: Any security that promises to pay a periodic nonvariable sum, such as a bond paying a fixed coupon amount per period.

fixed rate: An interest rate that does not vary during the life of the loan.

fixed-rate mortgage: A mortgage having a constant interest rate for the life of the debt.

flat: Term used to describe a type of bond trade; bonds trading for a net price that is not adjusted to reflect any accrued interest are said to trade flat. See accrued interest

flight away from quality: A market that becomes increasingly tolerant of risk and, as such, is willing to price lower-quality debt instruments at a smaller premium yield over higher-quality instruments than had heretofore been the case. See flight to quality.

flight to quality: A market that finds high-quality debt instruments such as governments increasingly attractive relative to lower-quality debt instruments. The result is a growing spread in their yields. See flight away from quality.

flipping: The act of quickly selling a recently acquired investment; thus an investor who subscribes to a new-issue IPO and then sells the shares in the immediate aftermarket would be described as a flipper.

floating rate notes: A type of debt security whose coupon rate is determined by a formula that is based on a function of market interest rates (e.g., treasuries). Typically the divided payment is ? as market interest rates rise.

floating rate preferred: A type of preferred stock whose indicated dividend rate is determined by a formula that varies its payment rate with moves in market interest rates.

floor agreement: A contract that, on each settlement date, requires the maker to pay the holder a sum determined by the difference (if positive) between the floor interest rate and the reference interest rate. Otherwise no payment is made.

floor trader: One holding a seat on an exchange who trades for his or her own account. Also called RCMM.

Florida land boom: A speculative real estate boom that took place in the 1920s and was followed by a crash in the price of Florida property.

flower bonds: Government bonds that may be used at their par value for estate tax payments.

flowthrough: A method of handling the reporting of investment tax credits in which benefits are taken into and reflected in the income statements as they are incurred rather than spread over the acquired asset's life (normalization).

FNMA (Federal National Mortgage Association): A financial corporation that was previously government-owned, but is now privately owned by its shareholders. FNMA operates a secondary market in mortgages. FNMA issues its own debt securities to finance its mortgage portfolio.

focal point: A round-number value that is generally agreed upon or recognized by market participants as such. For example, a price of $20 would likely by viewed as a focal point, whereas a number such as $19.83 would not.

footnotes (to a financial statement): Notes that explain or expand upon entries; an integral part of a financial statement.

Forbes: A popular, twice-monthly investment periodical famous for, among other things, its *Forbes* lists, such as the list of loaded laggers.

foreclosure: The process by which secured lenders seize the collateral underlying their loans. The "automatic stay" provision of the Bankruptcy Code initially prevents such foreclosures. If, however, the court later determines that the secured lenders are not receiving "adequate protection," the court may lift the automatic stay in favor of the secured lenders.

Form 10K: A detailed annual report that must, in a timely manner, be submitted to the SEC, to the listing exchange, and to any shareholders who request it.

Form 10Q: A detailed quarterly report that must, in a timely manner, be submitted to the SEC and the listing exchange, and may be sent to shareholders who request it.

Form 13D: A required SEC filing of any individual or group owning 5 percent or more of any public corporation; to be properly filed, the form must disclose a number of matters including the filer's actual ownership percentage, its cost, the intentions of the owner, and any relevant agreements of the owner with any other party.

forward contract: An agreement between a buyer and a seller that calls for the delivery of an asset at a prespecified price, amount, time, and place. Unique one-of-a-kind contract; not traded on an exchange.

forward rate: A short-term yield (interest rate) for a future holding period implied by the spot rates of two different maturity securities.

four-nine position: A holding of approximately 4.9 percent of the outstanding shares of a company; about the limit for a quiet holding. At 5 percent the holder must file a Form 13d with the SEC revealing his or her position.

fourth market: The market for direct trading of listed securities between institutions.

franchise factor: A unique competitive advantage that facilitates a firm earning excess returns on its capital. These excess returns tend to cause the firm's stock price to have a PE ratio above its base PE ratio.

fraudulent conveyances: Defined differently by the several uniform state statutes and the Federal Bankruptcy Statutes. All have their origin in the statute of 13 Elizabeth enacted in 1570 that provided that "Covinous and fraudulent feoffments, gifts, grants . . . devised and contrived of malice, fraud, coven, collusion or guile, to the end, purpose and intent, *to delay, hinder or defraud creditors* and others . . . shall be utterly void. . . ."

Freddie Mac (Federal Home Loan Mortgage Corporation): A government agency that assembles pools of conventional mortgages and sells participations in a secondary market.

free cash flow: The amount of cash flow remaining after funding required levels of capital expenditures.

front-end loading: Taking a large portion of the sales fee on the purchase from the early payments on that long-term purchase contract.

front running: An illegal trading strategy in which the trader (usually an employee of a brokerage or specialist firm) learns that a large order to trade is about to be entered (usually placed by a substantial customer) and runs ahead of that trade to place an order at the then-current market price just prior to the time that the market learns of the large trade intention. If the large order causes a major price change, the position established by the front runner can, shortly thereafter, be reversed at an attractive profit. The front runner is (illegally) trading on inside information (knowledge of the forthcoming trade).

full employment: The unemployment rate that is thought to be the minimum sustainable level that can be reached before inflationary pressures accelerate and the maximum level that the public will view as reasonable. Opinions on this level have over time varied from around 4 to 6 percent.

full faith and credit: The promise backing a debenture or other type of uncollateralized debt instrument; the borrower promises to pay and pledges its full faith and credit (best efforts).

full replicaton: Technique for constructing a passive index portfolio where all of the components of an index are purchased in proportion to their weights.

fundamental analysis: The evaluation of the stocks or other assets and their investment-attractiveness based on their underlying financial, competitive, earning, and managerial position or similar evaluation of other types of investments.

fundamental betas: Betas caculated from the firm's fundamental characteristics such as its operating leverage, sensitivity to market interest rates, etc.

fundamental indexing: Creates a set of index weights based on some nonmarket fundamental yardstick such as sales. Posposed as an alternative way of constructing an index fund.

GAAP (generally accepted accounting principles): A set of accounting principles that are supposed to be followed in preparing audited accounting statements.

gambler's ruin: The wiping out of an individual's original capital by one or a series of adverse events. Often used in the context of the risk of gambler's ruin.

gamma factor: The number of years of above-average growth at a rate equal to that of the recent past that is necessary to justify the current multiple on a high-PE growth stock.

general mortgage bond: A bond having a generalized claim against the issuing company's property.

general obligation: A municipal bond secured by the issuer's full faith and credit, but without any specific collateral or claim to a stream of tax payments.

general unsecured creditor: A creditor whose loan is not secured (is uncollateralized) by any specific assets; debts are evaluated based only on the creditworthiness of the borrower.

geometric mean return (GMR): The computed average return that, if earned over the entire set of periods, produces the same ending compound value as the separate per-period returns applied period by period; mathematically, the value obtained by taking one minus the nth root of the product of one plus each of the n per-period returns.

GIC (guaranteed interest contract): An investment sold by insurance companies that offers high yields plus the opportunity to earn similar returns on additions to the investment plan.

gift tax: A progressive tax on gifts; now integrated with estate taxes.

gilt-edge security: A very secure bond or other security.

gilts: Debt securities issued by the government of the United Kingdom.

give up: A now-prohibited practice whereby brokers making trades for the portfolios of mutual funds were directed by the fund to pay a portion of their commission fees to brokers who had sold the fund's shares.

Glass-Steagall Act: A 1933 (Depression era) federal act that required the separation of commercial and investment banking. Now largely repealed.

GNMA (Ginnie Mae) (Government National Mortgage Association): A government agency that provides special assistance on selected types of home mortgages; securities are backed both by GNMA mortgage portfolios and by the general credit of the government.

go-go fund: A type of mutual fund popular in the late 1960s. Such funds sought short-term trading profits. Also called a performance fund.

going concern: The concept of a firm continuing in business. Conversely, if a firm cannot continue as a going concern, it may need to liquidate. A company capable of continuing in business is usually (but not always) more valuable than one in liquidation mode.

going private: The process by which a heretofore public company buys back all of its publicly held stock so that ownership rests with a few owners and it thereby becomes a privately held company.

going public: The process by which a start-up or heretofore private firm sells its shares in a public offering and thereby becomes a publicly traded company.

golden handcuffs: An employment agreement that makes the voluntary departure prior to normal retirement age of upper-level managers very costly to such managers; these managers may lose attractive deferred compensation and unvested stock options if they leave prematurely.

golden handshake: A provision in a preliminary merger agreement in which the target firm provides the acquiring firm with an option to purchase its shares or assets at attractive prices or to receive a substantial bonus if the proposed takeover does not occur.

golden parachute: A very generous provisional termination payment that is paid to upper management if control of their firm's ownership shifts to another group (a takeover).

good till canceled order (GTC): A type of security market order (buy or sell) that remains in effect until it is either executed or canceled.

goodwill: The amount by which a firm's going concern value exceeds its book value.

governments: U.S. government bonds issued by the Treasury Department and backed by the full faith and credit of the federal government.

governments only fund: A type of money market mutual fund that invests exclusively in very-short-term U.S. government securities.

grace period: Time period (e.g., thirty days) in which offensive action (e.g., foreclosure or bankruptcy) is stayed, thereby providing a defaulting debtor with an opportunity to cure the default.

Graham and Dodd approach: A type of securities analysis that stresses the importance of an investment's current fundamentals as opposed to its future prospects. Its originator, Benjamin Graham, coauthored the investment text that dominated the college investment course market from the 1930s to 1950s. Also called the Graham approach.

grantee: The individual receiving property under a grantor deed.

grantor: The conveyor of property under a grantor deed; the one who transfers property to another.

Gray approach: An investment timing technique that seeks to identify overvalued and undervalued market phases on the basis of interest rates relative to market PE ratios.

Great Crash: 1929 stock market decline that preceded the Great Depression of the 1930s.

greater-fool theory: The tongue-in-cheek view that a still "greater fool" will come along to bail out a foolish investor's foolish investment.

greenmail: The practice of acquiring a large percentage of a firm's stock and then threatening to take over the firm in an effort to have the company buy the greenmailer out at a premium.

Gross Domestic Product (GDP): The sum of the market values of all final goods and services produced annually in the country, valued at their market prices.

gross income: Total income, either actual or estimated.

gross margin: The net sales of an enterprise minus its cost of goods sold.

growth fund: A common stock mutual fund that seeks to achieve price appreciation by assembling a portfolio of growth stocks.

growth share matrix: A relationship popularized by the Boston Consulting Group (BCG) that relates interfirm profit differences to the combined impacts of market share and growth.

growth stock: The shares of a company that are expected to achieve rapid growth; often carries above-average risks and PE ratios.

guarantee bond: A bond having a guarantee from a company other than the issuer.

guarantee preferred: A preferred stock having a guarantee from a company other than the issuer.

haircut: An economic concession suffered by a creditor in connection with a restructuring. The "haircut" may be implemented through a reduction in principal and/or interest owed, a "stretched out" payment schedule, or other mechanisms.

head and shoulders price formation: A technical pattern of historical stock prices that looks like a human head and shoulders (small price rise then a decline then a larger rise followed by a second decline and finally a second small rise followed by a decline: left shoulder, head, right shoulder) and is said to forecast a price decline.

hedge: A trading strategy in which derivative or other securities are used in an attempt to reduce or completely offset a counterparty's risk exposure to an existing asset position.

hedge fund: A type of investment company that operates with wide latitude in the management of its portfolio. This wide latitude permits the hedge fund to do things that standard investment companies such as mutual funds are generally not permitted to do: sell short, buy and sell futures and options, take a large concentrated position in a single company, take an active role in management, etc. Only sophisticated investors are allowed to purchase and hold units of these types of funds.

hedging: Taking opposite positions in related securities or other assets (e.g., common stock and bonds convertable into the same common stock) in an attempt to profit from relative price movements (risk hedging) or to reduce exposure to an existing risk (pure hedging).

hemline indicator: A whimsical technical market indicator that forecasts stock market moves on the basis of women's hemlines. The higher the hemline, the higher the market level. For, example in the 1920s, hemlines were high and the market was rising. In the 1930s, hemlines and stock prices fell.

high-yield bond: A bond that is rated below investment-grade (below BBB).

highest and best: In considering among alternatives (such as choosing the best bid), debtors, creditors, and the court need to consider a variety of factors. Bids frequently include a package of consideration, including equity and debt instruments, each of which need to be valued. Some bids may be unconditional. Others may be highly conditional due to financing and other contingencies. Under these circumstances, the highest nominal bid may not necessarily be the best. The parties will consider factors such as the need for cash versus speculative value, and the ability to close quickly versus needing to satisfy various conditions. Certainty of closure and consideration may be more valuable than nominal amount of consideration. As a result, the winning bid is frequently referred to as being "highest and best" rather than just the "highest."

highest and best use: The use of an asset to which the highest value attaches. For example, land used for farming may achieve its highest and best use if homes are built on it.

histogram: A discrete probability distribution display.

hockey stick: Projections depicting increasing profits after years of flat or declining performance. The graph of such trends is in the shape of a hockey stick.

holding company: A company that is set up to maintain voting control over other business enterprises.

holding period return (HPR): The rate of return over some specific time period.

holding period return relative (HPRR): The end period compound value for a specific holding period.

holdouts: In out-of-court restructurings, where consenting creditors agree to significant economic concessions, other creditors have a major incentive to hold out. They not only avoid having to take "haircuts," they benefit from having a more credit-worthy company (brought about by the other creditors' concessions).

horizontal integration: The process of a business buying or building from scratch a business that is complementary in nature to its existing lines of business.

horizontal spread: Short and long option positions on the same security with the same strike price but different expiration dates.

house call: A margin call in which the margin borrower's equity falls below the brokerage firm's minimum. This minimum is typically set at 35 percent, but some brokerage firms may set the minimum as low as 30 percent. See margin call, Fed call.

Hulbert Financial Digest: A publication containing ratings of investment advisory services.

hypothecation: The pledging of securities as loan collateral.

immediate annuity: An annuity contract that provides for income payments to the annuitant to begin immediately upon its purchase.

immunization: The process of buying bonds with durations equal to one's investment horizon or using interest futures to accomplish the same purpose. Such a program is designed largely to eliminate the risk inherent in the fluctuations of market interest rates.

impaired: A claim that is paid in full or is reinstated on its original terms will generally be deemed to be "unimpaired." Otherwise, the claim will be "impaired." Impaired claims are entitled to vote on its treatment in a plan of reorganization.

in and out: The purchase and subsequent sale of the same security within a short time period.

in play: The status of being an actively pursued target takeover candidate.

inactive post: NYSE trading post for inactively traded securities. See post.

income anticipation: An accounting practice in which a profit is reflected on the income statement before the corresponding revenues are received.

income approach: Valuing real estate or some other type of asset as the discounted value (present value) of its expected income stream.

income bond: A bond on which interest is paid if and only if the issuer has sufficient earnings.

income fund: A common stock mutual fund holding and managing a portfolio of stocks paying high dividends.

income statement: A financial statement of interim earnings; provides a financial accounting of revenues and expenses during a specified period, i.e., three months, one year, etc.

income stock: A stock with a high indicated dividend rate.

incorporation: The forming of a business enterprise into a legal body endowed with various rights and duties. Once formed, the corporation limits the exposure of its owners to the amount invested in the enterprise.

increasing rate notes: Bond issues whose coupon rates automatically increase by some predetermined amount at predetermined times.

indenture (bond): The statement of promises under the Trust Indenture Act that the company makes to its bondholders, including a commitment to pay a stated coupon amount periodically and return the face value (usually $1,000) at the end of a certain period (such as twenty years after issue). An indenture trustee, such as a bank, is charged with overseeing the issuing firm's commitments. See indenture trustee.

indenture trustee: The trustee named in the debt instrument's indenture who is charged with acting for the benefit of the holders of the debt represented by the indenture. This trustee represents the bondholders' interests in dealing with the bond issuer. See indenture.

independence (statistical): The relationship between two variables in the situation where knowledge of one's value does not help explain the other's value. Thus, if IBM and AT&T stock returns are totally unrelated, knowing that AT&T stock returned x percent over the most recent twelve months would not help explain IBM stock's return over the same period.

index arbitrage: A (program) trading strategy involving the simultaneous undertaking of offsetting positions in stock index futures contracts and the underlying cash market securities (stocks making up the index). If, for example, the index futures contract is priced above the stocks making up the index, the arbitrager would buy the stocks and sell the futures contract on the index. If, in contrast, the index was priced below its corresponding stocks, the arbitrager would short the stocks and buy the index contract. The index arbitrage positions would be reversed at contract expiration.

index fund: A mutual or closed-end fund that attempts to duplicate the performance of a market index such as the S&P 500.

indexing: A passive bond or stock portfolio management strategy that seeks to match the performance of a selected market index.

industry analysis: The evaluation of an industry's position and prospects as they relate to its component firm's investment attractiveness.

inflation: The rate of increase in the price level; for example, if on the average $1.06 will buy what $1 would buy a year earlier, inflation equal to 6 percent has occurred.

inflation hedge: An investment asset whose value varies directly with its price level.

informal workout: An approach to dealing with a troubled firm that seeks to avoid the problems and costs of a formal bankruptcy proceeding by obtaining sufficient lender concessions to allow the obligor to continue to function outside of the jurisdiction of the bankruptcy court.

initial public offering (IPO): A new issue of stock offered by a firm that has no prior public market or public trading of its stock.

input-output model: A mathematical model in the form of a grid that relates various industries' outputs to their derived demands for inputs from other industries.

insider trading: The buying or selling of traders having access to relevant nonpublic information relating to the company in question. Such trading is illegal.

insolvency: Can be defined in several different ways depending upon the particular statute to be applied. One common classification is a simple balance sheet insolvency (liabilities exceeding assets). A second test is the inability of a debtor to pay its debts as they become due.

installment sale: In general, any sale that calls for payments to be made over time rather than upon the closing of the transaction; in real estate transactions, an installment sale may reduce and postpone the seller's tax liability if the payments are stretched out over a sufficiently long period.

Instinet: An automated communications network among block traders.

institutional investor: A type of organization that invests the pooled assets of others; includes pension funds, mutual funds, bank trust departments, insurance companies, and investment companies.

intercorporate dividend: Dividend payment from one corporation to another; 70 percent of such dividends are not subject to the corporate income tax for the recipient.

interest: The amount a borrower pays for the use of a lender's funds; frequently expressed as an annual percentage of the principal balance outstanding; may be compounded monthly, quarterly, annually, or on some other periodic basis.

interest futures: A futures contract calling for the delivery of a debt security such as a T-bill or long-term government bond.

interest-on-interest: Income from reinvestment of interest payments. See compound interest.

interest rate anticipation: An active bond portfolio management strategy designed to preserve capital or take advantage of capital gains opportunities by predicting the direction of interest rates and their effects on bond prices.

interest rate collar: The combination of a long position in a cap agreement and a short position in a floor agreement, or vice versa.

interest rate parity: In an efficient market, the relationship that must exist between two countries' spot and forward foreign exchange rates and those two countries' respective interest rates.

interest rate risk: The risk to an investor that a market interest rate rise will take place, thereby reducing the market value of fixed income securities. Or the risk that market interest rates will decline, thereby reducing the return on coupon payments that are to be received and reinvested.

interest rate swap: An agreement calling for the periodic exchange of cash flows based on an interest rate that remains fixed and one that is linked to a variable-rate index.

interest spread: The cost of carry, measured in percentage points.

internal liquidity (solvency) ratios: Financial ratios that measure the ability of the firm to meet future short-term financial obligations.

internal rate of return (IRR): The discount rate at which the value of the expected cash outflows of an investment are equal to those of the expected cash inflows.

international fund: A mutual fund that invests in securities of firms based outside the fund's home country.

International Monetary Market: A futures exchange associated with the Chicago Mercantile Exchange. It lists futures contracts on gold, T-bills, Eurodollars, CDs, and several foreign currencies, stock index futures, and options on futures.

Internet brokers: Brokerage firms that implement securities trade orders entered on the internet and usually charge very low commission rates (e.g., $7 a trade).

in-the-money option: An option whose striking price is more favorable to option-holders than the current market price of the underlying security. For a call (put), the strike price would be below (above) the underlying stock's prices.

intraday dependencies: Nonrandom price movements of transactions taking place over the course of a single day.

intrinsic value (option): See exercise value.

intrinsic value (stock): The underlying value that a careful evaluation would produce; generally takes into account both the going concern value and the liquidation or breakup value of the company. An efficient market would always price stocks at their intrinsic values. An inefficient market would not necessarily do so.

inverted market: A futures market in which the futures price on a particular asset exceeds its corresponding spot price.

inverted yield curve: A market in which short-term interest rates are above long-term interest rates.

investment: The current commitment of dollars for a period of time in order to derive future payments that are expected to compensate the investor for the combined impact of the time the funds are committed, the expected rate of inflation, and uncertainty.

investment banker: A financial firm that (among other things) organizes a syndicate to underwrite or market a new issue of securities.

Investment Companies: Periodical that reports on mutual funds; published by Weisenberger.

investment company: A company that manages pooled portfolios for a group of owners; may be either a closed-end company whose fixed number of shares outstanding are traded like other shares, or an open-end company (mutual fund), whose shares outstanding change by the net amounts bought and sold.

Investment Company Institute: Organization of mutual funds and other institutional investors; publishes *Mutual Fund Forum.*

investment-grade (bond): A bond rated BBB or higher.

investment management company: A company, distinct from the investment company (e.g., mutual fund), that manages the portfolio and performs administrative functions for the fund.

investment manager: One who manages an investment portfolio.

Investor's Daily: A national business newspaper that competes with the *Wall Street Journal.*

involuntary bankruptcy: A bankruptcy petition filed by the creditors of a debtor that is designed to force the commencement of a case under Chapter 11 or 7 of the Bankruptcy Code.

IRA (individual retirement account): A retirement plan that allows employees to set aside up to $3,000 annually (2005) in a tax-sheltered investment instrument. Earnings in the retirement fund are not taxed until they are withdrawn. The contributed sum is also deductible from taxable income if the individual is not covered by a company pension or has a relatively low income. See Roth IRA.

itemizing: One of two basic options available to those filing income tax returns; involves taking deductions for specific allowed expenses rather than taking the standard deduction. Itemized deductions are subtracted from adjusted gross income in the process of computing taxable income. Taxpayers are permitted either to itemize or take a standard deduction amount. Itemizing is preferred when the total for itemized deductions exceeds that for the standard deduction. See deduction.

January effect: An empirical anomaly in which risk-adjusted stock returns (particularly of depressed stocks) in the month of January are significantly higher than those in any other month of the year. See anomalies.

January indicator: A technical timing device based on the assertion that as January goes, so goes the year. Empirical evidence is not supportive.

junk bonds: High-risk bonds (rated below investment-grade, below BBB) usually promising a very high indicated return coupled with a substantial default risk.

Kansas City Board of Trade: A futures exchange that lists contracts for the trading of wheat and Value Line stock index futures.

Keogh account: A retirement account that allows self-employed individuals to set aside (2005) up to $40,000 or 20 percent of their self-employment income (whichever is lower) in a tax-sheltered fund. Neither the contribution nor the accounts earnings are subject to tax until the funds are withdrawn.

key person life insurance: Life insurance on key employees, naming their employer as the beneficiary; designed to assure creditors, suppliers, and customers that the firm would survive the loss of the insured.

kickers: Investors sometimes seek an additional return beyond the rate promised through the interest rate on a bond. They negotiate with the issuer for additional securities to provide such returns. These instruments, called "kickers," may take the form of warrants or other equity securities that provide the investor with an upside reward if the company is successful.

Krugerrand: A South African gold coin containing exactly one ounce of gold. The coin is often used as an investment vehicle by gold investors and speculators.

kurtosis: The degree to which a distribution departs from the normal distributions; see also platokurtosis and leptokurtosis.

lagging indicators: A set of economic variables whose values tend to reach peaks and troughs after the aggregate economy has already done so.

law of one price: The principle that, whenever two assets offer equivalent payoff matrices, their prices must be identical.

leading indicators: Government-compiled data series whose movements are identified as tending to precede turns in the overall economy.

leakages: Spendable funds that, rather than being spent on domestically produced goods or services, "leak" into savings, import purchases, or taxes during each round of stimulatory spending or tax-reduction, reducing each spending round relative to its prior level, thereby reducing the power of fiscal policy to stimulate the economy.

leap: A long-term option contract (put or call).

learning curve: A relationship popularized by the Boston Consulting Group which hypothesizes that manufacturers are able to reduce per-unit costs substantially as they increase their cumulative volume; in one formulation, costs are said to decrease by 20 percent with each doubling of cumulative volume.

leg on: The process of assembling an option spread trade or other combination investment position one side at a time.

legacy costs: Expenses that will need to be paid in the future to current and past employees for their current and past service (pension, medical, etc.) or other future costs such as for environmental cleanup that firms are liable for resulting from prior operations. In other words, future costs that existing companies are saddled with because of their history of past operations. A new start-up company would not be saddled with these types of costs.

legal lists: Lists of stocks authorized by various states for investing by fiduciaries.

lender liability: Claims against prebankruptcy lenders relating to the lender group's inappropriate and actionable activities that contributed to the company's failure.

leptokurtosis: The characteristic of a population distribution that differs from the normal by having a greater amount of its probability in the peak and tails and less in the two intermediate zones.

lettered stock: Newly issued stock sold at a discount to large investors prior to a public offering of the same issue; in accordance with SEC Rule 144, buyers agree not to sell their shares for a prespecified period after purchase.

leverage: Using borrowed funds or special types of securities (warrants, calls) to increase the potential return relative to the amount invested; usually increases both the risk or loss and the expected return.

leveraged buyout (LBO): The takeover of a company financed largely through the use of debt that is secured by the acquired firm's own assets.

liabilities: Debts; appear on right side of a balance sheet.

LIBOR: London Inter-Bank Offered Rate. A floating rate contained in many borrowing arrangements. It is frequently offered to borrowers as an alternative to the prime rate. Typically, companies borrow at a spread over LIBOR. Weaker credits pay higher spreads.

lien: A charge against or interest in property designed to secure payment of a debt for performance of an obligation.

life annuity: An annuity that pays a fixed income for the life of the annuitant.

LIFO (last in, first out): An accounting method that, for income-reporting purposes, values items taken out of inventory at the most recent unused invoice cost. See FIFO.

limit order: An order to buy or sell an asset at a prespecified price (or better).

limited liability: Property that under most circumstances protects shareholders from exposure to their corporation's debts in a bankruptcy.

line of credit: A prearranged agreement from a lender to supply up to some maximum loan amount at prespecified terms.

linear model: A method for estimating portfolio risks that requires only alpha and beta estimates of the components.

liquidation: The process of selling all of a firm's assets and distributing the proceeds according to the priority of their claims, first to creditors beginning with the highest priority, and then any residual to shareholders (first preferred, then common).

liquidation value: The total value of a going concern's assets (in excess of its debts) if those assets are sold piecemeal.

liquidity: The ease with which an investment can be converted into cash for approximately its original cost plus its expected accrued interest.

liquidity preference hypothesis: The term structure of interest rates hypothesis, which asserts that most borrowers prefer to borrow long and most lenders prefer to lend short; implies that long-term interest rates generally exceed short-term interest rates. See unbiased expectations, segmented markets hypothesis.

liquidity ratio: A ratio (e.g., current or quick) designed to reflect a firm's short-run financial situation.

liquidity risk: The degree to which an asset's holding period return varies with interest rate moves in the marketplace.

listed bonds: Bonds authorized for trading on one or more exchanges.

listed stocks: Stocks authorized for trading by one or more of the stock exchanges.

listing: The act of obtaining exchange approval for trading on that exchange.

listing requirements: The criteria that a company must meet in order to have its securities listed for trading on an exchange.

load: The selling fee applied to a load mutual fund purchase; typically 6 percent of the amount invested.

load fund: A type of mutual fund sold through agents who receive fees. Such fees are typically 6 percent on small purchases and somewhat less on investments above $10,000.

loaded lagger: A stock of a company whose assets, particularly its liquid assets, have high values relative to the stock's market price.

lock-up agreement: An agreement between an acquirer and its intended takeover target that is designed to make the target unattractive to any other acquirer; similar to a golden handshake. Usually, both the target and would-be acquirer commit to use their best efforts to obtain approval of the merger agreement. If either side fails to do so, it agrees to pay the other side a substantial sum of money: the breakup fee.

long interest: The number of futures or options contracts outstanding (owned and sold). For such contracts, long interest equals short interest.

long position: The ownership of stocks or other securities as opposed to a short position, in which the investor has sold securities that he or she does not own.

long-term assets: See fixed assets.

long-term capital gain (loss): Gain (loss) on a capital asset held for at least a year.

long-term liabilities: Liabilities for which payment is not due for at least a year or until the end of the next operating period, whichever is shorter; usually includes outstanding bonds, debentures, mortgages, and term loans.

loss: Net revenues minus costs when costs exceed revenues. See profit.

low-load fund: A mutual fund that imposes a small front-end sales charge; typically 2 to 4 percent. See load fund, no-load fund.

low PE stocks: Stocks whose price-earnings ratios (PEs) are well below the market average; sought out by value-oriented investors.

LTM: Last Twelve Months, or the four most recent quarters of operating results.

LYON: A complicated type of zero coupon convertible debt security that is both callable and redeemable at prices that escalate through time.

M1: The basic money supply; includes checking deposits and cash held by the public.

M2: A broader-based money supply definition than M1; includes everything in M1 plus most savings and money market deposit accounts. See M1.

M3: A still broader-based money supply definition than M2; includes everything in M2 plus large certificates of deposit and money market mutual funds sold to institutions. See M1 & M2.

M&A: Abbreviation for "mergers and acquisitions."

MAC: Acronym for "material adverse change."

maintenance capital expenditures: The amount a business must spend in order to do no more than preserve the efficiency and appearance of plant and equipment. No net additions to plant and equipment are contemplated.

maintenance margin: The required proportion that the investor's equity value must be in relation to the total market value of the portfolio in order to avoid a margin call. The investor will receive a margin call if the percentage drops below this level (typically 35%). See margin call.

management control: A situation in which no investor group owns enough of the firm's stock to exercise control and thus control is abdicated to the company's senior managers.

management fee: Compensation paid to the investment management company for its services to the fund. The average annual fee for a mutual fund is about 0.75 percent of assets for actively managed funds and 0.20 percent for index funds.

management-oriented company: A firm that is operated largely in the interest of management as opposed to that of the shareholders.

mandatory convertible notes: See equity notes.

manufactured call: A call-like position generated by a combination of a put and a long position in the underlying stock; position with a similar payoff matrix to a call.

manufactured put: A put-like position generated by a combination of a call and a short position in the underlying stock; position with a similar payoff matrix to a put.

margin (borrowing): Borrowing to finance a portion of a securities purchase; regulated by the Fed. For example, if a 60 percent margin rate is set, $10,000 worth of stock may be purchased with up to $4,000 of borrowed money. Only securities of listed and some large OTC companies qualify for margin loans.

margin (sales): Profit as a percentage of sales revenues.

margin call: A demand by a brokerage firm for additional collateral or cash needed to support existing margin debt; such a call is issued when the borrower's equity position falls below a preset percentage (e.g., 35%) of the value of margined securities. See house call and Fed call.

margin maintenance: The minimum percentage of equity that a margin account must maintain in order to avoid triggering a margin call (e.g., 35%).

margin rate: The minimum percentage of the cost of a purchase of marginable securities that must be paid for with the investor's own money. Currently (2005) set at 50 percent.

marginal tax rate: The percentage that must be paid in taxes on the last increment of taxable income.

mark to market: The practice of recomputing the equity percentage in a margin account (stock or futures) on a daily basis.

market: The means by which buyers and sellers are brought together to trade goods and/or services for money.

market approach: Estimating the value of properties (particularly real estate) based on what similar properties have been selling for in the marketplace.

market clearing price: The price at which quantity supplied for an item equals its quantity demanded. At that market clearing level, no unsatisfied seller is available at or below the market price and no unsatisfied buyer is available at or above that market price.

market indexes: An average of security prices designed to reflect overall market performance. The Dow Jones Industrial Average, the best known and most closely followed, is calculated by adding up the market prices of thirty leading industrial companies and dividing by a divisor; the divisor is changed periodically in order to offset the impact of stock splits. Dow Jones Inc. also compiles averages for utility and transportation stocks. Standard & Poor's investor service, the NYSE, NASD, and AMEX all compute their own indexes. Indexes are also compiled for bonds, commodities, options, and various other types of investments (e.g., artwork).

market indicator: See technical market indicator.

market maker: One who creates a market for a security by continuously quoting a bid and asked price. Most market makers are members of NASD.

market model: Relating the price of individual security returns to market returns with a linear equation of the form: $R_{it} = \alpha_i + \beta_i R_{mt}$ where R_{it} = return of security i for period t; R_{mt} = market return for period t; and α_i and β_i are firm i parameters.

market-on-close order: An order that is to be held until just before the close of the market and then executed.

market order: An order to buy or sell an asset at the current market price; requires immediate execution at the best currently available price.

market portfolio: A hypothetical portfolio representing each investment asset in proportion to its relative weight in the universe of investment assets.

market price: The current price at which willing buyers and willing sellers will transact. Determined by the interplay of supply and demand.

market risk: The return variability associated with general market movements; not diversifiable within the market. Also called systematic risk.

market risk premium: The increment of expected return above the risk-free rate that investors demand from the market as compensation for accepting exposure to systematic risk.

marketability: The ease with which an investment can be bought or sold without appreciably affecting its price; for example, blue chip stocks are usually highly marketable because they are actively traded.

master limited partnership (MLP): A type of business organization that combines some of the advantages of a corporation with some of the advantages of a limited partnership. Shares of ownership trade much like corporate stock yet the MLP is taxed like a partnership; that is, the partnership's pro rata profits are imputed to its owners and taxed only once.

matched and lost: Term applied to the outcome for the loser when two traders simultaneously arrive at the relevant trading post with equivalent orders, only one of which may be filled within the current market situation; they flip a coin to determine whose order is to be filled.

maturity: The length of time left until a security (e.g., bond or derivative) must be redeemed by its issuer.

maturity date: The date at which a security's principal must be redeemed.

mean: The average or expected value of a sample or distribution.

me-first rules: Restrictions in a bond's indenture that limit a firm's ability to take on additional debt with similar standing to that of the bonds in question.

merger: The act of combining two firms into a single company.

MGIC (Mortgage Guarantee Insurance Corporation): One of a group of companies that, in exchange for a fee, guarantee the timely payment of a portion of certain mortgages' obligations.

middle-of-the-road fund: A mutual fund that assembles and manages a balanced portfolio of stocks (some blue chips and some more speculative).

MIS: Management information system. The computing resources that hold and allow access to the information owned by an organization.

mode: The high point or most likely outcome of a distribution; for a symmetrical distribution, the mode and mean (average value) are identical.

modern portfolio theory (MPT): The combination of the capital asset pricing model, efficient market hypothesis, and related theoretical models of security market pricing and performance.

Monday–Friday stock pattern: The observed (if weak) tendency of stock prices to decline on Mondays and rise on Fridays.

monetarists: A group of economists that emphasizes the powerful role of monetary (as opposed to fiscal) policy in its influence over the level of economic activity. See fiscalists.

monetary asset: An investment that is denominated in dollars.

monetary policy: Government policy that utilizes growth in the money supply to affect the level and direction of economic activity; implemented by the Fed through its control over bank reserves and required reserves, especially though the use of open market operations.

money fund: See money market mutual fund.

money illusion: Failure to take account of inflation's impact; thus an individual who received a 10 percent raise and thought his or her financial situation had improved in spite of the fact that prices had risen by 20 percent would suffer from money illusion.

Money **magazine:** A monthly personal finance periodical published by Time Inc.

money market: The market for high-quality, short-term securities such as CDs, commercial paper, bankers' acceptances, Treasury bills, short-term tax-exempt notes, and Eurodollar loans.

money market account: A type of bank or thrift institution account that pays money market rates and seeks to compete with money market mutual funds.

money market mutual fund: A type of mutual fund that invests in and holds a portfolio of short-term highly liquid securities. Also called a money fund.

money multiplier: The ratio of a change in reserves to the resulting change in the money supply; thus a money multiplier of five would imply that a $1 billion increase (decrease) in reserves would result in a $5 billion increase (decrease) in the money supply.

money supply: Generally defined as the sum of all coin, currency (outside bank holdings), and deposits on which checklike instruments may be written. See M1, M2, and M3.

monkey with a gun (strategy): A negotiation tactic where one very aggressive party to the negotiations attempts to convince the other parties that they are so irrational that unless their demands are met, they will do something that hurts everyone.

mood indicators: Technical market indicators designed to reflect the market's degree of pessimism or optimism.

Moody's Industrial Manual: An annual publication containing detailed historical information on a very large number of publicly traded firms.

Moody's Investor Service: A firm that publishes manuals containing extensive historical data on a large number of publicly traded firms. Moody's also rates the riskiness of bonds and assigns ratings (e.g., AA).

mortgage: A loan collateralized by property, particularly real estate; the lender is entitled to take possession of the property if the debt is not repaid in a timely manner.

mortgage-backed security: A debt instrument representing a share of ownership in a pool of mortgages (e.g., GNMA passthroughs) or backed by a pool of mortgages (e.g., FNMA bonds).

mortgage bond: Debt security for which specific property is pledged as collateral.

mortgagee: The lender under a mortgage loan (see mortgagor).

mortgages (secured claims): The law governing real property mortgages and mortgages on chattel; are governed by various laws and different statutes in various jurisdictions. No central federal bankruptcy law exists on the subject.

mortgagor: The borrower under a mortgage loan (see mortgagee).

multi-index model: A method for estimating portfolio risk that utilizes a market index as well as indexes for various market subcategories.

multiplier: The ratio of the change in the level of government spending to the resulting change in the level of GNP.

municipal bond fund: A mutual or closed-end fund holding a portfolio of municipal bonds.

municipals: Bonds issued by state and local governments. Most such bonds pay interest that is tax-free to the recipient.

mutual fund: A pooled investment in which managers buy and sell assets for a common portfolio. The portfolio's income and gains and losses accrue to the owners; may be either load (with sales fee) or no-load (no sales fee); stands ready to buy back its shares at their net asset value (sometimes less a redemption fee) on a continuous basis.

mutual fund cash position: A technical market indicator based on mutual fund liquidity; high (low) fund liquidity is said to be associated with a subsequent market rise (fall).

naked option writing: Writing call options without owning the underlying shares; if it is exercised, the naked writer satisfies the contract with the option-holder by buying the required shares on the market.

NASD (National Association of Securities Dealers): The self-regulator of the OTC market. The NASD sponsored the NASDAQ trading system. These two, NASD and NASDAQ, are now separate organizations.

NASDAQ (National Association of Securities Dealers Automated Quotations): An automated information system that provides brokers and dealers with price quotations on securities that are traded OTC. See NASD.

NASDAQ Composite Index: A value-weighted index of OTC issues.

NASDAQ National Market System List: The primary list of OTC issues carried in most newspaper stock quotations. Membership is determined by criteria similar to the AMEX listing.

National Association of Investment Clubs (NAIC): Organization that fosters and assists in the setting up and operating of investment clubs.

NAV (Net Asset Value): The per-share market value of a mutual fund's portfolio.

NBER (National Bureau of Economic Research): A private nonprofit research foundation that establishes the dates for business cycles and sponsors economic research.

near money: Assets such as savings accounts and Treasury bills that can quickly and easily be converted into spendable form.

net equity value: The stated accounting value of a firm obtained after subtracting the value of its outstanding debt obligations.

net-net: A stock whose market price is very low relative to the value of its liquid assets; more specifically, stock whose per-share price is less than the company's net per-share liquid assets, where net liquid assets equals gross liquid assets less the pro rata amount of both short- and long-term debt.

net present value (NPV): A measure of the value of the excess cash flows expected from a potential investment project. NPV is equal to the present value of the cash inflows from the project, discounted at the investment's required rate of return, minus the present value of the investment's cash outflows also discounted at the investment's required rate of return.

net worth: The dollar value of assets minus liabilities; the stockholders' residual ownership position. Also called equity.

new issue: An initial stock sale, usually of a company going public; also an initial sale of a bond issue.

new listing: A stock that has recently been listed on an exchange; may be the company's first listing on the particular exchange or first on any exchange.

New York Curb Exchange: The name that was once applied to the stock exchange that is now called the American Stock Exchange.

nifty fifty: A list of about fifty companies, with high current PE multiples and rapid recent growth rates, that were preferred by many institutional investors in the 1970s.

noise trader: One who buys and sells securities without having any specific knowledge or superior analysis relating to its underlying value (an uninformed trader).

no-load (mutual) fund: A mutual fund whose shares are bought and sold directly from the fund at its NAV. Unlike a load fund, no agent or sales fee is involved.

nonmarket risk: Individual risk not related to general market movements; the total risk of an investment may be decomposed into that associated with the market (market risk) and that which is not (nonmarket risk). Also called unsystematic risk.

non-normal distribution: A distribution, such as a skewed distribution of returns, that differs from the normal shape. See kurtosis, leptokurtosis, skewness, and platokurtosis.

nonparticipating insurance: A type of insurance policy sold by a stockholder-owned company as opposed to participating insurance that is sold by an insurance company owned by its policy-holders (mutual).

normal distribution: A population distribution corresponding to the precisely defined normal bell-shaped curve.

normal yield curve: A bond market in which bond yields to maturity rise with their terms to maturity.

normalization: Spreading the benefits of investment tax credits or other types of credits across the life of the asset that produced the credits. See also flowthrough.

notes: Intermediate-term debt securities issued with maturity dates of one to ten years.

notional principal: The principal value of a swap transaction, which is used as a scale factor to translate interest rate differentials into cash settlement payments.

NOW (negotiable orders of withdrawal) accounts: A special type of deposit account that earns interest and allows checklike instruments to be written against it.

NYFE (New York Futures Exchange): A futures exchange associated with the NYSE; lists futures and option contracts on the NYSE Composite Index.

NYSE (New York Stock Exchange): The largest U.S. stock exchange. The vast majority of large U.S. companies list their stocks on the NYSE.

NYSE Composite Index: A value-weighted index of all NYSE-listed securities.

odd-lot short ratio: A technical market indicator based on relative long-short trading by small investors; when such trading is heavy, the market is said to be near a bottom.

odd lot trade: A transaction involving less than one round lot of stock; usually 100 shares, although a few stocks are traded in 10-share lots.

odd-lotter: One who trades shares of stock in odd lots.

off-board trading: Trading that takes place off an exchange, particularly OTC trading in NYSE-listed securities.

one-decision stocks: A now largely discredited concept popular the early 1970s that certain high-quality growth stocks should be bought and held; supposedly, the only decision necessary was to buy (like the old saying: "Buy but do not sell Manhattan real estate").

open-end investment company: A mutual fund or other pooled portfolio of investments that stands ready to buy or sell its shares at its NAV or NAV plus load if the fund has a load.

open interest: The number of option or commodity contracts outstanding; analogous to the number of shares outstanding for a stock.

open market committee: The Federal Reserve committee that decides on open market policy; consists of all seven of the Federal Reserve Board governors plus five of the presidents of the regional Fed banks, including the president of the New York bank.

open market operations: Fed transactions in the government bond market (Treasury bills). These operations are designed to affect bank reserves and thereby influence the money supply, interest rates, and economic activity.

operating company: A firm with active ongoing business activities.

optimal portfolio: The portfolio that has the highest utility for a given investment. It lies at the point of tangency between the efficient frontier and the curve with the investor's highest possible utility.

option: A put, call, warrant, right, or other security giving the holder the right but not the obligation to purchase or sell a security or other asset at a set price for a specific period.

Options Clearing Corporation (OCC): A company whose job is to guarantee performance of, monitor margin accounts for, and settle exchange-traded option transactions.

ordinary least squares: A method of estimating regression parameters by choosing linear coefficients that minimize the squares of the residuals.

organizational slack: Wasted firm resources resulting from managerial deadwood, lack of aggressiveness, carelessness, and so on.

OTC (over the counter): The market in unlisted securities and off-board trading in listed securities.

out-of-the-money option: An option whose striking price is less attractive than the current market price of its underlying stock. For a call (put) the strike price is above (below) the stock price.

overbought: An opinion that the market has risen too high too rapidly and is therefore poised for a downward correction.

oversold: An opinion that the market has fallen too far too rapidly and is therefore poised for an upward correction.

Pac Man defense: Tactic designed to avoid a takeover by attempting to acquire the attacking firm. Named after a video game.

paper: See commercial paper.

paper loss: An unrealized loss.

paper profit: An unrealized gain.

par (bond): The face value at which the bond issue matures.

par (common stock): A stated amount below which per-share equity (net worth) may not fall without barring any future dividend payments.

par (preferred stock): The stated value on which the security's dividend and liquidation value is based.

Par ROI equation: An empirically estimated profitability equation of the Strategic Planning Institute.

parking: The illegal practice of holding a security in the name of one (sham) owner for the benefit of another (true owner) in an attempt to conceal the beneficial owner's true identity. Sometimes stock is parked during the period prior to launching a takeover attempt.

participating bond: Bond that may pay an extra coupon increment in years in which the issuing firm is especially profitable.

participating life insurance: Life insurance sold by a mutual company, which is owned by and shares its profits with its policy-holders.

participating preferred: Preferred stock that may pay an extra dividend increment in years in which the issuing firm is especially profitable.

passed dividend: The omission of a regular dividend payment.

passthrough: A share of ownership in a mortgage pool whose interest and principal payments are flowed through to the owners.

payback period: The length of time until the amount originally invested in a project is recaptured via earnings from the project.

payment default: A failure to make scheduled payments of interest or principal that are due on a debt obligation.

payout ratio: Dividends per share as a percentage of earnings per share.

PE (price-earnings ratio): The stock price relative to the most recent twelve-month's earnings per share (or sometimes relative to the company's next twelve months' forecasted earnings).

PE ratio model: An empirical model designed to explain price-earnings ratios as a function of various fundamental factors.

penny stock market: A market for low-priced stocks (under $1 per share); especially active in Denver.

penny stocks: Low-priced stocks usually selling for under $1 per share; normally are issued by small speculative companies.

pennying: Entering a limit order (either to buy or sell) with a threshold price a penny better than the best current offer level.

pension: A periodic or lump sum payment to a person following retirement from employment or such a payment to surviving dependents of a deceased former employee.

percentage order: A market or limit order that is entered once a certain amount of stock has traded.

performance fund: See go-go fund.

per-period return (PPR): The return earned for a single period.

physical: The underlying physical delivery instrument for a particular futures contract.

PIKs (payment in kind securities): Securities whose yields are, at the issuer's option, payable in additional securities of like kind to the existing securities; thus a preferred stock may choose to pay the dividend in additional preferred shares.

pink sheet stocks: OTC stocks not traded on the NASDAQ system; issued by very small, obscure, and often speculative companies.

pink sheets: Quotation source for most publicly traded OTC issues, especially non-NASDAQ issues.

pit: Name of the physical location where specific commodity contracts are traded.

planning horizon (portfolio management): Time frame in which a portfolio is managed.

platokurtosis: The characteristic of a distribution that differs from the normal by having less of the distribution concentrated at the peaks and tails; see kurtosis, leptokurtosis.

point (stocks and bonds): Pricing unit; for stocks, a point represents $1 per share; for bonds, a point is equivalent to $10.

point and figure chart: A technical chart that has no time dimension. An x is used to designate an up move of a certain magnitude while an o denotes a similar size down move. The x's (o's) are stacked on top of each other as long as the direction of movement remains up (down); a new column is begun when direction changes.

points (real estate): A fee charged for granting a loan, especially for a mortgage on real estate. One point represents 1 percent of the amount of the loan.

poison pill: Antitakeover defense in which a new diluting security is issued if control over some prespecified percentage of the firm (e.g., 20%) is about to shift.

policy statement: A statement in which the investor specifies investment goals, constraints, and risk preferences for the benefit of the manager.

Ponzi scheme: An investment scam promising high returns that are secretly paid out of the money coming in from "investors"; usually exposed when incoming funds are insufficient to cover promised out-payments. The scam depends upon fresh investor money being brought in to pay its promised return.

pooling of interest accounting: A type of merger accounting in which an acquired firm's assets and liabilities are transferred to the acquiring firm's balance sheet without any valuation adjustment.

portfolio: A collection of investment asset holdings in an investment-like account by a single owner (institution or individual).

portfolio insurance: An investment service in which the "insurer" endeavors to place a floor under the value of the "insured" portfolio. If the portfolio's value falls to a prespecified threshold level, the portfolio insurer attempts to neutralizes it against a further decline by purchasing an appropriate number of index puts or selling an appropriate number of index options.

portfolio risk: Risk that takes account of the diversifying impact of portfolio components.

position trader: A commodity trader who takes and holds a futures position for several days or more (as opposed to a day trader).

post: One of eighteen horseshoe-shaped locations on the NYSE floor where securities are traded. Also called trading post.

postponable expenditures: Purchases of long-term assets such as consumer durables.

preemptive rights: Shareholder rights to maintain their proportional share of their firm by subscribing proportionally to any new stock issue. Such rights are reserved for the shareholders of some publicly traded companies, but many companies do not provide preemptive rights to their shareholders.

preferences: In general, a transfer of the debtor's property to or for the benefit of a creditor on account of an antecedent debt at a time in which the debtor was insolvent, the purpose or result of which was to facilitate the creditor receiving more than the creditor would receive in a bankruptcy proceeding.

preferred habitat: One of four hypotheses, designed to explain the term structure of interest rates based on a tendency for borrowers and lenders to gravitate toward their preferred loan lengths.

preferred stock: Shares of equity in a corporation whose indicated dividends and liquidation values must be paid after creditors, but before common shareholders receive any dividends or liquidation payments.

premium (bond): The amount by which a bond's market price exceeds its par value.

premium (option): The market price of an option; confusingly, the term is also sometimes used to refer to an option's time value.

premium over conversion value: The amount by which a convertible's market price exceeds its conversion value.

premium over straight-debt value: The amount by which a convertible bond's market price exceeds its value as a nonconvertible debt security.

prepackaged bankruptcy: A bankruptcy proceeding in which the debtor and major creditors have worked out the terms of the reorganization plan prior to the bankruptcy filing so that the legal process can move along quickly.

prepayment penalty: The fee assessed for early liquidation of an outstanding debt if so provided in the loan agreement.

prepetition: Referring to events or the status that existed prebankruptcy; that is before the bankruptcy petition was filed.

present value: The value today of a dollar to be received at some future point in time, using appropriate discount rates.

present value factor: The number used when deriving the present value of a future cash flow. For the first year it is calculated as one divided by one plus the discount rate, or $\{1/(1 + \text{discount rate})\}$. For subsequent years it is calculated as one divided by one plus the discount rate raised to the power of the year in question. For example, in year five the present value factor would be $\{1/((1 + \text{discount rate})^5)\}$.

price dependencies: Price movements that are related to (correlated with) past price movements.

price floor: The support level of a convertible bond provided by its straight-debt value.

price momentum: A strategy in which an investor acquires stocks that have enjoyed above-market stock price increases.

price stability: The absence of inflation or deflation.

primary distribution: The initial sale of a stock or bond (new issue).

primary market: The market for the initial sale of a security; subsequent trades of the security are said to take place in the secondary market.

prime: One of the two component securities created when appropriate shares are deposited into an Americus Trust. The prime receives the stock's dividends and up to some prespecified liquidation payment at the termination date; the score receives any value in excess of the amount assigned to the prime.

prime rate: The interest rate that banks advertise as the best (lowest) rate that they will charge their very good/excellent creditworthy customers. Some very secure borrowers may, however, be able to borrow at a still lower super prime rate.

principal (in a trade): The person or institution for whom the broker acts as an agent.

principal (of a bond): The face value of a bond.

priorities: Certain claims such as claims for back taxes, debtor in possession financing, and the costs of administering a bankrupt estate are paid ahead of the general claims of other creditors, all as particularized in the Bankruptcy Code.

private equity: Investing in entire companies (not public) or divisions purchased from other companies. The exit for such investments is often to take them public after enhancing their value.

private market value: The value that a private buyer would pay for an entire company in order to control the disposition of its cash flow. Determined using discounted cash flow analysis.

private placement: A direct sale of a security issue to a small number of large, qualified buyers.

probability distribution: A display of possible events along with their associated probabilities.

professional corporation pension plans: Pension plans as a means to shelter income from taxes; set up by professionals such as doctors, lawyers, and architects after organizing their businesses as corporations. The 1982 tax act severely limited the amount of tax-sheltered contributions that may be put into such plans.

profit: Net revenues minus costs when revenues exceed costs. See loss.

profit and loss statement: See income statement.

profitability models: Models designed to explain company profit rates.

profitability ratio: A ratio such as return on equity and return on sales designed to reflect the firm's profit rates.

program trading: A type of mechanical trading in large blocks by institutional investors; usually involves both stock and index futures contracts as, for example, in index arbitrage or portfolio insurance. Also called programmed trading.

programs: The actual trades instituted by a program trader. Market watchers might, for example, see a series of large trades in stocks making up the S&P 500 and conclude that programs are moving the market in a particular direction.

proof of claim: A document that creditors seeking to participate in the distribution of the proceeds of a bankrupt estate must file with the court within the time periods provided in order thereby to be eligible to receive a payment and distribution from the bankrupt estate.

proprietorship: The condition of ownership of a business entity, usually referring to sole ownership.

prospectus: An official document that all companies offering new securities for public sale must file with the SEC prior to proceeding with the offerings; spells out in detail the financial position of the offering company, what the new funds will be used for, the qualifications of the corporate officers, and any other material information.

protective put: A strategy in which a put option is purchased in order to protect a long position in an underlying asset or portfolio of assets.

proxy: A shareholder ballot.

proxy fight: A contest for control of a company.

proxy material: A statement of relevant information that the firm must supply to shareholders when they solicit proxies. See proxy.

public offering: A security sale made through dealers to the general public and registered with the SEC.

pump and dump: A market manipulation strategy (illegal) wherein a trader who has accumulated a substantial position in a stock or, less often, another security, recommends an investment in it to others (pump) while quietly unloading his or her position (dump).

purchase accounting: An accounting procedure used to consolidate the financial statements of two merged companies in which the net assets of the acquired firm are entered on the books of the acquiring firm at amounts that sum to the firm's acquisition price. As opposed to the "pooling of interest" method of accounting for a business combination, the purchase method allows assets to be written up to their fair market values. Under the pooling method, assets of the acquired firm continue to be carried over to the books of the acquiring company at their historical basis. Earnings under the purchase method are included only from the date of acquisition, whereas under the pooling method they are restated as far back as necessary. See pooling of interest accounting.

pure arbitrage: An arbitrage trade that involves no element of risk. See arbitrage.

pure hedge: A hedge whose sole purpose is to reduce the risk on an existing position. See hedge.

pure risk aversion: A desire to avoid risk and willingness to trade off expected returns in order to reduce risk.

pure risk premium: The portion of the promised yield in excess of the riskless rate that is due to pure risk aversion as opposed to that which reflects the expected default loss.

put: An option to sell a specified amount of stock or other asset at a specified price over a specified time period.

put bond: A bond with an indenture provision allowing it to be sold back to the issuer at a prespecified price.

put-call parity: A theoretical relationship between the value of a put and the value of a corresponding call on the same underlying security with the same strike and expiration date.

quarterly earnings: Interim profits, usually per-share profits, for a three-month period.

quarterly report: A report to shareholders containing three-month financial statements and certain other information.

quick ratio: See acid test ratio.

raider: A hostile (unfriendly to present management) outside party that seeks to take over control of a target company.

rally: A brisk general rise in security prices.

random walk: The random motion of stock prices, analogous to the movement of a drunk who at any time is as likely to move in one direction as another; implies that the next price change is as likely to be up as down regardless of past price history. This type of behavior is called Brownian motion in the physical sciences.

rate of return: The profit rate on an investment that takes into account both dividends and capital appreciation (increases in the price of the security); for example, a 9 percent rate of return implies that the owner of $100 worth of stock will earn a total of $9 in dividends and capital appreciation over the forthcoming year.

rating (bond): A credit quality or risk evaluation assigned by a rating agency such as Standard & Poor's or Moody's.

ratio analysis: Balance sheet, income statement, and other types of financial analysis that utilize ratios of financial aggregates.

RCMM (registered competitive market maker): See floor trader.

reaffirmation agreement: An agreement by a debtor to pay a debt that would otherwise have been dischargeable in a bankruptcy proceeding. Under state law and the bankruptcy code, all prebankruptcy property of the debtor generally becomes property of the estate. However, an individual is permitted to exempt certain properties. These properties are called "exempt property." Property designated through certain exemption statutes cannot be reached by creditors through judicial collection efforts.

real estate limited partnership (RELP): A type of investment vehicle that is organized as a limited partnership and invests directly in real estate properties.

real estate sales company: A firm that sells property, especially at marketing events such as complimentary dinners; the property is often in a distant location (Florida, Arizona) and part of a projected retirement or vacation development.

real options: Options embedded in a firm's real tangible assets that provide managers with valuable decision-making flexibility, such as the right to abandon an investment project rather than sink more money into it.

real return: A return calculation adjusted for the impact of changes in the price level; for example, if the nominal rate of return was 7 percent, a 3 percent inflation rate would correspond to a real rate of return to 4 percent $(7 - 3 = 4)$.

real risk-free rate (RRFR): The basic interest rate with no reflection of inflation or uncertainty. The pure time value of money.

realized capital gains: Gains that result (and generally become taxable) when an appreciated asset is sold.

realized yield: The expected component yield on a bond that is sold assuming the reinvestment of all cash flows at an explicit rate.

rebate: The return of a portion of a payment.

receivership: A prejudgment collection remedy that exists outside of the Bankruptcy Code. The court appoints a receiver as an equitable remedy in order to prevent the deterioration or impairment of the value of the property of a debtor.

recession: An economic downturn categorized as a recession by the National Bureau of Economic Research (NBER); historically, two successive quarters of decline in real (in noninflationary dollars) GDP have signaled the start of a recession.

record date: The shareholder registration date that determines who is to receive that period's dividends. Or a similar date for a bond and its coupon payment.

red chip stocks: Stocks of intermediate quality. See blue chip stock, white chip stock.

red herring: See registration statement.

redemption fee: A charge (typically 2%) that is assessed of those who cash in their shares of certain mutual funds.

redemption price: See call price.

refinancing: The selling of new securities in order to finance the retirement of others that are maturing or being called.

regional exchange: A U.S. stock exchange located outside New York City.

registered bond: A bond whose ownership is determined by registration as opposed to possession (bearer bond).

Registered Competitive Market Maker (RCMM): See floor trader.

registered representative: A full-time employee of a NYSE member firm who is qualified to serve as an account executive for the firm's customers.

registered trader: An exchange member who trades stocks on the exchange floor for his or her own account (or account in which he or she is part owner).

registrar: A company such as a bank that maintains the records of share ownership.

registration statement: A form that must be filed with the SEC before a security can be offered for sale; must contain all materially relevant information relating to the offering. A similar type of statement is required when a firm's shares are listed for trading. Referred to in the trade as a "red herring" due to the disclaimers written in red ink on its cover. Describes the terms of the bond issue, business operations of the company, and other relevant information required by the SEC.

regression: An equation that is fitted to data by statistical techniques; computers are generally used to perform the calculations. In the simplest case, a regression will have one variable to be explained (dependent variable) and one variable to explain it (independent variable) and would take the form: $x_t = a + by_t$ (where x_t = dependent variable; y_t = independent variable; and a and b are parameters determined by the computer that best fits the data). Graphically, one can envision a scatter diagram relating x_t and y_t with a line drawn through the points close to line on the average as the regression line. The "a" is the intercept and "b" the slope coefficient of this line. More complicated multiple regression equations of the form $x_t = a + by_t + cz_t + dw_t + ev_t \dots$ containing more than one explanatory variable may also be estimated. Again the computer can be used to select the best values for a, b, c, etc.

regression toward the mean: The tendency of many phenomena to migrate toward their average values over time.

regulated investment company: A company such as a mutual fund or closed-end fund that qualifies for exemption from federal corporate income tax liability as a result of meeting the requirements set forth in Subchapter M of the Internal Revenue Code.

Regulation Q: A Fed rule that at one time limited interest rates that banks and thrifts could pay on certain types of deposits/investments; rendered inoperative by deregulation.

Regulation T: A Fed rule that governs credit to brokers and dealers for security purchases.

Regulation U: A Fed rule that governs margin credit limits.

reinvestment risk: The risk associated with reinvesting coupon payments at unknown future (market-determined) interest rates. The yield to maturity on a bond is generally computed under the assumption that coupons will be reinvested at the same rate as the bond's current yield to maturity; if, however, market interest rates decline prior to the bond's maturity, the reinvested coupons will not generate the expected return and the actual realized yield to maturity will be lower.

REIT (real estate investment trust): Companies that buy and manage rental properties and/or real estate mortgages and pay out more than 95 percent of their income as dividends; no corporate profit taxes are due on their income.

relative strength: A technical analysis concept based on an assumption that stocks whose market prices have risen relative to the overall market exhibit "relative strength," and this relative strength tends to carry them to still higher price levels. Tests of the concept are largely negative.

release: A canceling of litigation claims, frequently granted pursuant to the plan of reorganization to various entities involved in the case.

REMIC (Real Estate Mortgage Investment Conduit): A type of mortgage-based debt security that restructures the payment streams of a portfolio of mortgages into bondlike components. Thus the short-term REMICs receive most of the initial cash flows in a pattern similar to a short-term debt security. Similarly, the longer-term REMICs are promised a cash flow much like a long-term bond. The uncertain portion of the cash flow stream is left largely with a residual security called the resid.

reorganization: Restructuring a firm's capital structure and operating facilities in the face of a default, near-default, or bankruptcy.

replacement cost approach: The valuing of real estate or other asset on the basis of the cost of producing equivalent assets.

repo: See repurchase agreement.

repurchase agreement (repo): A type of investment in which a security is sold with a prearranged purchase price and date designed to produce a particular yield.

required rate of return: The expected return that is designed to compensate investors for the passage of time, the expected rate of inflation, and the uncertainty of the return.

reserve requirement: The percentage of reserves that each bank is required to maintain on deposit with the Fed relative to each increment of demand or time deposits.

resid: The residual security left as the various cash flows are assigned to the various-term REMICs.

residual asset value: The present value of the amount in which the assets of a business are to be sold at some specified future date.

resistance level: A price range or level that, according to technical analysis, tends to block or at least restrict further price rises.

retained earnings: An entry on the income statement equal to annual after-tax profits less dividends paid; also an entry on the balance sheet, the sum of annual retained earnings to date.

retrade: When a buyer of assets takes advantage of the vulnerability of a distressed seller to insist on new more advantageous terms, at the last minute, for a deal already agreed to. Or, more generally, when one party to a negotiation seeks to alter the terms of an agreement to the disadvantage of the other party.

return on assets (ROA): Profits before interest and taxes as a percentage of total assets. Also called return on investment (ROI).

return on equity (ROE): Profits after taxes, interest, and preferred dividends as a percentage of common equity.

return on investment (ROI): Profits before interest and taxes as a percentage of total assets. Also called return on assets (ROA).

return on sales (ROS): Profits as a percentage of sales; also called sales margin.

revenue bond: A municipal bond backed by the revenues of the project that it finances.

reverse crack: A commodity trade involving buying heating oil and gasoline and selling an equivalent amount of crude oil.

reverse crush: A commodity trade involving buying soybean oil and meal and selling a corresponding amount of soybean futures.

reverse merger: An acquisition structure whereby the acquirer first acquires control of the target by, for example, purchasing majority ownership of its stock. Then the acquirer causes the target to merge the acquirer into the target. This transaction is typically accomplished to take what is currently a shell corporation (the target) that has a prior history as a public company and use it as a vehicle for turning the acquirer (a heretofore private company) into a public company without the expense of an IPO. The surviving company usually goes forward with the name and history of the target.

reverse mortgage: A type of mortgage in which the mortgagor uses his or her home as a vehicle to obtain a periodic (e.g., monthly) income. Typically a relatively old person (e.g., sixty-five years or older) owns his or her home and has no outstanding mortgage. This person pledges the home in exchange for a promise of a monthly income for as long as the homeowner continues to live in the home. A debit balance is built up against the house. When the house is sold, the maker of the reverse mortgage receives the balance due from the proceeds of the sale.

reverse split: A security exchange transaction in which each shareholder exchanges his or her existing shares for a reduced number of shares but retains the same proportional ownership; thus a 10-for-1 reverse split would exchange 10 new shares for each 100 old shares. Reverse splits are generally motivated by a desire to raise the company's per-share market price.

revolving credit facility: Similar to working capital facilities, but may be used for other corporate purposes. Similar in nature to credit cards in that they typically provide for some minimum repayment schedule.

riding the yield curve: A bond portfolio management strategy that seeks to take advantage of an upward-sloping yield curve by purchasing intermediate-term bonds and then selling them as they approach maturity.

right: A security allowing shareholders to acquire new stock at a prespecified price over a prespecified time period, generally issued proportional to the number of shares currently held; normally exercisable at a specified price that is usually below the current market price. Rights generally trade in a secondary market after they are issued. Some rights are not transferable and as such they do not trade.

risk: The variance of the expected return, i.e., the degree of certainty associated with the expected return. See also systematic and unsystematic risk.

risk arbitrage: An investment strategy in which offsetting positions in the securities of an acquisition target and its would-be acquirer are taken when the combined position is computed to show a profit if the merger takes place at the announced terms.

risk averse: The property of preferring security and demonstrating a willingness to sacrifice some amount of expected return in order to achieve a more secure yield.

risk-free rate: The interest rate on an investment, such as a Treasury bill, that is viewed by investors as devoid of risk.

risk hedge: A hedge position undertaken from scratch that is designed to profit from relative price moves in the underlying positions; option spreads are an example.

risk neutral: The property of preferring the highest expected return available without regard to risk; indifference to risk.

risk premium: The expected return in excess of the risk-free rate reflecting an extra increment of return to compensate for the investment's risk.

risk return trade-off: Tendency for more risky assets to be priced to yield higher expected returns than less risky assets.

risk-reward ratio: A measure of the amount of risk assumed in seeking a specific level of profit.

riskless investment: An investment having an expected return that is certain to be realized; that is, if a riskless asset is expected to yield 6 percent, the probability of its earning exactly a 6 percent return is 100 percent.

risky asset: An asset whose future returns are uncertain.

Robert Morris Associates: An organization of bankers that compiles averages of financial ratios for various industry groups.

rollover: A change from holding one investment asset in the investor's portfolio to holding another. For example, replacing a maturing bond with a new bond.

rollup: An amalgamation of a group of failed firms into a newly reconstituted entity shorn of its component's legacy costs.

Roth IRA: A type of IRA for which the contributions deposited into the account are in the form of after-tax dollars (no tax deduction), but the funds that are withdrawn emerge without a tax liability attached. Thus all of the account's earnings are tax-free. See IRA.

round lot: The basic unit in which securities are traded; usually 100 shares, although some stocks trade in 10-unit lots.

Rule 144: An SEC rule restricting the sale of lettered stock.

Rule 390: A NYSE rule restricting members of the exchange from off-board trading (trades not taking place on an exchange).

Rule 415: An SEC rule allowing shelf registration of a security, which may then be sold periodically without separate registrations of each part.

Rule of 20: A market timing rule based on the proposition that the sum of the Dow Jones Industrial Average's PE and the inflation rate generally tend toward a value of 20; thus, according to those who advocate the validity of this rule, departures in either direction tend to forecast a market move.

run: An uninterrupted series (usually daily) of price increases or an uninterrupted series of price decreases.

S corporation: See Subchapter S corporation.

Sallie Mae (Student Loan Market Association): A federal government agency that facilitates education-lending and raises funds by selling notes backed by government-guaranteed student loans.

Sarbanes-Oxley: Reform legislation requiring CEOs to vouch for the fairness and accuracy of their firm's financial statements.

saturation effect: The impact on profits and revenues when a heretofore rapid-growth firm or industry largely satisfies what had been the market's pent-up demand.

savings bonds: Low-denomination Treasury issues designed to appeal to small investors. Such securities do not trade in a public market.

scalper: A commodity trader who seeks to profit from very short-run (intra-day) price changes.

scorched-earth defense: An antitakeover tactic in which the defending company's management engages in practices designed to reduce the firm's value to such a degree that it is no longer attractive to the potential acquirer.

seasoned equity isssues: New equity shares offered for sale by firms that already have publicly traded stock outstanding.

seasoning: The process by which new issues of securities acquire market acceptance in their post-issue trading.

seat: Membership on an exchange.

SEC (Securities and Exchange Commission): The government agency with direct regulatory authority over the securities industry.

secondary distribution: A large public securities offering that is made outside of the usual exchange or OTC market. Such an offering is used in order to sell a larger quantity of the security than those making the offering believe can be easily absorbed by the market's usual channels. A secondary offering facilitates spreading out the period for absorption.

secondary market: The market for already-issued securities. May take place on the exchanges or OTC market.

secondary stocks: Relatively obscure stocks not favored by institutional investors, thus individual investors are the principal market for these stocks; secondary stocks may trade on the AMEX, NASD, and regional exchanges or be among the smaller companies listed on the NYSE market. See tertiary stocks.

second mortgage: A mortgage debt secured by a property's equity but subordinated to the first mortgage-holder's claim on the property.

Section 341 hearing: An organizational meeting early in a bankruptcy case involving unsecured creditors, the U.S. Trustee, and the company.

Section 363 sale: A bankruptcy auction sale. Debtors can sell assets two ways: through a plan, and through the exemptions provided under Section 363. Sales are allowed pursuant to Section 363 if certain tests are met, such as if the asset's value is sinking rapidly or the company will not be able to afford the cash burn-through consummation of a plan.

Section 382: A Tax Code provision in relation to cancellation of indebtedness (COD) income. When a company pays off prepetition debt at the discount (a common event in a bankruptcy), the haircut can be recognized as taxable gain. The company often will have incurred net operating losses, or "NOLs," over a period of years. Such NOLs can be utilized to offset the gains from discharge of indebtedness. Section 382 limits the use of such NOLs to shelter COD income if a "change of control" of the company's equity has occurred.

sector fund: A type of mutual fund that specializes in a narrow segment of the market; for example, an industry (chemicals), region (Sunbelt), or category (small capitalization).

sector rotation strategy: An active investment strategy that involves investing in the stocks of companies that operate in specific industries or stocks with specific characterisitics (low P/E, growth, value) that are anticipated to outperform the market. Then shifts in sector concentrations occur as their relative attractivenesses changes.

secured (senior) bond: A bond backed by a legal claim on specified assets owned by the issuer.

securities: Paper assets representing a claim on or interest in something of value. Examples include stocks, bonds, mortgages, warrants, rights, puts, calls, futures contracts, and certain warehouse receipts (e.g., ADRs).

Securities Amendment Act of 1970: An act restricting the front-end loading fees that mutual funds can charge their investors.

securitization: The process of turning the ownership of an asset with relatively poor marketability into a security with substantially greater market acceptability; for example, a portfolio of mortgages can be turned into a security that looks like a standard bond but is derived from real estate mortgage loans, auto loans, or credit card balances.

security: A financial instrument, such as indebtedness, common stock, preferred stock, rights, or warrants.

security agreement: An agreement that creates or provides for a security interest (e.g., collateral).

security interest: A lien created by an agreement.

security market line: The theoretical relationship between a security's market risk and its expected return.

segmented markets hypothesis: A theory designed to explain the term structure of interest rates as due to the supply and demand of each maturity class. See liquidity preference and unbiased expectations hypotheses.

self-tender: A firm tendering for the purchase of its own shares; sometimes used as an antitakeover defense. A self-tender may be used as an alternative to paying a dividend.

seller financing: A procedure in which the real estate seller finances part of the property's purchase price by accepting the buyer's note as partial payment.

selling short: The act of selling a security that belongs to someone else and is borrowed; the short seller covers his or her short position by buying back equivalent securities and restoring them to the original owner. The short seller hopes that the securities prices will fall while he or she is short.

selling short against the box: Selling short securities that the seller already owns. Usually done to defer a gain for tax purposes.

semistrong form of the efficient market hypothesis: The view that market prices quickly and accurately reflect all public information; implies that fundamental analysis applied to public data is a useless waste of time.

semiweak form of the efficient market hypothesis: The view that market prices cannot be successfully forecast with technical market indicators.

senior obligation: A claim that is not subordinated to another claim. Such obligations may come behind secured obligations.

SEP (Simplified Employee Pension) plan: Pension plan in which both the employee and the employer contribute to an individual retirement account (IRA).

serial bond: A bond issue, portions of which mature at stated time intervals rather than all at once.

serial correlation: Correlation between adjacent time series data.

shark repellent: Antitakeover provisions such as a poison pill.

shelf registration: An SEC provision allowing the preregistration of an amount of a security to be sold over time without specific registration of each sale; permitted by SEC Rule 415.

short against the box: The short selling of stock that the short seller also owns; usually employed as a tax device for extending the date of realizing a gain.

short covering: Buying an asset to offset an existing short position.

short interest (futures and options): The number of futures or options contracts written and outstanding for a particular contract. For these contracts, short interest always equals long interest.

short interest (stocks): The number of shares sold short.

short position: To have sold an asset that is not owned with a promise to repurchase it later, hopefully at a lower price.

short sale: The sale of borrowed securities with the intention of repurchasing them later at a lower price.

short-short fund: A type of bond mutual fund holding a portfolio of very-short-term debt instruments (but longer than that of a money market mutual fund).

short squeeze: The result when powerful forces driving up the price of a stock have the effect of squeezing a substantial short interest. The squeezed shorts are forced to cover by buying in the shares that they have sold short, usually at inflated prices, thereby driving prices still higher.

short-swing profit: A gain made by an insider on stock held for less than twelve months; such gains must be paid back to the company.

short-term gains (losses): Gains (losses) on capital assets held for less than six months.

short-term trading index: A technical market indicator based on the relative percentage of advancing versus declining stocks.

short-term unit trust: A unit investment trust made up of an unmanaged portfolio of short-term debt securities; usually self-liquidating within six months of issue.

simple interest: Interest paid and computed only on the principal. No compounding takes place.

single-index model: A method of estimating portfolio risk that utilizes only the market index and market model as opposed to the full variance-covariance matrix.

single-premium deferred annuity contract: An annuity with a defined future value; sold by insurance companies.

sinking fund: An indenture provision calling for a specified portion of a bond issue to be redeemed, periodically; required by many bond indentures in order to provide that all of the issue's outstanding debt will not come due at one time but rather will be spread out over a number of years.

SIPC (Securities Investors Protection Corporation): A federal government agency that guarantees the safety of brokerage accounts up to $500,000, no more than $100,000 of which may be in cash.

skewed distribution: A nonsymmetrical distribution; it's probabilities are spread out more on one side of its mode than the other.

skewness: The degree to which a distribution is nonsymmetrical.

skunk at the picnic (strategy): An approach in a negotiation where one party is extremely aggressive in seeking to gain an advantage vis-à-vis the other parties to the negotiation.

SMA (special miscellaneous account): A sum associated with a margin account; normally equal to the account's (margin) buying power. The SMA account is increased when stock is sold and decreased when stock is purchased. At times the SMA of an account can become inflated (above the account's buying power) when the equity of the account is near or below the minimum for margin maintenance.

small-firm effect: An empirical anomaly in which risk-adjusted stock returns for companies with low market capitalization tend to be above those returns generated by high market capitalization firms.

smokestack companies: Companies in basic industries (e.g., steel, chemicals, paper, etc.) whose profits and sales revenues tend to move cyclically with the economy.

social responsibility fund: A type of mutual fund that avoids investments in companies whose activity it views as socially undesirable. For example, those involved with tobacco, alcohol, pollution, defense, guns, and so forth would likely be avoided by such a fund.

social irresponsibility fund: A type of mutual fund that assembles a portfolio of the stocks of the very types of companies that social responsibility funds avoid.

source and application of funds statement: An accounting statement reporting a firm's cash inflows and outflows. Now called changes in financial position statement.

S&P (Standard & Poor's Corporation): A major firm in the investment area that rates bonds (level of risk), collects and reports financial data, and computes market indexes.

S&P 500 Index: A value-weighted stock index based on the share prices of 500 large firms. Many index funds select this representative index as their benchmark.

special offering: A large block of stock offered for sale on an exchange with special incentive fees paid to the brokers whose customers are purchasers. Also called a spot secondary.

Special Purpose Acquisition Company (SPAC): A blind pool investment company that plans to acquire one or more companies for investment purposes.

specialist: An exchange member who makes a market in assigned listed securities on an exchange.

specialized dependencies: Predictable return patterns related to some specific type of event such as a new issue or tax-loss trading.

speculating: The act of committing funds for a short period of time at high risk in the hopes of realizing a large gain.

split: An exchange of securities whereby each shareholder ends up with a different number of shares (usually more but sometimes less) but the new number of shares represents the same percentage of the firm's ownership as before the split. In a two-for-one split, a shareholder with 100 old shares would receive an additional 100 shares. See stock split (forward split); reverse split.

spot market: The market for immediate delivery of some commodity such as wheat or silver.

spot secondary: See special offering.

spread (bid-ask): The difference between the bid and the ask price.

spread (interest rate): The different between two market yields such as the spread between BB (junk) bond yields and that of equivalent maturity govenments.

spread (trade): A type of hedge trade such as a vertical or horizontal spread (options) or some comparable combination trade in the futures market; offsetting positions taken in similar securities in the hope of profiting from relative price moves.

stalking horse: In connection with an auction sale, sellers generally find a "stalking horse," or "lead bidder," to be beneficial. Such a stalking horse provides a minimum price that the company will receive for its asset in the sale.

Standard & Poor's Corporation Reports: An investment periodical containing quarterly updated analyses of a large number of publicly traded firms.

Standard & Poor's Encyclopedia: A book published periodically that contains analyses of S&P 500 stocks.

Standard & Poor's Investor Service: A major firm in the investment area that rates bonds (risk level); also computes market indexes, compiles investment information, and publishes various investment periodicals.

Standard & Poor's Stock Guide: A monthly publication with a compact line of data containing information on most publicly traded corporations.

standard deviation: A measure of the degree to which the distribution of a random variable is compact or spread out. For a normal distribution, about two times out of three the variable's actual value will be within one standard deviation on either side of the mean value; about 19 out of 20 times it will be within two standard deviations. One standard deviation is the square root of the variance (which see).

standstill agreement: A reciprocal understanding between a company's management on one side and an outside party that owns a significant minority position in the company's stock on the other side. Each party gives up certain rights in exchange for corresponding concessions by the other party. For example, the outside ownership group may agree to limit its ownership position to some prespecified level. In exchange, management may agree to allow some minority board representation by the outside group.

stays: A restraining of creditors (in a bankruptcy proceeding) from taking action to collect on their claims against the debtor and enforce security interests against the debtor or the debtor's property.

Stein estimators: Statistical techniques for estimating a variable that assumes a regression toward the mean tendency and makes a corresponding adjustment in the estimated value of the variable.

Stock Clearing Corporation: A NYSE subsidiary that clears transactions for member firms.

stock dividend: A distribution to shareholders paid in the form of additional shares of stock; similar to a stock split, although usually proportionately fewer new shares are distributed. Stock dividend payments do not alter each stockholder's percentage of ownership.

stock exchange: An organization established for trading a specific list of securities during specific trading hours, usually at a single location.

stock split (forward split): The division of a company's existing stock into more shares (say, 2-for-1, or 3-for-1); usually undertaken in order to reduce the price per share with the objective of improving the shares' marketability. See also reverse split.

stock split (reverse split): See reverse split.

stockholder-oriented company: A company whose management is particularly responsive to the interest of its stockholders; a large ownership group may exercise effective control, or management itself may own a large block of the company's stock.

stop limit order: A type of securities market order that turns into a limit order when (if) the market price reaches a certain prespecified threshold level where the market price is moving adversely.

stop loss order: An order to sell or buy an asset (usually stock) at the current market price immediately after a certain prespecified threshold price is reached where the market price is moving adversely.

straddle (in commodities): Another name for a spread, where offsetting positions are taken in similar contracts such as adjacent expirations of the same physical.

straddle (in options): A combination put and call on the same stock at the same striking price.

straight debt: Bonds without a conversion feature or other equity-like features.

straight-debt value: The underlying value of a convertible bond if it were to be stripped of its conversion feature and thus was valued only as a straight-debt (nonconvertible) bond.

straight-line depreciation: A method of writing off the recorded balance sheet values of long-lived assets at a constant dollar rate over their estimated lives.

stranded costs: Previously incurred costs for plant and equipment that, while still carried on the books, are no longer useful and now need to be written off.

strangle: Combination put and call position where the two options have different strike prices.

strap: A combination of two calls and one put, each having the same strike and expiration date.

street name: Securities held in customer accounts at brokerage houses but registered in the brokerage firm's name.

strike: See striking price.

striking price: The amount that an option holder (call) is required to pay in order to exercise an option. For a put the price that the put-writer must pay in order to purchase the stock if the put-holder exercises his or her option to sell. Also called strike, strike price, or exercise price.

strip: A combination of two puts and one call, each having the same strike and expiration date.

strip bond: A coupon bond with its coupons removed. A strip bond returns only principal at maturity and thus is equivalent to a zero-coupon bond.

strong form of the efficient market hypothesis: The view that market prices quickly and accurately reflect all public and nonpublic information; implies that inside information is useless in security selection.

style analysis: An effort to explain the variability in the observed returns of a portfolio in terms of the movements in the returns to a series of benchmark portfolios designed to capture the essence of a particular security characteristic such as its size, value, and growth.

subaccounts: Stock, bond, and money market funds used as part of a program to invest money in an annuity.

Subchapter M: The section of the Internal Revenue Code that sets forth the criteria that must be met in order to qualify as a regulated investment company.

Subchapter S: The section of the Internal Revenue Code that sets forth the criteria that must be met in order to qualify as a Subchapter S corporation. See Subchapter S corporation.

Subchapter S corporation: A classification whereby a corporation may be taxed as a partnership under the provisions of the Internal Revenue Code. See Subchapter S.

subordinate (junior) bonds: Bonds that, in case of default, entitle holders to claims on the issuer's assets only after the claims of holders of more senior creditors (bank debt senior debentures and mortgage bonds) are satisfied in full.

subordination provisions: Bond indenture provisions that assign a bond issue a lower priority than other (senior) bond issues.

sum of the years' digits depreciation: A method of calculating accelerated depreciation that each year assigns depreciation charges equal to the ratio of the number of years remaining in the asset's estimated useful life to the total of the years in the asset's estimated life.

Super Bowl indicator: A whimsical technical market indicator whose signal is based on whether the Super Bowl (football) is won by a former member of the old American Football League (AFL) or the National Football League (NFL). An NFL victory forecasts an up market for the coming year; an AFL victory forecasts a down market. No forecast is derived from an expansion team win.

super Dot system: See DOT.

SuperNOW account: An interest-bearing checking account.

support level: A floor price that, according to technical analysis, tends to restrict a stock's downside price moves.

surrender charges: A penalty assessed for withdrawing money from a annuity prior to the prespecified time allowed for withdrawals.

Survey Research Center: Research institute located at the University of Michigan that surveys consumers and publishes statistics on consumer sentiments.

swap fund: A type of mutual fund that allows investors to purchase its shares using the shares of other companies as currency; valuing those exchanged shares at their market prices.

sweep account: A type of bank account that sweeps the portion of the balance exceeding some preassigned minimum into a money market account on a daily basis.

syndicate: A group of investment bankers organized to underwrite a new issue or secondary offering.

systematic risk: See market risk.

tactical asset allocation: A portfolio strategy that adjusts the investor's mix of stocks, bonds, and cash by increasing (decreasing) the allocation to the asset class that is believed to be relatively undervalued (overvalued).

takeover bid: A tender offer designed to acquire a sufficient number of shares to achieve working control of the target firm.

tangible investments: A broad group of assets that includes precious metals, gemstones, artifacts, and some types of collectibles.

tangibles: See tangible investments.

tax basis: The cost of capital assets that is subtracted from the selling price in order to determine the gain or loss for tax purposes.

tax credit: Sums derived from various types of activities (e.g., purchase of solar energy equipment) that can be applied to offset computed taxes on a dollar-for-dollar basis, thereby reducing the amount of taxes otherwise due.

tax-loss carry forward: Unutilized prior-period reported losses that may be employed to offset the tax liability of subsequent income.

tax-loss trading: Year-end selling of depressed securities designed to establish a tax loss.

tax-managed fund: A type of investment company that sought to convert dividend income into capital gains; prior to IRS rulings disallowing the practice, such funds organized themselves as corporations rather than as mutual funds and reinvested their portfolios' dividends.

tax shelter: An investment that produces deductions that can be applied against the investor's other income with a resulting savings in income taxes. The Tax Reform Act of 1986 severely restricted most types of tax shelters.

tax swap: A type of bond swap in which one bond issue is sold in order to yield a tax loss and replaced with an equivalent (similar but not identical) bond issue.

taxable income: Adjusted gross income less deductions and allowance for exemptions; the income figure on which one's income tax liability is computed.

T-bill: See Treasury bill.

TEBF (Tax-Exempt Bond Fund): A mutual or closed-end fund that invests in municipal bonds, thereby providing tax-free income to its holders.

technical analysis (broad form): A method used for forecasting general market movements with technical market indicators.

technical analysis (narrow form): A method used for evaluating securities' investment attractiveness based on past price and volume behavior; largely debunked by evidence favorable to the weak form of the efficient market hypothesis.

technical default: A default related to a breach of a financial covenant or other such promise as distinct from an actual payment default, where the company fails to make a principal or interest payment.

technical market indicator: A data series or combination of data series said to be helpful in forecasting the market's future direction. Also called a market indicator.

Templeton approach: A fundamental approach to investment analysis named after renowned mutual fund manager John Marks Templeton; emphasizes a worldview to finding undervalued issues.

tender offer: An offer to purchase a large block of securities made outside the general market (exchanges, OTC) in which the securities are traded; often made as part of an effort to take over a company.

term insurance: A type of life insurance not having a savings feature; unlike whole life, where annual premium rates are fixed, premiums rise with the age of the insured in order thereby to reflect the greater probability of death; see also whole life insurance.

term loan: Bank loans that are generally of a longer-term nature (several years) than most bank loans and have preset amortization schedules and a stated maturity.

term structure of interest rates: A pattern of yields for differing maturities (risk controlled). See also segmented markets, unbiased expectations, and liquidity preference hypotheses.

term to maturity: Length of time until the maturity (final payment date) of a debt instrument.

tertiary stocks: The most obscure classification of stocks; much less popular than even secondary stocks; often trade only in the pink sheets. See secondary stocks.

testator: See testor.

testimonium: The concluding portion of a will.

testor: A person who leaves a will in force at his or her death. Also called testator.

thin market: A market in which trading volume is low and transactions relatively infrequent.

third market: The over-the-counter market in listed securities.

363 Motion: Section 363 of the Bankruptcy Code allows companies in Chapter 11 to sell all or a significant portion of their assets in a bankruptcy auction sale. The court can give buyers assurances regarding clear title.

three-step top-down approach: A type of approach to fundamental analysis that focuses on: (1) economic, (2) industry, and (3) firm factors, performed in that order.

thrifts: Banklike depository institutions other than commercial banks that accept savings deposits, especially savings and loan associations, mutual savings banks, and credit unions.

tick: The minimum-size price increment on a futures contract.

ticker symbols: Symbols for identifying securities on the ticker tape and quotation machines; listed in *S&P Stock Guide* and several other publications.

ticker tape: A device for displaying relevant information on stock market trading.

Tigers (Treasury Investment Growth Receipts): Zero-coupon securities assembled by Merrill Lynch and backed by a portfolio of Treasury issues.

tight money: Restrictive monetary policy.

time value (option): The excess of an option's market price over its intrinsic value.

time value (present value): The value of a current as opposed to a future sum.

times-interest-earned ratio: Gross (before-tax, before-interest) profit relative to a firm's interest obligation.

TIPS: Treasury Inflation Protected Securities. Government bonds whose values are adjusted twice a year to offset the effects of changes in the consumer price index.

title search: A process whereby the validity of a title to a real estate parcel is researched and evaluated.

TOLSR (Total Odd-Lot Short Ratio): A technical market indicator that relates odd-lot short sales to total odd-lot trading.

top-down approach: An approach to fundamental analysis that begins with economic analysis, then industry analysis and finally company analysis. See three-step top-down approach.

top-tier stocks: Established growth stocks preferred by many institutional investors.

total return: Dividend return plus capital gains return (stocks). On an analogous concept for other types of investments such as bonds.

total risk: The sum of market and nonmarket risk.

tracking error: The difference in returns between an active investment portfolio and its benchmark portfolio.

trade creditor: A supplier or vendor who has provided goods, services, or raw materials to a company and has not yet been paid.

trading post: See post.

trading rule: A formula approach used to decide whether or not to undertake a particular transaction based on relationships observed in historical data.

transaction cost: The cost of executing a trade; includes commissions and the impact of the bid-ask spread.

transfer: Every mode, direct or indirect, absolute or conditional, voluntary or involuntary, for disposing of or parting with either property or an interest in property.

transfer agent: The agent who maintains the records for and keeps track of changes in security-holder ownership.

transfer tax: A New York State tax applied to the transfer of equity securities.

Treasury bill: Government debt security issued on a discount basis by the U.S. Treasury. Also called a T-bill.

Treasury bond: A U.S. government bond issued with an initial maturity greater than ten years.

Treasury note: A U.S. government bond issued with an initial maturity of one to ten years.

treasury stock: Previously issued stock reacquired by the issuing company.

trust: A property interest held by one person for the benefit of another.

trustee: See bankruptcy trustee; also under an indenture, a bank, or other third party that administers the provisions of a bond indenture; see also indenture trustee.

turnover: Trading volume in a security or in the market as a whole.

Turov's formula: A formula for computing the amount by which a stock price must change in order to produce returns equivalent to the returns on its call options.

12b-1 fund: A type of mutual fund that does not charge an up-front load but does withdraw a selling fee from the fund's assets on an annual basis.

two-tier tender offer: A takeover tactic in which an initial offer is made for a controlling interest in the target (usually cash), and a second, generally less attractive offer (usually securities) is made for the remainder. Such an offer structure is designed to put pressure on holdout shareholders to take advantage of the front end of the offer.

ugly duckling: A business unit whose surface characteristics make it unattractive, but which can become very valuable (become a swan) under certain circumstances.

unbiased expectations hypothesis: A theory designed to explain the term structure of interest rates as reflecting the market consensus of contiguous forthcoming short rates. See liquidity preference and segmented market hypotheses.

underwriter: An investment banker who agrees to buy part or all of a new security issue with the expectation of selling the securities to the public at a slightly higher price. Or, an investment banker who performs a similar function for a tender offer.

underwriting fee: The underwriter's selling fee earned as the difference between the price paid to the seller of an underwritten issue and the price paid by the buyer.

unemployment rate: The percentage of those members of the labor force who are actively seeking employment but are currently out of work.

unit investment trust: A self-liquidating unmanaged portfolio in which investors own shares and receive distributions.

United Shareholders of America (USA): A shareholder rights organization that was sponsored by T. Boone Pickens; USA advocated such issues as equal voting rights for all classes of stock, secret proxy votes, and prohibition of poison pills. Established in 1986. Dissolved in 1994.

United States Trustee: An employee of the Department of Justice who attends to certain administrative functions in the administration of bankruptcy cases. This person is different from a bankruptcy trustee, who is an individual assigned to manage and run a debtor's estate, and an indenture trustee, charged with enforcing the rights of the bondholders.

universal life: A type of life insurance policy in which the cash value varies with the policy-holder's payments and the company's investment returns.

Unlisted Market Guide: An investment periodical that covers small companies that are not reported on by larger periodicals such as *Value Line* and Standard and Poor's.

unlisted security: A security that trades only in the OTC market.

unrealized capital gains: Paper gains that reflect the price appreciation of currently held unsold assets.

unsecured obligation: A claim against the firm that is not backed by any specific collateral interest.

unsystematic risk: See nonmarket risk.

uptick: A transaction that takes place at a higher price than the immediately preceding price.

uptick-downtick ratio: A ratio of the number of uptick block transactions relative to the number of downtick block transactions.

urgent selling index: A technical market indicator based on the volume of advancing relative to declining issues.

usable bond: A bond that may be utilized at its face value in order to exercise corresponding warrants of the issuing firm.

VA (Department of Veterans' Affairs): Federal government agency concerned with the affairs of veterans and, among other things, guarantees mortgage loans for qualifying veterans.

Value Line: A finance/investments periodical that publishes quarterly analyses on about 1,700 firms and compiles the *Value Line Index*; owned by Arnold Bernhard and Company.

Value Line Index: An equally weighted, broadly based stock price index.

value oriented investor: A type of investor who seeks to assemble and own a portfolio of stocks that sell at low prices relative to their tangible underlying values; that is, a low price relative to their earnings, cash flows, book values, breakup values, and liquid asset values.

value stock: The stock of a company whose market price is low compared to earnings, net worth, sales, and other fundamental characteristics.

variable annuity: An investment vehicle similar to a mutual fund, but sold by insurance companies.

variable life: A type of life insurance policy in which the cash value varies with the return on the policy-holder's portfolio.

variable rate mortgage: A mortgage in which the interest rate applied to the mortgage is structured to vary with market interest rates.

variable rate note: A bond whose coupon rate is reset periodically according to a formula based on the current level of market interest rates.

variance: The expected (average) value of the square of the deviation from the mean of a distribution; variance of $X = E(X - \bar{x})^2$; where $\bar{x}$ is the mean of X and $E(x)$ is the expected value operator of x. Used as a measure of the risk of a return distribution.

variance-covariance model: A method of estimating portfolio risk that utilizes the variances and covariances of all of the potential components.

Vasicek adjustment: A method of adjusting estimated raw betas based on the uncertainty of the mean and specific raw beta estimates.

venture capital: Risk capital extended to start-up or small going concerns.

venture capital fund: An investment company that invests in venture capital opportunities.

versus purchase order: A type of sales order used to identify the specific purchase date and price of securities to be delivered for sale. Used to minimize the current tax liability of the transaction.

vertical integration: The process of a business either buying or building from scratch a further stage of the production process: supplier or customer.

vertical spread: Short and long option positions on the same security with the same expiration but different striking prices.

vested benefits: Pension benefits that are retained by the employee even if the individual leaves his or her employer.

volume: The number of shares traded in a particular period (e.g., day).

WACC: Weighted Average Cost of Capital. A company's cost for its blend of debt and equity. The WACC rate may be used to discount a company's future cash flows back to the present value.

wallpaper: Worthless securities that can be more effectively used for wallpapering one's house.

Wall Street Journal, **the:** A widely read business/investment newspaper published five (now six) days a week by Dow Jones Inc.

Wall Street Week **(WSW):** A popular and long-running weekly business news television program. Carried by the Public Broadcasting Corporation.

warrants: Certificates offering the right to purchase a specified amount of stock (or, in rare cases, bonds) in a company at a specified price over a specified period. If exercised, to be satisfied by the issuance of additional shares of the warrant-issuing company.

wash sale: A sale and repurchase made within thirty days, thereby failing to establish a reportable loss for tax purposes.

weak form of the efficient market hypothesis: The theory that market prices move randomly with respect to past price-return patterns; implies that technical analysis, as practiced by the chart-readers, is useless.

Weighted Average Life (WAL): A measure of a bond's maturity. It takes into account principal payments made over time, so that a bond making interim principal payments will have a WAL shorter than the actual maturity. See duration.

Weisenberger: A major publisher of mutual fund investment information, including *Investment Companies.*

whack-up: The process of allocating the finite pie of a restructuring firm's value among the various constituencies.

when-issued trading: Trading in as-yet-unissued securities that have a projected future issue date. Payment is due upon issuance.

white chip stock: A stock of low quality. See blue chip, red chip stocks.

white knight defense: Finding an alternative and presumably more friendly acquirer (the white knight) than the immediate takeover threat.

white squire defense: Finding an important ally who will acquire a substantial minority position of the firm now controlled by existing management but threatened by an outside group; presumably the white squire will oppose and hopefully help block the efforts of the outsider to take control of the vulnerable company.

whole life insurance: A type of life insurance policy that couples life insurance protection with a savings program. Annual premiums are established and fixed at the time of the initial purchase. A surplus account is built up in the policy's early years for the purpose of meeting claims that exceed premiums when the policyholders are older and death rates are higher.

will: A legal document stating a person's intentions with regard to the disposition of his or her property or estate at the time of death.

Wilshire 5000 Index: A value-weighted stock index based on a large number of NYSE, AMEX, and OTC stocks.

winnowing: The process of eliminating certain potential buyers who have expressed interest in specific assets or properties that may be for sale. This is done in an attempt to maximize the efficiency of the sale process and eliminate the merely curious.

wire house: An exchange member electronically linked to an exchange.

withholding tax: A portion of an employee's income withheld by the employer as partial payment of the employee's income tax liability.

working capital (gross): The sum of the values of a firm's short-term assets.

working capital (net): The difference between the values of a firm's short-term assets and its short-term liabilities.

working capital facilities: Those portions of a company's bank credit agreement usually reserved for the acquisition of working capital such as to finance its inventory or accounts receivable.

working control: The ownership of a sufficient number of shares to elect a majority to the company's board of directors.

work-out: Another term for a restructuring (usually undertaken out of court).

writer (of an option): One who sells and thereby assumes the short side of a put or call contract and therefore stands ready to satisfy the potential exercise by the long side.

yankee bonds: Bonds denominated in U.S. dollars but issued by a foreign firm or government.

yield: The return on an investment expressed as a percentage of its market value.

yield (current): Current income (dividend, coupon, rent, etc.) divided by the price of the asset.

yield curve: The relationship between yield to maturity and term to maturity (or duration) for equivalent risk debt securities.

yield curve note: A type of debt security whose coupon rate is structured to move inversely with market rates; thus when market interest rates decline the coupon rate on the yield curve notes will rise, and vice versa.

yield spread: The difference between the promised yields of particular bonds or classes of bonds at a given time relative to yields on Treasury issues of equal maturity.

yield to earliest call: The holding-period return under the assumption that the issue is called as soon as the no-call provision in the bond's indenture expires.

yield-to-maturity: The yield calculation that takes proper account of both the coupon return and the principal repayment at maturity.

yield-to-worst: The lowest of (1) the current yield, (2) the yield-to-maturity, and (3) the yield-to-call.

zero-coupon bond: A bond issued at a discount from its par or face value that matures at its face value.

zero tick: A transaction immediately preceded by a transaction at the same price.

zone of insolvency: A financial situation in which the company's position has deteriorated to the point where creditors may be adversely affected. Bankruptcy is possible but not certain.

Resources and Suggested Readings

This book like all books is limited in how much it can cover on any one topic. You may wish to learn more about a variety of topics than I have covered herein. Accordingly, this section will provide you with a list of suggested readings on various topics.

In addition, you will probably want to obtain current information on various matters. This section is also designed to provide you with help in that area. Note, however, that this section is by no means comprehensive. What follows is just a small taste of what is available.

BOOKS

General Investing

A Random Walk Down Wall Street
Completely Revised and Updated 8th Edition
Burton G. Malkiel
W. W. Norton, 2004 (paperback)

An excellent book by a great scholar.

Against the Gods: The Remarkable Story of Risk
Peter L. Bernstein
Wiley, 1998 (paperback reprint)

Fascinating reading, but as one reviewer put it, the book is "long on history but short on risk management strategy." In other words, not very practical.

A Non-Random Walk Down Wall Street
Andrew W. Lo and A. Craig MacKinlay
Princeton University Press, 2001 (paperback reprint)

Like Malkiel's, another very worthy book, but not a practical guide for amateur investors. This is a book with an academic tone. It has a lot of good stuff but is way beyond the typical non PhD reader.

Investing for Dummies
3rd Edition
Eric Tyson
For Dummies, 2002 (paperback)

Value Investing: From Graham To Buffett and Beyond
Bruce C. N. Greenwald, Judd Kahn, Paul D. Sonkin, and Michael van Biema
Wiley, 2004 (paperback reprint)

The Intelligent Investor: The Definitive Book On Value Investing
Revised Edition
Benjamin Graham, updated with new commentary by Jason Zweig
Collins, 2003 (paperback)

Motivation

Think and Grow Rich
Napoleon Hill
Ballantine, 1987 (paperback)
The Original Version, Restored and Revised, Aventine, 2004 (paperback)

This is more of a motivational, Dale Carnegie–type book.

The Automatic Millionaire: A Powerful One-Step Plan to Live and Finish Rich
David Bach
Broadway, 2003 (hardcover)

This book focuses on how to save and through the power of compound interest grow your nest egg.

The Richest Man in Babylon
George S. Clason
Signet, 2002 (paperback reissue)

Another largely motivational book.

Mutual Funds

Common Sense on Mutual Funds: New Imperatives for the Intelligent Investor
John C. Bogle
Wiley, 2000 (paperback reprint)

Mutual Funds for Dummies
Eric Tyson
For Dummies, 2004 (paperback)

Bonds

Investing in Fixed Income Securities: Understanding the Bond Market
Gary Strumeyer
Wiley, 2005 (hardcover)

Junk Bonds

Investing in Junk Bonds: Inside the High-Yield Debt Market
Edward I. Altman and Scott A. Nammacher
Beard, 2002 (paperback reprint)

Bankruptcy Investing

Bankruptcy Investing: How to Profit from Distressed Companies
2nd Edition
Ben Branch and Hugh Ray
Beard, 2002 (paperback)

Distressed Securities: Analyzing and Evaluating Market Potential and Investment Risk
Edward I. Altman
Beard, 1999 (paperback)

Corporate Financial Distress and Bankruptcy: Predict and Avoid Bankruptcy, Analyze and Invest in Distressed Debt
3rd Edition
Edward I. Altman and Edith Hotchkiss
Wiley, 2005 (hardcover)

Options

Options Made Easy: Your Guide To Profitable Trading
2nd Edition
Guy Cohen
Financial Times Prentice Hall, 2005 (hardcover)

Getting Started in Options
5th Edition
Michael C. Thomsett
Wiley, 2005 (paperback)

Futures Markets

Trading Commodities and Financial Futures: A Step-by-Step Guide to Mastering the Markets
3rd Edition
George Kleinman
Financial Times Prentice Hall, 2004 (hardcover)

Real Estate Investing

Investing in Real Estate
4th Edition
Andrew James McLean and Gary W. Eldred
Wiley, 2003 (paperback)

WEBSITES

Individual Investor Services
American Association of Individual Investors (AAII)
www.aaii.com

National Association of Investors Corporation (NAIC)
www.betterinvesting.org

The Motley Fool
www.fool.com

National Association of Securities Dealers
www.nasdaqtrader.com

NEWSPAPERS

Wall Street Journal
www.wsj.com

Investor's Business Daily
www.investors.com

MAGAZINES

Business Week
www.businessweek.com

Forbes
www.forbes.com

INVESTOR-ORIENTED JOURNALS

AAII Journal
www.aaii.com

Financial Analysts Journal
www.aimrpubs.org/faj/

Journal of Portfolio Management
www.iijournals.com/JPM/

INVESTMENT NEWS SOURCES

Bloomberg
www.bloomberg.com

PC Quote
www.pcquote.com

CNN
money.cnn.com

INVESTMENT-RELATED CREDENTIAL SERVICES

Chartered Financial Analyst
www.cfainstitute.org

Certified Financial Planner
www.cfp.net

Chartered Alternative Investment Analyst Association
www.caia.org

Keir Educational Resources
www.jackkeirine.com

ALTERNATIVE INVESTMENTS

Center for Interventional Securities and Derivative Markets
cisdm.som.umass.edu

Index

About the Author

BEN BRANCH is Professor of Finance at the University of Massachusetts, Amherst, where he has taught finance, investment, banking, and industrial organization for over 30 years. He was previously on the faculty at Dartmouth College, the University of Michigan, and the University of Texas, and has served on the boards of several corporations, including the First Republic Bank, BankEast, Bank of New England, and Proactive Technologies. Currently serving as associate editor of the *International Review of Financial Analysis*, he has published dozens of journal articles and book reviews, and is the coauthor of *Bankruptcy Investing* and author of *Fundamentals of Investment for Financial Planning*.